D1575590

PUBLIC RELATIONS

James S. Norris

Jacksonville Junior College

PUBLIC RELATIONS

LIBRARY
FORSYTH TECHNICAL COMMUNITY COLLEGE
2100 SILAS CREEK PARKWAY
WINSTON-SALEM, NC 27103-5197

PRENTICE-HALL, INC., Englewood Cliffs, New Jersey 07632

Library of Congress Cataloging in Publication Data

NORRIS, JAMES S. (date)
PUBLIC RELATIONS.

Bibliography: p.
Includes index.
1. Public relations. I. Title.
HM263.N68 1983   659.2   83-16140
ISBN 0-13-738401-7

Editorial/production supervision and interior design: **Joan Foley**
Cover design: **George Cornell**
Manufacturing buyer: **Ed O'Dougherty**

© 1984 by Prentice-Hall, Inc., Englewood Cliffs, New Jersey 07632

All rights reserved. No part of this book may be
reproduced, in any form or by any means,
without permission in writing from the publisher.

Printed in the United States of America

10 9 8 7 6 5 4 3 2 1

ISBN 0-13-738401-7

PRENTICE-HALL INTERNATIONAL, INC., *London*
PRENTICE-HALL OF AUSTRALIA PTY. LIMITED, *Sydney*
EDITORA PRENTICE-HALL DO BRASIL, LTDA., *Rio de Janeiro*
PRENTICE-HALL CANADA INC., *Toronto*
PRENTICE-HALL OF INDIA PRIVATE LIMITED, *New Delhi*
PRENTICE-HALL OF JAPAN, INC., *Tokyo*
PRENTICE-HALL OF SOUTHEAST ASIA PTE. LTD., *Singapore*
WHITEHALL BOOKS LIMITED, *Wellington, New Zealand*

9, 2

4

For *Katie,* My Love

CONTENTS

10   HOW PEOPLE SEE THINGS, THINK ABOUT THEM, AND ACT ON THEM, 140

11   SPORTS, 152

12   CORPORATE PUBLIC RELATIONS, 184

PREFACE

The time is long gone since public relations was only for the rich and powerful. It is no longer the special preserve of corporations that can afford public relations departments as part of their marketing effort, or can indulge themselves in the retention of "consulting firms." In fact, it has not been that way for some time now.

Today, public relations is everyone's business. Up and down Main Street, there is not a private enterprise or a nonprofit organization to which the techniques of public relations cannot be applied. From car dealer to children's home, from bookstore to public library, from paper mill to ballet theater— *all* demand the nourishment of well-managed public relations. Lacking it, these enterprises often wither before our eyes.

It seems to me that today every business student should go forth armed with a working knowledge of public relations. Though the student may never see Madison Avenue or the public relations department at General Motors, an understanding of public relations can add measurably to what he or she brings to an organization. If a person envisages a career in marketing, a knowledge of public relations techniques and methods is likely to be welcome in most firms.

In a world of work that is becoming increasingly skill-conscious, especially as far as recent college graduates are concerned, public relations is a salable skill. Just how salable can be demonstrated by a visit to a local manufacturing plant, a bank, a hospital, a department store, a museum, or an art gallery. (A chat with the leading politician in town might be instructive too.) The visitor will quickly discover that there is no coordinated public relations program, or that any effort in that direction is in the hands of a well-meaning amateur.

Cities of under 750,000 possess hundreds of businesses and institutions, every one of which might profit from being "thought better of." Yet a glance at the Yellow Pages of the local phone book will disclose that there are relatively few public relations counselors offering their services. The list of specialists becomes even shorter when one takes into account the local advertising agencies, which often claim a public relations capability.

The need, and thus the opportunity, is there—whether it be as a full-time public relations consultant, a company public relations director, or a member of the marketing department with an extra skill possessed by no one else.

But there is another need the person with public relations knowhow is going to have to satisfy, and that is the understanding and appreciation of what properly applied public relations can do for an organization. Lack of understanding of the uses of public relations along Main Street is astonishing and disheartening. It is, as they say, a challenge and an opportunity.

One would hope then that many more colleges and universities will *insist* that business students gain a grasp of the subject. That is why this text has been constructed to meet the requirements of a wide spectrum of students, from two-year college students whose focus is business-related to MBA candidates. The first 10 chapters are devoted to the mechanics of public relations—the skills and knowledge that must be commanded before one can properly function as a public relations person. We then examine five areas—sports, business, entertainment, education, and product promotion—to see how public relations functions in each.

Every chapter begins with an *overview and goals* preview of the chapter and concludes with a *summary* and a list of *key terms.* Each chapter also includes a real experience *(The Way It Happened)* that illustrates public relations principles in action, as well as a *personal project* that will enable students to apply the lessons they have learned. *Readings* for each chapter have been selected to broaden understanding.

ACKNOWLEDGMENTS

I am grateful to the many people who offered their suggestions, particularly Joe Luter—a public relations professional typical of the many who serve the small, local business.

The editorial staff of the *Florida Times-Union* has been most generous in supplying samples of releases. The dozens of organizations and businesses that have granted permission to reproduce the public relations material deserve thanks as well.

I would also like to thank acquisitions editor Read Wickham, production editor Joan Foley, and copyeditor Jeannine Ciliotta of Prentice-Hall for their efforts in putting together this book.

PUBLIC RELATIONS

1

THE "HOW DO THEY FEEL ABOUT US" BUSINESS

OVERVIEW AND GOALS

In this chapter we seek to gain a sense of what the business of public relations is all about. When you have completed this chapter, you will be able to

> ***Appreciate*** *the dimensions of public relations.*
>
> ***Understand*** *why relations with our publics are so important to all of us.*
>
> ***See*** *the vital relationship between public relations and performance.*
>
> ***Understand*** *the roles played by attitudes, perceptions, and opinions.*

Public relations is concerned with how people feel about issues, products, and individual or corporate personalities. Perhaps a better term for it would be *public relationship,* because what we are doing is building relationships—quite intimate relationships sometimes—with a great many dif

FIGURE 1-1   Publicizing a state for industrial purposes is a special kind of public relations work demanding a high level of creative ability. The organization responsible for selling the state for industrial development usually works under the state department of commerce, in this case, it is the Florida Division of Economic Development. Letters, brochures, advertisements—all communications material—sent out by this division will go to sophisticated prospects that include some of the largest and most successful corporations in the United States. Anything less than "first class" simply will not do when approaching these people. Here the Florida Division of Economic Development reprints three of its award-winning ads, which ran in such publications as *Business Week* and the *Wall Street Journal*.

Credit: Florida Department of Commerce.

ferent kinds of people. Because our subject is so broad, if we define it at all, we must define it in simple terms.

Who are the people who wish to build relationships? Almost any person or institution you can think of: the Republican party, your local town council, U.S. Steel, a pop singer, the NAACP, the Ku Klux Klan, your own college. With whom do we wish to build our relationships? Registered voters, stockholders, members of Congress, alumni—in short, "the public" in all its infinite variety. How do we go about building relationships with these people? That, you will discover, is what this book is about. And here too, there is great variety. So let us apply a broad brush. *Public relations* is having relationships with people.

Given this definition, it can be said that we are all in public relations. The student sitting in front of you who has not done his homework has a concern. He would like the teacher and the rest of the class not to get the impression that he is a numbskull. The student to your right may have a public relations problem too. She is going to present a report, and wonders if it will go well. She is on the alert for comments and responses. She will be delighted if one of her friends says to her, "Marge, you certainly speak well— and I liked what you said." That's a very good "relation" to have with your public.

Of course, we *all* want people to think well of us. As Maslow and other psychologists have found,[1] the *need* for love, esteem, affection, and respect is as real and natural as breathing. When others, in their words and actions, accord us love and respect, we feel good. It's nice to feel good about yourself, isn't it? And it's not nice to feel bad. Therefore we tend to act in relation to our public in ways that will gain us affection and esteem, and thus make us feel good. How do we do this? By offering love and respect to others! In what we say and what we do—in everything that touches the lives of others—we behave in such a way as to deserve their esteem and affection. It is as though each person in our lives were a mirror, and in that mirror is reflected back to us a picture of that person who deserves to be so highly thought of. No wonder public relations people are so concerned with "images"!

Companies, too, tend to act like people in their relations with their respective clienteles. Your local bank wants your affection and esteem, and it works for it. (It did take banks a little longer than most retail businesses to discover that it is good *business* to be nice to people.) That is why the teller is bright and cheerful and gives the impression that you are one of the bank's favorite customers and that the bank is delighted to be able to serve you. From the bank president down to the youngest employee, all are aware of the importance of your feelings about them and the bank. They hope you will walk out the door feeling very good about them.

[1] Abraham H. Maslow, *Motivation and Personality* (New York: Harper & Row, 1954).

"Feeling Good" Is Just the Beginning

As you discovered quite some time ago, when people care for you—that is, regard you as a nice person—everything seems to go smoothly. Your relationships with them are likely to be much more relaxed and rewarding. Mutual trust and respect, and even affection, make it far easier for us to get along with one another. On the other hand, we are apt to be reserved with someone we either don't know, or instinctively distrust.

I'm sure you can see how this principle applies just as readily to business organizations as it does to individuals. If a business gains your respect and affection, you feel good about that firm. It will then be just that much easier for the business to get along—that is, do business—with you. If the firm performs badly, it is likely to lose a customer. We need to be liked and respected not simply so that we can bask in the glow of being "popular" or "highly regarded," but also because we see beyond the immediate need and recognize that there are consequences as well. So it is with business firms. Westinghouse seeks to "keep your trust" (that is, your respect) because consumer acceptance of its products is important. The bank seeks to gain your friendship because when it begins a drive for Christmas Club memberships, you are going to be a logical and, it hopes, willing customer. At Sears, your returned merchandise will be accepted cheerfully and efficiently not just to make you "feel good" about the company, but to help keep you as a loyal customer.

Images Lead to Perceptions

Whether as persons or as business institutions, these carefully nurtured images we reflect cause others to perceive—to "see us"—in certain ways. We carry with us our *perception;* that is, what we see, of a certain event, place, or person. In public relations, this is something we have to be careful about. We are in the business of creating images and reflecting them, but sometimes people look in our mirrors and see things we do not expect them to see. Sometimes of course they see things we do not want them to see.[2] So part of your job is to make certain that your mirror reflects you or your clients accurately and does not distort you or them.

If you do not believe that people all see things somewhat differently, you might ask the members of your class what they think of the Cadillac car. You will find that what they *perceive* ranges from delightful to detestable. Almost everyone will use a different word or phrase to describe what he or she sees in a Cadillac. A Cadillac dealer of course hopes all of us will perceive the Cadillac as being "the very best."

---

[2]It is widely held that the television camera is the most pitiless of "mirrors." It reveals not only our skin blemishes, but our blemishes of character as well.

Sometimes Perceptions Are Prepackaged

Occasionally it is easy for us to accept ready-made perceptions. We think things or people ought to be a certain way, and that becomes the way they are. The trouble is, frequently they are not.

We tend to cut things from the same pattern. We create *stereotypes.* Star football players are "dumb jocks." Professors are absent-minded. And little old ladies are sweet, kindly, and gentle. But as you have observed, there are plenty of athletes who go on to graduate school; there are professors with all the facts at their fingertips; and how about that sweet little old lady down the street? It may be that she has a penchant for shoplifting, violates the health code by keeping 25 cats, and has never paid a cent of income or property taxes.

"Preformed" perceptions are something the public relations person has to deal with every day. There are many ways of dealing with them, as you will learn. But there is another kind of perception that gives us the most trouble of all, and that stretches our ingenuity to its utmost. This is the perception that is "cast in iron."

Cast-Iron Perceptions

You will often meet people whose perceptions are almost immovable. No matter how much proof you present, they will still refuse to believe that the moon is *not* made of green cheese. They do not want their perceptions changed—and often for very good reasons. We do not wish to perceive our football team as a bunch of dirty players. We do not want to see our favorite singer in an unfavorable light.

Galileo once got himself into a great deal of trouble with the hierarchy of the Catholic Church. Despite his scientific proof, it was simply inconvenient for the Church at that time to accept the perception of the earth as revolving around the moon. And you remember the trouble Columbus had with his sailors? They had the unshakable perception of the world as being flat, and had no desire to discover where the outer edge was.

In Chapter Three we discuss some of the characteristics of the people with whom we have public relations. There we will learn that there are often deep-seated psychological reasons for resisting change in perceptions. That pal of yours who insists that *his* brand of beer is best, and won't even sample another brand, is not just being stubborn.

Attitudes Affect Perceptions

Very often hardened perceptions result in hardened attitudes. These are extremely difficult for the public relations person to change, as one famous marketing psychologist has pointed out: "No successful advertising can ignore

FIGURE 1-2 **In this news release from the Florida Game and Fresh Water Fish Commission, we see an excellent example of how in public relations we have to "make things happen." The competition to select an artist and subject for the year's waterfowl stamp is of good reader interest, especially for sportsmen, and should get a good play on the sports page. Note that 146 entries were received, indicating considerable interest on the part of artists. It is interesting, too, that this annual competition is well established in its third year, and apparently assured of continuing and growing interest.**

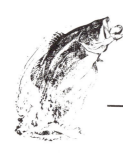

for immediate release

1/20/82

NEWS RELEASE

florida game and fresh water fish commission

Office of Informational Services • Tallahassee, Fla. 32301 • (904) 488-4676

Contact: Trisha Spillan (904) 488-4676

CABLE'S RINGNECKS
CAPTURE STAMP

TALLAHASSEE - When the votes were cast, it was a Florida resident this year whose work was selected to grace the 1982-83 Florida Waterfowl Stamp.

Tampa-based artist Lee Cable's painting of three ring-necked ducks was selected as the winning design by members of the Game and Fresh Water Fish Commission. Some 146 entries were received in the competition, now in its third year. The selection was made at the January meeting in Tampa.

Thompson Phillip Crowe of Nashville, Tenn, took second place with his painting of a Labrador retriever holding a ring-necked duck while Bob Binks of Daytona Beach placed third in the overall ratings with a portrait of a blue-winged teal.

Cable will receive no monetary remuneration from the Commission for his painting. However, judging by the experience of past winners, he should receive substantial financial gain from sale of limited edition prints of the design.

A native of Ohio, Cable came about his love for the outdoors from hunting and fishing jaunts taken with his father around the family farm.

He had formal art instruction with Martin Wogaman, a noted figure painter. After a stint in the Air Force, he and his wife settled in Greenville, Ohio where he worked as an art director. They later moved to Florida where he worked for a time with a Lakeland advertising firm and then with the Tampa Times.

While at the Tampa-based newspaper, Cable's interest in wildlife art began to flourish. He started writing and illustrating stories on wildlife which appeared in publications like Florida Sportsman and the Tampa Tribune.

In 1975 he made the decision to turn fulltime to wildlife art and his decision has been a good one. He has had several successful shows and won several state awards. Each summer, the couple and their three children travel to Colorado where the artist spends time photographing and painting animals in their native setting.

(MORE)

Credit: Florida Game and Fresh Water Fish Commission.

the stable, enduring attitudes of the consumer public. Since attitudes affect the way a product is seen, affect the very perception of facts, facts alone cannot combat hostile attitudes. Opposition to an attitude tends to strengthen it."[3]

Recently I watched a politician being interviewed on TV. I was under the impression that he was a member of a party whose ideas, for the most part, I don't agree with. "How mealy-mouthed and evasive he is!" I said to myself as the interview went on. But then I discovered I was mistaken; he was from my party. Almost immediately it began to seem to me that his answers were all to the point and well-taken.

Think of your own perceptions, which have been formed as a result of your own attitudes. You will not sniff, smoke, or shoot certain things in your arms because your attitude toward them is that they are harmful and dangerous, and that you would have to be crazy to use them. You may have a very positive attitude toward modern jazz, whereas your perception of Dixieland is that it is old-fashioned and boring. As difficult as these hardened attitudes are for the public relations person, his or her job is made even more complicated by another fact: Attitudes keep shifting.

Changing Attitudes

If attitudes, and thus perceptions, did not change, public relations people would not have such a hard time. There would not be so many moving targets to shoot at. Because we do know attitudes and perceptions change, we try to anticipate these changes, or at least try not to be taken off guard when they occur.

Style and fashion offer an immediate and typical example of how quickly perceptions and attitudes about dress can change. Just one glance at the person teaching your class will indicate that he or she and you may have very different ideas about dress. From your point of view, his jacket may be too narrow-shouldered, his tie too wide, and his shirt too white. But he sees himself as being well and neatly dressed. Why the difference in attitudes? It often results because his perception of being "well dressed" was formed some years ago. He *likes* the way he looks and is not about to jump into the latest designer clothes.

Have you been to the movies lately? Our perception of what constitutes bad taste has certainly shifted radically in the past few years. Our attitude toward the motion picture as family entertainment has shifted with it. Four-letter words and explicit love scenes are normal fare these days. Yet one generation ago, Hollywood had a "code" so strict it would be considered ludicrous today.

[3]Ernest Dichter, *Handbook of Consumer Motivations* (New York: McGraw-Hill, 1964), p. 396.

FIGURE 1-3   Attitudes can be affected by the way in which a news release is handled. Here, a company has some not particularly pleasant news to report. It might have ignored it. It might have tried to "paper it over" with platitudes. Instead, it bit the bullet and gave a frank and honest report of the situation. The reader is likely to form the attitude that "these are frank and honest people."

WYLE LABORATORIES ELECTRONICS MARKETING GROUP

ACKNOWLEDGES NATIONAL SEMICONDUCTOR CANCELLATION

IRVINE, CALIFORNIA, JANUARY 28, 1982. The Electronics Marketing Group of Wyle Laboratories (NYSE) acknowledged today that National Semiconductor Corporation was cancelling Wyle franchises for Santa Clara, El Segundo, Irvine and San Diego, California and Seattle, Washington. The cancellation is expected to be effective as of February 22, 1982. The announcement was made in Irvine, California by Lauren L. Pond, Jr., President of the Electronics Marketing Group.

Pond said that Wyle facilities at Phoenix, Arizona, Denver, Colorado, and Salt Lake City, Utah will remain franchised at this time, but are expected to be cancelled at a later date.

"While we were aware that National Semiconductor was concerned about our recent franchise agreements with Texas Instruments, we did not expect the cancellation," Pond said.

Pond added that, "If the National Semiconductor franchises are cancelled, this action is expected to have a negative short term effect on the Wyle Electronics Marketing Group. However, we believe that in the longer term we will recover any lost sales through the newly acquired Texas Instruments Semiconductor product line and support from our other major semiconductor suppliers, including AMD, Fairchild Semiconductor, Intel Corporation, RCA and Signetics."

Wyle Laboratories is a diversified high-technology company operating in the fields of electronic components and systems marketing; research, engineering services, and testing; industrial manufacturing; and transportation. The company has offices and facilities in principal locations throughout the U.S.

#   #   #

Technical Contact: John L. Lovett

Credit: Wyle Laboratories.

There was a time, not too long ago, when crewcuts were in and long hair (to say nothing of beards) was out. Perceptions of long hair had created some very hardened negative attitudes. Anyone with shoulder-length hair, a beard, or a mustache was regarded as untrustworthy. Many young men quickly found that a job interview without a fresh haircut was guaranteed to be a failure. Today, attitudes are quite different. Long hair is not only acceptable, it's stylish. And if you do not think attitudes and perceptions keep changing, just look at some Civil War photographs. *Every* officer had a beard. General George Armstrong Custer, who ran into all that trouble at the Little Big Horn, wore his blond curls down to his shoulders—a fact that must have delighted his scalpers. Public relations people must always keep in mind this important fact: In such broad categories as marriage, work, leisure time, life styles, and social and political attitudes, vast and dramatic changes are constantly taking place.

Knowledge Shapes Beliefs and Attitudes

In the next chapter, when we talk about communications, you will see how important it is for us to talk in terms our public understands. Today's public understands a great deal more than any public ever did before. In short, the public relations practitioner today is faced with an audience that is more knowledgeable, and thus more sophisticated, than was the case a generation or so ago. People are more discriminating, more questioning, less likely to accept things at face value. This means that you, as a public relations person, are going to have to watch your step. The "masses" are not gullible rubes, and we had better not act as though they were.

Today, in your classroom, you are almost sure to find several people who have lived or traveled abroad. They have eaten foreign foods and gotten to know foreign people. In the spring, when school ends, the roads of Europe are filled with student hikers and their bright backpacks. Sewed to their packs are the flags or insignia of dozens of different countries. Travel gives us a far different outlook (or attitude) on many things. This phenomenon was not so evident a generation or two ago. Until relatively cheap transportation made it possible, going to a strange country was like going to the moon. Our perspectives were limited, and so was our thinking. Motion pictures and television have taken us into many strange and unusual places as well. The fact that more people are traveling, reading newspapers and magazines, and listening to TV and radio has had a tremendous impact on perceptions and attitudes. Tons of information on a great variety of subjects are being supplied us each day. We have the opportunity to form opinions—and we often do. The Reagan administration arrived in Washington with some interesting economic theories. Before long, thousands of us were talking glibly about Adam Smith, Milton Friedman, supply-side economics, and the politics of the "Fed."

FIGURE 1-4   **This is not only an excellently executed ad, it is a beautiful example of a company tackling a delicate problem head on. It is easy to be cynical about this sort of thing, but distillers do not want to be the cause of accidents. The subject of drunk driving is getting more and more attention. Communities are voting on Sunday as well as earlier nighttime closings. DWI penalties are getting tougher and tougher in an effort to cut down on driving fatalities. The House of Seagram wants to be on the right side, and this institutional ad puts it there. Note that reprints are available. Many undoubtedly found their way to company bulletin boards.**

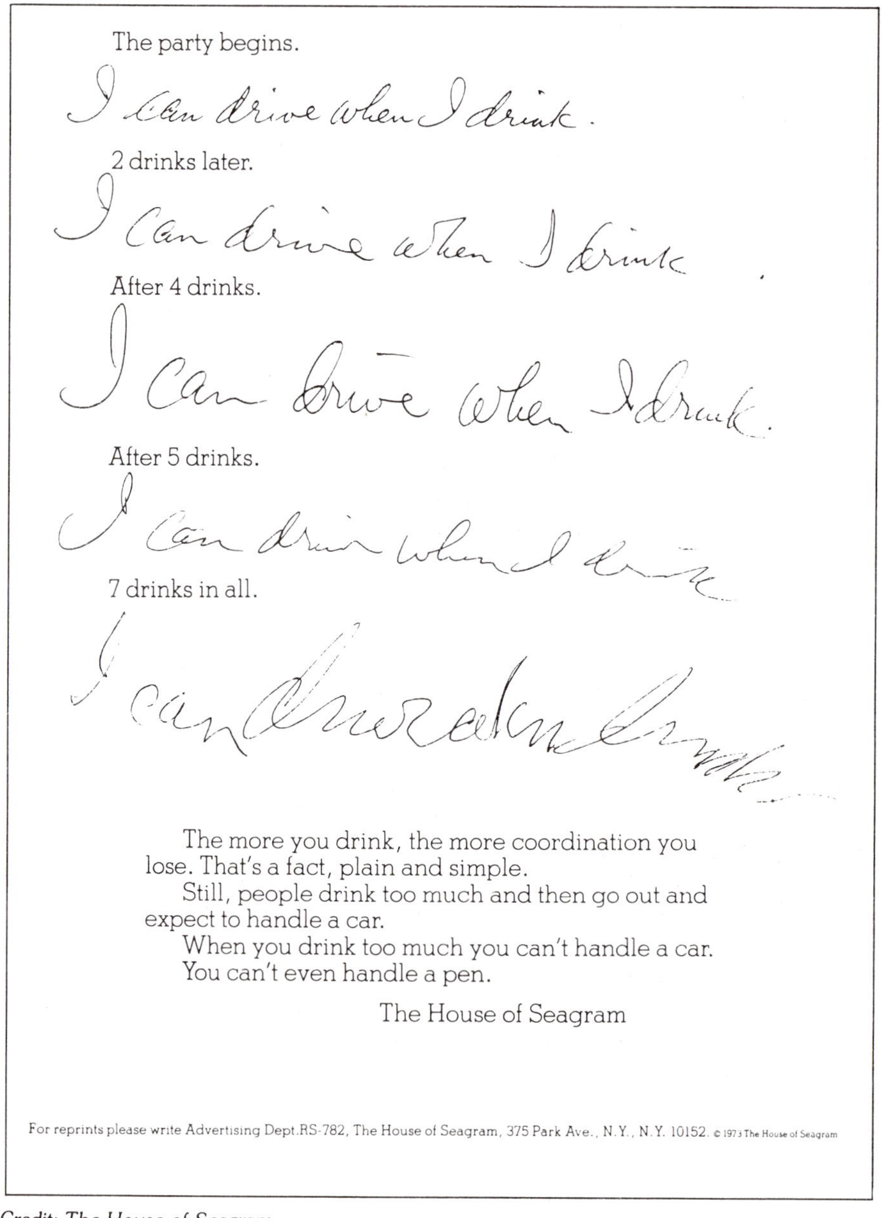

The party begins.

I can drive when I drink.

2 drinks later.

I can drive when I drink

After 4 drinks.

I can drive when I drink.

After 5 drinks.

I can drin when I d —

7 drinks in all.

I can drve dn m —

The more you drink, the more coordination you lose. That's a fact, plain and simple.

Still, people drink too much and then go out and expect to handle a car.

When you drink too much you can't handle a car. You can't even handle a pen.

The House of Seagram

For reprints please write Advertising Dept.RS-782, The House of Seagram, 375 Park Ave., N.Y., N.Y. 10152. © 1973 The House of Seagram

Credit: The House of Seagram.

FIGURE 1-5   All states employ public relations people who are concerned with the promotion of both industry and tourism, which are so important to the prosperity of the state. Here is a page from a brochure produced by Florida's Division of Industry Development.

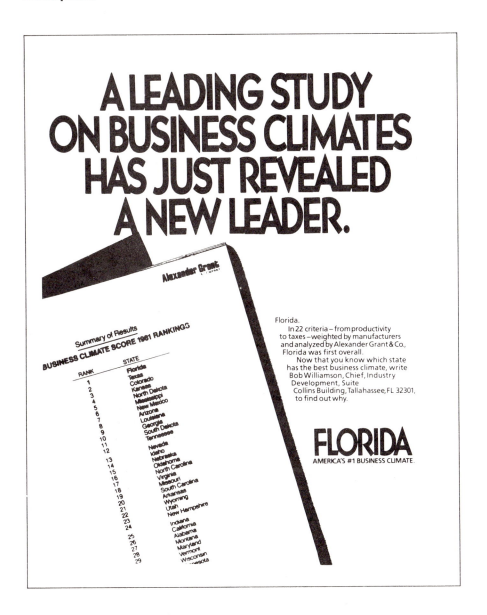

Credit: Florida Department of Commerce.

This broadening and deepening of knowledge and interests has resulted in another phenomenon with which the public relations people must deal— the single-issue lobby. These lobbies are made up of people who have focused their attitudes and perceptions on a single subject. Whether it is gun control, abortion, ERA, or school prayer, they bring to their cause great intensity of purpose and belief. The public relations problems they bring with them are just as intense. Single-issue lobbies are, to a great extent, products of public relations programs. Their opponents must fight them with the same methods.

We Want People to See Things Our Way

We have been talking about images and attitudes and perceptions, so I think you see what it all adds up to. Quite literally, we want people to see things "our way." We wish to be seen in the most favorable light. The local art museum wishes to be seen as making a real contribution to the community, and thus as deserving of support. Politicians wish to be seen as wise and honest. Oil companies wish to be seen as solvers of the energy problem, and at the same time as actively concerned with the environment. In short, we are in the business of creating relationships with people and institutions by means of which favorable images, attitudes, perceptions, and beliefs may be projected.

Who are these people? How do we create our relationships? How do we go about helping to shape the way they "see" us? That is what the rest of this book is all about. But before we can build a relationship, we must bridge the gap between us. I must *communicate* with you. Because if I cannot communicate with you, then the seed that will grow into a relationship can never be planted. Therefore, we begin examining the business of making relationships with the most basic, fundamental act of all—*communication.*

SUMMARY

Public relations is "having relationships with people," a great variety of people. We want people to "feel good" about us. When they do, it makes everything else we do—including selling to them—that much easier.

All of us gain perceptions of things because they reflect an image. Sometimes our images and perceptions are precast. We call these stereotypes, "cast-iron perceptions." Attitudes are closely controlled by our perceptions. As our perceptions, or images, of things change, so do our attitudes and beliefs. As we learn, our perceptions change, and our beliefs change too.

As a public relations person, you are going to be dealing with a public with more learning—and therefore with far more beliefs—than ever before.

Our business is one of creating learning relationships with people so that our image will reflect favorable attitudes and beliefs on their part.

KEY TERMS

Relationships	Stereotype
Need to "feel good"	Attitudes
Image	Opinions
Perception	Beliefs

THE WAY IT HAPPENED: THE BEEF FOLKS

It is a well-known rule in the chain store food business that the store with the best meat counter attracts—and holds—the most customers. In display, service, variety, and quality of product, all of us strive to put our best foot forward. As the meat counter goes, you might say, so goes the rest of the store.

At Fine Bros., a successful regional chain, we looked hard for the device that would position us as the leader in meat. We hit on the tactic of referring to ourselves as "The Beef Folks." In other words, *we* were the authorities and leaders. Notice that we didn't say "Lamb Folks" or "Pork Folks." That's because in most people's minds, we have found, a good *steak* means everything else is good.

So in our advertising, on our letterheads, in store windows and back counters, on the sides of our delivery trucks we tell the world that *we* are "The Beef Folks." We are buying an image of excellence.

Michael Claire
Advertising and Public Relations
Fine Bros.
Jacksonville, Florida

A PERSONAL PROJECT

The Scot Robert Burns wrote a wonderful poem entitled "To A Louse." In the poem, he asks if it wouldn't be nice if we had the power to see ourselves as others see us.

O wad some power the giftie gie us
To see oursels as others see us!
It wad frae monie a blunder frne us,
An' foolish notion:
Wat airs in dress an' gait wad lea'e us,
An' ev'n devotion!

Do you agree with Burns? Do you know people whose self-perceptions are way off target? Seeing *themselves* as others do might come as quite a shock.

Prepare a personality index, a set of paired characteristics: "happy–sad," "ambitious–lazy," "outgoing–reserved," and so on. Prepare a scale of pluses and minuses, 1 to 5, for each characteristic. Select a subject—one of your classmates, perhaps—and ask his or her friends to rate the person's personality characteristics. Then ask your subject to rate himself or herself on the same scale.

Does the subject "see himself" as others do? Do his friends agree on how they see him?

READING TO BROADEN UNDERSTANDING

BERNAYS, EDWARD L. *Biography of An Idea: Memoirs of Public Relations Counsel Edward L. Bernays* (New York: Simon and Shuster, 1965), HM 263, B 394. Bernays was one of the creators and major figures of this business, and his book is a broad history of public relations as he lived it. Particularly fascinating is his account of his relationship with his uncle Sigmund Freud.

———. *Public Relations* (Norman: University of Oklahoma Press, 1952), HM 263, B 415. This is more of a "how to" book. See p. 7, "Why Public Relations Knowledge Is Vital Today" and p. 77, "The Rise of a New Profession."

CUTLIP, SCOTT M., AND ALLEN H. CENTER. *Effective Public Relations*, 5th ed. (Englewood Cliffs, N.J.: Prentice-Hall, 1978), HM 263, C 78. See pp. 4, 5 for comments on definitions of public relations. The authors conclude: "The game goes on. Meantime, *public relations defines itself by what it does.*"

OSKAMP, STUART. *Attitudes and Opinions* (Englewood Cliffs, N.J.: Prentice-Hall, 1977), HM 261, O 75. A rewarding book in gaining an understanding of what it is we are trying to move and change in public relations. See particularly p. 49, "Structure and Function of Attitudes and Beliefs," and p. 119, "Formation of Attitudes and Opinions."

It is suggested that the following three publications be subscribed to or otherwise made available to the class. They will include material appropriate to the understanding of every chapter in this book:

Public Relations Journal (Public Relations Society of America, 845 Third Avenue, New York, N.Y. 10027).

Public Relations News (127 East 80 Street, New York, N.Y. 10021). A newsletter.

Public Relations Quarterly (44 West Market Street, Rhinebeck, N.Y. 12572).

2

COMMUNICATION: THE ART OF GETTING ACROSS

OVERVIEW AND GOALS

We now look at an essential part of public relations: communication. We examine the process of communication and see how it takes place. We discuss the vehicles by which our communications are carried. We will also look at the concept of "publics"—the kinds of people who receive public relations messages. When you have completed this chapter, you will be able to

> ***Appreciate*** *the importance of communication in public relations.*
>
> ***Understand*** *the process of communication.*
>
> ***Perceive*** *how communications can break down.*
>
> ***Command*** *some basic rules for successful communication.*

I don't know whether public relations has a patron saint. If not, a German monk by the name of Gutenberg, who lived in the fifteenth century, is as good a candidate as anyone. Later we'll discuss the more modern folk heroes, such as Ida Tarbell, George Creel, and Edward Bernays.

When Gutenberg figured out a way to mold a letter, ink its surface, and press it to paper, the real breakthrough in communications began. Quite literally, he changed the world. Until the idea of movable type took hold, communication was a slow and painful process. Travelers brought "news." Documents had to be laboriously handwritten and relatively few people could read them, for only a very few people knew how to read. With the advent of printed words, a whole new world was open to anyone who could read. So people learned to read.

When William Tyndal, an English clergyman, translated the Bible into English, it made the basis of their faith accessible to Christians in their own language. If you could read, you were almost dragged to the church, where the whole community listened avidly. It is said that the great printed Bibles had to be chained to the pulpits so people couldn't take them home. Printed notices began to appear on walls. Pamphlets and "news sheets" were read in coffeehouses. People exchanged their hopes, aspirations, and dreams. In eighteenth-century America, Ben Franklin and Tom Payne began to write and print the words that would create a nation. In London, bankers scored the communications beat of the century when they flew carrier pigeons out of Waterloo with the news of the battle. It was the fulfillment of a gambler's dream—getting the results before the results were posted.

History is replete with communication stories as, time after time, "the word" has turned the course of events.[1] And through all our history, communication has been taking quantum jumps. It is exciting to speculate where we will go from the computer that stores libraries full of information and retrieves in an instant, and from the communications satellite that puts me at your ear in an instant, though you may be in the remotest corner of the world.

The Importance of Communication

It is impossible to exaggerate the importance of communication. Great events have taken place when it worked well; great tragedies have occurred when communications broke down. The religions of the world spread and were established through the communications process. There is hardly a business manager today who does not strive to improve communications between himself or herself and subordinates (in both directions). If management is to function properly, clear lines of communication must be established vertically between subordinate and superior, and laterally between departments of the enterprise.

A sales story, whether written or spoken, is a communication. The very

---

[1] Later in this book we will discuss the role of historians, novelists, and poets in shaping our attitudes and perceptions.

lifeblood of the marketplace depends on communication between buyer and seller. Great corporations wish to be "understood" by people. Indeed, as individuals, most of us wish to avoid being misunderstood. It is little wonder, then, that scientists, scholars, and businesspeople have devoted great effort to understanding the process of communication. To increase understanding and to minimize misunderstanding many investigations have analyzed the process to see how it works. We in public relations must do the same. For if we do not understand how ideas "get across" to people, we are talking in an empty hall. Our audience is silent and invisible. *We* are silent and invisible.

The Process of Communication

When you communicate with someone, and someone in turn communicates with you, this is what happens: You have determined to have a little talk with your classmate Joe regarding his habit of borrowing your notes and forgetting to return them. You've been thinking about speaking to Joe for some time now, and you have carefully considered what you are going to say to him. After all, you don't want to hurt his feelings and lose a friend. On the other hand, you do want to get your message across. You want to make him understand that although you are glad to help him all you can, his failure to get your notes back to you is causing you some inconvenience and extra work. This whole thing is slightly embarrassing to you, and you've probably spent some time going over in your mind the words you are going to use in your message to Joe.

The *means* you will use in getting your message across to him may also have occurred to you as an important factor to consider. You might write him a note; you might call him on the phone; you could stop him in the hall after class. You could even have a mutual friend intercede and carry the message for you. You decide to put your thoughts in a note, and the next day Joe gets your message. He sees what you are talking about right away and appreciates the friendly way you have expressed yourself. The next day, having framed his own reply very carefully (he doesn't want to lose a friend, either), he tells you how sorry he is to have inconvenienced you. The chain has been completed. A successful communication has taken place.

Communications Breakdown

The story of Joe had a happy ending, but it does not always happen that way. Sometimes communications break down. In the case of Joe, several things might have happened. You might have spent so much time working on your message that it got complicated and involved. Joe could not understand what you were talking about. While reading your letter, he may have received an important phone call, put the letter down, and forgotten all about it.

We refer to any interference with the communications process as *noise.* It is as though you were listening to a radio broadcast: Suddenly the set begins

FIGURE 2-1   **Brevity, clarity, and frankness are qualities much to be desired when writing a news release.**

```
FROM:   JOS. SCHLITZ BREWING COMPANY
        235 West Galena Street
        Milwaukee, Wisconsin 53212
        Contact:  John A. Rourke
        Vice President -- Public Relations
        Telephone:  (414) 224-5028
             Home:  (414) 271-4565



                                    FOR IMMEDIATE RELEASE


        MILWAUKEE, Jan. 28 -- In response to an inquiry from

the New York Stock Exchange, a Jos. Schlitz Brewing Company

spokesman said:  "We have no explanation for the recent activity

in the company's stock."



                        - 0 -
```

Credit: Jos. Schlitz Brewing Company.

to crackle with static, and you are unable to hear the program. When you were deciding just how to word your letter in the best way, communicators would say you were *encoding* it. When Joe received your message and extracted the meaning from it, we say he was *decoding* it. Both sender and receiver have to encode and decode properly for successful communications.

You expect a reply to your message to Joe. You hoped his reaction would be pleasant and agreeable, as it was. This is what your communication effort was all about. This reaction or *feedback* is very important; it is often how we measure our success or failure in getting across. People sometimes communicate silently through gestures or facial expressions. The movement of a hand, the tilting of an eyebrow, can often speak volumes. This is called *body language* because our bodies do the talking for us. Sometimes our bodies express our feelings without our realizing it. Suppose, instead of writing Joe a letter, you had confronted him in the hall after class. And suppose, as you began to talk, he had folded his arms across his chest and regarded you with a cold, steady gaze. He would have been telling you something, wouldn't he?

Some people are blessed with a built-in antenna that is sensitive to even the slightest changes in people's attitudes and feelings. We call this sensitivity *empathy.* It is a wonderfully helpful ability for the public relations person to have. He or she knows how the wind is blowing even when it is only a gentle whisper on the cheek. Lacking it, we can charge about with one foot in our mouths, trampling feelings right and left.

Of course, it is possible for someone's reaction to our message to be somewhat different from the response fed back to us. Joe might have felt hurt and resentful that it was necessary for you to write him about the notes. But he kept his feelings to himself and presented you with a good "face." This is another reason why that "sixth sense" of empathy is so important in public relations. We must be sure we are reading the right message from our public.

The Medium and the Public

The medium you choose to transmit your message and the people you wish to receive it are tied very closely. Let us consider them together.

The *mediums* as we understand them in public relations are far broader than the familiar advertising media: radio, newspapers, TV, magazines, and outdoor posters. We use these mediums all the time. But we also use a wide range of other devices, such as annual reports, bulletin board announcements, songs, and newsletters. In short, we choose the means of carrying our message that will reach our public most effectively. In marketing terms, the public relations person's public closely resembles a *market segment*—a specifically defined group of people to whom a sales story can be addressed most profitably. Although in public relations we sometimes want to take to "everyone," more often than not our message is targeted to well-defined groups: the faculty, stockholders, members of ERA, members of a union local. We consider these our public and choose or devise the way of reaching them that is most effective and economical.

In considering publics, the public relations person must always keep in mind the phenomenon of the *thought leader*. These are persons of authority or reputation or demonstrated wisdom who have gained the respect of others. We sometimes seek their advice, and we listen carefully to what they have to say. We are influenced by their opinions.

Surely, these people are very important to us. For in winning them to our side, we may be winning dozens or hundreds of others. So we go to some trouble to identify them or pay attention when they identify themselves. Professional people such as doctors, teachers, and ministers are often thought leaders. So are experts and people of great accomplishment in the arts, sports, and business. Even different *types* of people can lead the crowd. Elaine's, a popular restaurant for literary people in New York, knew exactly the kind of clientele it wanted and went out of its way to attract the people other people like to be seen with. A "sporting" restaurant and bar will often pick up the tab for a popular ball player—if he just shows up regularly.

How to Get across Successfully

If you cannot encode your public relations message so that it is easily understood by the public at which it is aimed, you are lost before you start. If your message leaves your audience confused, resentful, or bored, you might as well have stayed in bed that morning. A great many professionals other than public relations professionals have been concerned for years with this business of "getting across" to readers or listeners. We have worked hard at it because the stakes are high.

News editors, book editors, advertising copywriters, direct mail experts—all these have learned the value of being understandable and how to achieve it.

Here is some of our hard-won experience:

1. *Keep it simple.* This is easy to say, but hard to do. People seem to *want* to say it the hard way. Given the choice between being direct and plain or verbose and obscure, they choose the latter every time. A teacher of mine once told me that everything of importance that ever had been said, had been said simply:

    > *God is love.*
    > *Win this one for the Gipper.*
    > *Layfayette we are here.*
    > *I love you.*
    > *He can run but he can't hide.* [2]

    Note that in these quotations, aside from proper names, only five words have more than *four* letters. That this kind of simplicity pays off is attested

[2] Joe Louis before the Billy Conn fight, Polo Grounds, New York, June 19, 1946. Conn was ahead on points till the eighth round, when he made the mistake of trying to mix it with Joe.

FIGURE 2-2   **In this release, the public relations person for the TPA tour seeks to generate interest with a story of the "young tigers" on the tour—an approach likely to catch the interest of an editor or sports columnist.**

Tournament Players Association
Sawgrass · Ponte Vedra, Florida 32082 · 904-285-3700

RELEASE: Immediately   January 15, 1982 (3-82)

BOBBY CLAMPETT TALKS ABOUT HIS GAME
AND THE GAMES OF HIS PALS ON THE TPA TOUR

When Bobby Clampett officially became a member of the TPA TOUR in the late summer of 1980, those in the know knew he would be something special.

He could play this game of golf; there was no question about that. Even at the tender age of 20 years and five months when he earned his TOUR card, he exhibited the skills of a veteran.

He is a prominent member of the new breed, the young fearless players who are expected to form the heart of the TOUR in the not too distant future. You know the names already, John Cook, Mark O'Meara, Gary Hallberg, Fred Couples.

They pal around together and, at times, you almost can imagine that they are plotting their strategy to take over the headlines of the TOUR.

A year ago, Clampett won $184,710 to finish 14th on the money list. He did not taste victory, but twice he lost in playoffs. The first was to Cook in the Bing Crosby National Pro-Amateur and the other was to Hale Irwin in the Buick Open.

The 24-year old Cook earned $127,608, a lot of that coming in the rain-shortened Crosby. O'Meara was named the rookie-of-the-year, even though the long-hitting Couples nosed past him on the money list in the year's final event.

"I'm very happy with the results I had in 1981," Clampett said as the new year dawned. "I've put a lot of effort into golf for many years. It hasn't come easily but it basically means being dedicated to my job.

"I spend a lot of time at it, but the key is knowing what you need to work on," he continued. "Anyone can hit balls for five hours, but you need to know at all times what type of practice you need and regulate your schedule accordingly.

(more)
The leading money-winner on the TPA TOUR is CHARITY

Credit: Sawgrass—An Arvida Resort Community.

FIGURE 2-3 This is a nice example of a well-designed release form. Though probably as strapped for dollars as any other public enterprise of this kind, this organization has been wise enough to retain a good graphic artist to design the release form. The "thank you" in the lower righthand corner is a good touch. The lesson to be learned here is that you need not be a big corporation to have a good-looking release form.

FOR IMMEDIATE RELEASE

**Alexander Brest Planetarium
1025 Gulf Life Drive
Jacksonville, Fla. 32207
Contact: Philip Groce, 904-396-7062**

December 16, 1981

"STELLAR HEAT"
New Cosmic Concert at Brest Planetarium

Starting January 1st, the Alexander Brest Planetarium presents "STELLAR HEAT".

This is a hot new cosmic concert featuring the music of FOREIGNER, BILLY SQUIRE,

GENESIS and FLEETWOOD MAC performing to LASER's, stars and hundreds of special

effects.

Showtimes are 9 p.m., 10 p.m. and 11 p.m. every Friday and Saturday in January.

Admission is just $2.50 for adults and $1.50 for children under 12 years.

******************FOR INSTANT PROGRAM INFORMATION CALL 398-STAR (7827)****************

All proceeds go to the support of the Jacksonville Museum of Arts and Sciences.

thank you

Credit: Alexander Brest Planetarium.

to by an expert in direct mail messages: "For every 100 words you write, make sure that 75% of them are words of five letters or less." There's no doubt in this authority's mind—*plain talk sells.*[3]

2. *Keep it short.* Or rather, say or write no more than you need to make your point. Knowing when to sit down and shut up takes a lot of practice and discipline. At Gettysburg, President Lincoln had a few well-chosen words to say. He said them so briefly the photographer never got a chance to set up his camera. And he said them so well the world will never forget them. The featured orator at the dedication of the military cemetery at Gettysburg was actually Senator Everett of Massachusetts. You remember Senator Everett's speech, don't you?

3. *Avoid gobbledygook.* Whoever invented that word was a genius. Doctors, lawyers, politicians, even teachers are often guilty of using "gobbledygook." Frequently, it takes the form of trade talk or "standard" phrases. Recently I received a letter from a school administrator that began, "Referring to the above referenced matter. . . ." I don't know what the rest of it said. I wadded the memo into a ball and shot it at the wastebasket. And what about football coaches who tell you how well they "defensed" the opposition?

4. *Stay in your audience's ball park.* If you are going to talk about the fine points of archeology, it is well to have an audience of archeologists. Otherwise, you may find your listener's eyes beginning to glaze over. Be careful of the age trap, too. For an eighteen-year-old, something that happened in the 1950s is ancient history. Most of your publics, you will find, have definite limits to their understanding. They are fenced in by their experience and learning.

5. *Tell it like it is.* Like Caesar's wife, a public relations person must be above suspicion. Your credibility is your most precious asset. You will not often get a second chance to lead a newspaper editor down the garden path. The *source* plays an important part here. Good public relations people do not conceal the truth—they reveal it in the most favorable light for their clients.

6. *Make sure the equipment works.* Obvious? Perhaps, but equipment failure has sent many a public relations person screaming into the night. Test all equipment, especially electronic equipment. Know where the light switches are and how they work. Tape wires down so a vice-president cannot trip over them. Be sure the pictures for the projector are in order. Do not leave your notes in the hotel room.

I once saw a representative of a newspaper publisher's group get in a terrible mess. He was describing newspaper ads, and the illustration flashed on the screen upside down and out of order. In desperation, the speaker ordered the projector turned off, declaring that he would describe each of the remaining ads "from memory." He did, too. It was a magnificent job, and when he finished we gave him a standing ovation. Later, I mentioned this great performance to a friend of mine, and he said, "Oh yes, the projector breaks down like that *every* night. And he *always* gets a standing ovation!"

[3]Maxwell C. Ross, *Advertising Age,* November 11, 1974.

FIGURE 2-4   **Compare this release with the one on p. 93. The opening of the new Armstrong office in Jacksonville is legitimate news. But the last paragraph, though plugging the company, also rates, under these circumstances, as legitimate information for those who might not be familiar with Armstrong's business. Thus, the whole release got printed.**

CORPORATE INFORMATION ARMSTRONG WORLD INDUSTRIES INC P O BOX 3001 LANCASTER PA 17604 TELEPHONE 717/397-0611

Armstrong

FOR RELEASE   ON RECEIPT   February 3, 1982

Armstrong World Industries, Inc. has announced plans to open a new Floor Division District Office in Jacksonville "to better serve flooring consumers in the state of Florida."

This office will be situated at Deerwood Center, Executive Center 3-- Suite 220, 7948 Baymeadows Way, Jacksonville 32216. The phone number will be 904/739-1395. The office will begin activities effective February 15.

Armstrong, with headquarters at Lancaster, Pa., manufactures and markets a comprehensive range of interior furnishings, including floor coverings (resilient flooring and carpets), ceiling systems, and furniture; and a variety of industrial specialty products for the building, automotive, textile, and other markets.

* * * * * * * *

Credit: Armstrong World Industries, Inc.

FIGURE 2-5   As a public relations writer you will often use, or create yourself, the "special ingredient" promotional device. Note how the writer has kept us on the hook about ESP until the last paragraph. You have seen this device used lots of times before. Crest toothpaste has "Fluoristan," most barbecue sauces are made with a "secret family recipe," and Exxon once had a "tiger" you could put in your tank.

CITYCENTER News

315 North Julia Street, Post Office Box 958, Jacksonville, Florida 32201

Release: Florida Times Union   *City:* Jacksonville

Re: New Program   *Source:* Mary Shugart

Business   Director of Public Relations

Jacksonville, Florida – It's official. The Holiday Inn CityCenter now has E.S.P.* Mr. James St. John, General Manager, says this special E.S.P. program is a real savings for companies with travel expenditures that are eating up profit. "Unless you are reviewing actual figures, it's hard to believe how exorbitant travel costs are. Our E.S.P.* program will help cut the cost of hotel accommodations as much as 30%." said Mr. St. John.

The Holiday Inn CityCenter is offering full American breakfast buffet in the Palm Beach Cafe, a cocktail in the Big Apple Lounge, local telephone calls, newspapers, and free valet parking---all free of charge. Plus, the Holiday Inn CityCenter is accessibly located in the heart of downtown Jacksonville in the business district.

The guests, Extra Special People*, are offered this program Monday through]Friday only. For more information, call Carolyn (904) 356-6000, or 800-874-8327 anywhere in the USA except Florida. Call today and increase your 1982 profit.

A Holiday Inn like none you've ever seen.

Credit: Holiday Inns.

FIGURE 2-6   **This is an example of just about the most basic "news release" you can find.**

February 4, 1982

Please print the following at your earliest convenience:

Kent Schmidt & Associates, Inc., an ERA member broker
has announced the addition of two broker-salesmen to its
sales staff. Phyllis Isham and Marcia Morales are welcomed.

Thank you.

Sincerely,

Frankie Shelley
Chairman
ERA Public Relations Committee

FS:jg

KENT SCHMIDT & ASSOCIATES, INC.
9850-7 San Jose Blvd.
Jacksonville, Florida 32217   904-268-7576

Each office independently owned and operated.

Credit: Kent Schmidt & Associates, Inc.

The Flesch Scale

There is a mechanical scale with which you can measure the readability of copy. It was invented by Rudolph Flesch.[4] Take the average number of affixes per 100 words (*delight*ed are affixes), subtract the average number of personal references per 100 words (such as the New York Yankees), and divide by 5. Then add the number of words per sentence. Easy is anything under 29. Most textbook and popular magazine editors use this scale and take pains to keep their readability at the level of their target audience.

Here is the opening paragraph of a direct mail letter selling steak knives to a mailing list of thousands.

> *Two years ago, I wrote a letter telling the story of how on a trip to Japan I was invited to a Japanese businessman's house and saw something that made my eyes pop! It was a new-fangled kind of knife.*

Note the number of two- and three-letter words. Notice the absence of prefixes and suffixes.

Now read this excerpt from a university report. It is addressed to educators.

> *For the purpose of this study, higher education encompasses post-secondary education in an accredited institution designed to provide educational opportunities which lead to a bachelor's, master's or doctoral degree.*

This short paragraph contains eight words of three or more syllables.

In the next chapter, we will take a closer look at the target audiences, or "publics" as we call them here.

SUMMARY

With the advent of printing, a new era in communications was born. Its importance cannot be exaggerated. Communications is a process that sometimes breaks down. It can be hindered by noise (any kind of interference). Communication is encoded by the sender and decoded by the receiver. Feedback tells you how well your message has been understood. Body language enables us to communicate nonverbally, through movements and gestures. Empathy is a kind of awareness or sensitivity to what goes on around us.

[4]Rudolph Flesch, *The Art of Plain Talk* (New York: Harper & Row, 1946), p. 65.

Communications are transferred by means of mediums—mail, radio, newspapers, and so on. Thought leaders are those whose word is accepted and followed. In public relations, we hope to communicate well with thought leaders and have them accept our messages. "Getting across" often depends on simplicity and brevity.

KEY TERMS

Gutenberg

Communication breakdown

Noise

Encoding

Decoding

Feedback

Body language

Empathy

Mediums

Thought leaders

Gobbledygook

Flesch scale

THE WAY IT HAPPENED:
"WITH A 12-STRING GUITAR"

How do you communicate with people who barely communicate with themselves? We had received a grant under the old Manpower Development Training Act to set up auto mechanic and body repair classes for the "disadvantaged"—unemployables, many illiterate.

How do you get the word to them that here's a shot at making something of yourself and earning a decent living? Not through the usual media, that's a cinch. Besides, most of these people have gotten tired of listening to promises. They don't believe anybody.

I guess we went far out in our communications process, but it worked. One of the members of our faculty played a 12-string guitar. That's a lot of guitar, in case you've never heard one. This teacher, who stood about six feet five, sounded like a combination of John Lee Hooker and B. B. King.

We went around to all the little country churches in the county and asked for a few minutes of their time. The pastors were all agreeable when we told them what we were up to. My friend with the 12-string guitar got up and sang some slow blues, a work song from the track-laying days, and a couple of songs of hope. Then he told the congregation how he could help their children overcome their hopelessness and discouragement if they would send them to him. He gave them a phone number and address. We filled our classrooms.

J. Miller
Tifton, Georgia

A PERSONAL PROJECT

Putting a message into a form that will be readily understood is not easy for everyone. Just ask your teacher to show you some of the memos he or she receives as part of the normal functioning of your college.

You can find examples of badly expressed thoughts almost everywhere: books, newspapers, even textbooks.

Select one of these passages and see if you can rewrite it in more understandable English.

But be careful: There is another side to this coin. Someone once revised Lincoln's Gettysburg Address as a modern newspaper editor might have handled it: "Four score and twenty years ago our forefathers. . . ." *Editor:* For clarity say, "Sixty years ago our relatives. . . ."

READING TO BROADEN UNDERSTANDING

BERLO, DAVID K.   *The Process of Communication: An Introduction to Theory and Practice* (San Francisco: Rinehart Press, 1960), P 90, B42. High-level stuff as compared to Diekman (see below). But look at Chapter Seven, "The Meaning of Meaning." See p. 177, the "But I Told Him" effect. The author says: "Communication breaks down because the source believes that meanings are in words, rather than in people."

DIEKMAN, JOHN R.   *Get Your Message Across: How to Improve Communication* (Englewood Cliffs, N.J.: Prentice-Hall, 1979), P 90, D 5. A practical and useful book. You can read the whole thing in an hour, and should. His chapter on "how to make it happen" suggests seven "means" for more effective communication.

HOVLAND, CARL I., IRVING L. JANIS, AND HAROLD H. KELLEY   *Communication and Persuasion: Psychological Studies of Opinion Change* (New Haven, Conn.: Yale University Press, 1953), P 90, H 69. Report of probably the first extensive research study of ". . . the experimental modification of attitudes and opinions ... will open your eyes." The experiments revealed what *kind* of people (personalities) are most and least receptive to attitude-changing communication.

MONTAGU, ASHLEY, AND FLOYD MATSON. *The Human Connection* (New York: McGraw-Hill, 1979), P 90, M 545. A more sophisticated look at communication. How studies in the fields of sociology, anthropology, psychology, biology, and philosophy have contributed to the "new wave" in communications.

SCHRAMM, WILBUR. *Men, Messages and Media: A Look at Human Communication* (New York: Harper & Row, 1973), P 90, S 375. A good overview of the subject. See particularly Chapter Six, "The Pathways of Communication: Who Talks to Whom." The author points out that a great deal of our time is spent talking to *ourselves*.

3

OUR PUBLICS—AND WHAT MAKES THEM TICK

OVERVIEW AND GOALS

We will look now at the people to whom we direct our messages. We will break these people down into categories. We will then observe some of the forces that cause these "publics" of ours to behave in the way they do. When you have completed this chapter, you should be able to

> ***Differentiate*** *the various types of "publics."*
>
> ***Understand*** *some of the important factors that shape human behavior.*
>
> ***Appreciate*** *the role of the needs-motivation concept.*
>
> ***Understand*** *what is behind learning theory.*

The "publics" toward which we direct our public relations messages can be of almost infinite variety. Sometimes we are trying to reach a wide range of people, such as the readers of daily newspapers in cities of over 500,000 population; often our target is small and closely defined, such as the members of the school board of Baton Rouge, Louisiana. But whether large or small, loosely or tightly defined, the character of that public is going to determine what we say, how we say it, and where we say it.

The Variety of Publics

The more common groups to whom we appeal in business can be divided into *inside* and *outside* publics. The former are the ones we are associated with in our daily business. The latter are those who make up the "environment" in which we operate. More specifically, we can identify:

1. *Employees.* These are certainly "part of the family," and every company is acutely conscious of its relationship with its employees. Most large companies have an employee relations director whose primary concerns are the morale, attitudes, and perceptions of those who work for the company. Ever since the days of such management innovators as Henri Fayot and Mary Parker Follet, industry has been aware of the importance of its relationships with its workers. The Japanese, West Germans, and Scandinavians are currently showing the world what that relationship can mean in terms of productivity.

   This employee public can be divided into a number of other publics: top management, middle management, front-line management, and the general work force. Each differs somewhat in direction from the other. Each requires a somewhat different approach if communication is to be successful.

2. *Stockholders.* Stockholders are people who have reached down into their pockets and demonstrated a "rooting interest" in a company. Their interest may be very practical. But the more friends we have, and the closer the friendship, the better off we are. The annual report, which we will examine in detail later, is a major way of reaching stockholders. It is often a major part of the work of many industrial public relations departments.

3. *Suppliers.* The relationship between industrial buyers and sellers and consumer buyers and sellers is quite different. Industrial buyers and sellers operate on a professional level. As vital as customers are to a company, suppliers are literally its life blood. A supplier whose prices, quality standards, and delivery schedules are not dependable can destroy a company. Dependability and a mutual respect based on a solid and lasting relationship is a highly desired state. Proper public relations can help achieve and maintain a mutually beneficial situation.

4. *The Neighbors.* All of us want to be "good neighbors"—and to be recognized as such. We keep the dandelions out of our lawns and turn the TV down after 11 P.M. When tragedy occurs, we are there with help and sympathy. When good works need to be done, we often attempt to do them. It is the same with any business institution, from the biggest plant in town to the used car dealer down the street. We want our reputation with the "home folks" to be the very best. Many companies have a tremendous social and financial stake in the community. Hundreds of local families may depend on company paychecks. Company taxes may be an important part of the city's revenue. The relationship between company and community is often a fragile one. Public relations not only helps to keep peace in the family, it helps create a spirit of friendly neighborliness.

FIGURE 3-1   This institutional ad from Gannett newspapers is interesting because of the theme: the "freedom of expression" allowed—and presumably encouraged—in its family of newspapers. Note particularly the next to last paragraph, where it states that "freedom rings . . . in news coverage, in editorial opinions, in community service. . . ." Note too that the source of this ad is Corporate Communications.

© 1982 Gannett

DIFFERENT VOICES MICHIGAN STYLE

When Gov. William G. Milliken announced withdrawal of his support for 1982 property tax relief, the reaction of Michigan residents was sharply divided. And so were the editorial opinions of the Gannett newspapers in that state.

To the Port Huron Times Herald, the action taken by the governor had "unexpectedly but decisively made him completely expendable here." It accused Milliken of "closing his eyes to reality" and to the "groundswell of near rebellion against property taxes" that had already struck California and Massachusetts.

To the Battle Creek Enquirer and News, however, Milliken "made the right decision in withdrawing his proposal." The Enquirer and News felt that broader public understanding of the state's problems should precede any tax reform measure.

To the Lansing State Journal, which came down between these poles, the move was merely a "risky political gamble," but one that had been made "inevitable by the continuing decline in the state's economy."

Those different points of view were arrived at individually by publishers and editors of those newspapers exercising their independent professional judgment and local understanding built on decades of newspapering experience in the state.

Such diversity is not unusual for Gannett member newspapers. As a matter of principle, every Gannett voice is free to express its own opinions, serve its own community and meet its professional obligations as its local managers see fit.

That freedom rings throughout Gannett, from Nashville to Oakland, from St. Cloud to St. Thomas, from Olympia to Burlington. It rings in news coverage, in editorial opinions, in community service, as each member serves its own audience in its own way.

For more information about Gannett, write: Gannett Co., Inc.; Corporate Communications, Lincoln Tower; Rochester, N.Y. 14604, or call (716) 546-8600.

GANNETT
A WORLD OF DIFFERENT VOICES
WHERE FREEDOM SPEAKS

91

Credit: Gannett Company, Inc.

FIGURE 3-2   The number of publications you never see can be numbered in the hundreds. Yet there is a magazine (sometimes several) for every trade, hobby, sport, industry, or avocation you can think of. In fact, there are many you would not think of. If you are a beekeeper, or a water skier, or a raiser of Poland China hogs, there is a magazine for you. Although the editorial matter in these publications might not interest you, the articles are of intense interest to the magazine's clientele. *Oral Surgery* is just such a magazine. Its contents are fascinating, if you are a dentist. In public relations we have to remember that there are such publications and that articles about our clients and their products can be of real interest to them.

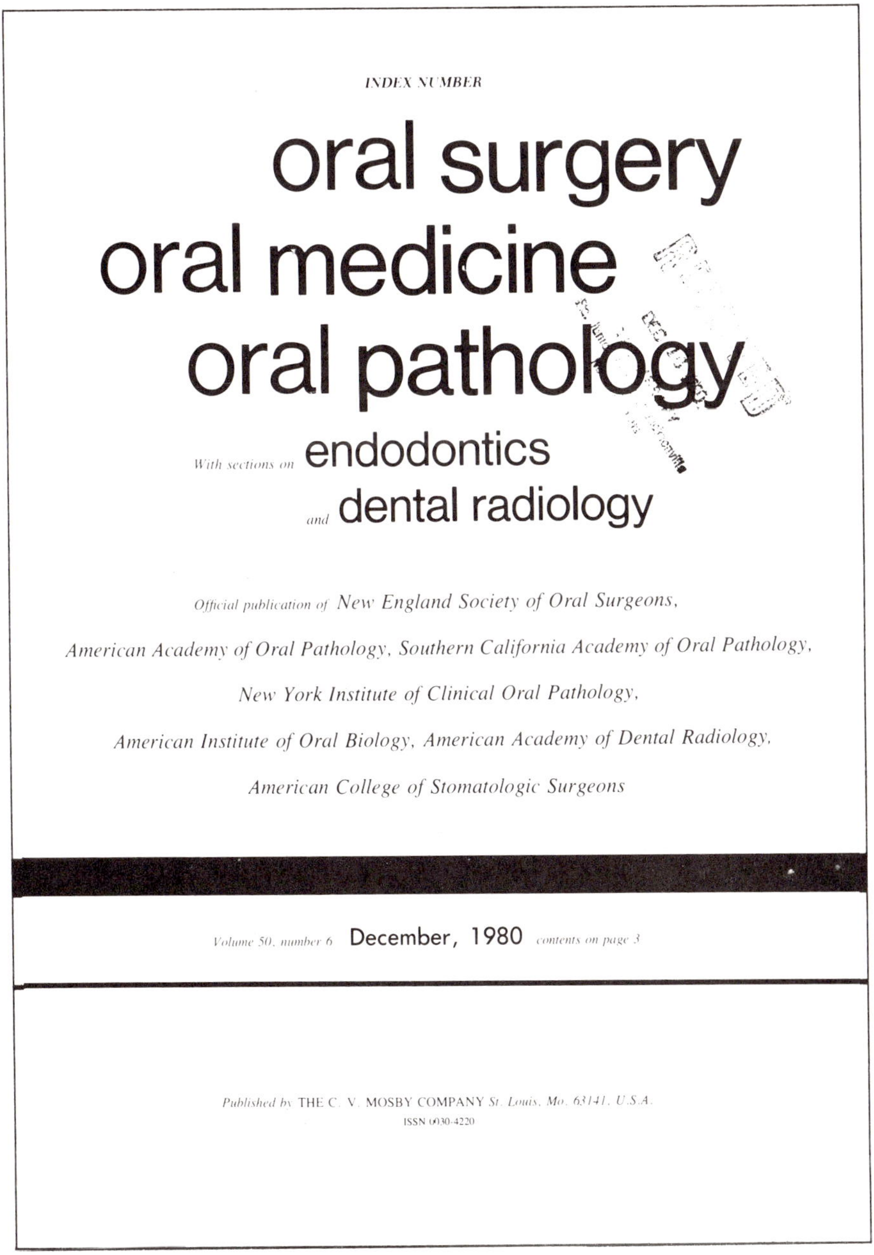

INDEX NUMBER

oral surgery
oral medicine
oral pathology

With sections on endodontics
and dental radiology

Official publication of New England Society of Oral Surgeons,

American Academy of Oral Pathology, Southern California Academy of Oral Pathology,

New York Institute of Clinical Oral Pathology,

American Institute of Oral Biology, American Academy of Dental Radiology,

American College of Stomatologic Surgeons

Volume 50, number 6 December, 1980 *contents on page 3*

Published by THE C. V. MOSBY COMPANY St. Louis, Mo. 63141, U.S.A.
ISSN 0030-4220

Credit: Oral Surgery, 50, 6 (December 1980).

5. *The Middlemen.* The people who handle the retail and wholesale distribution of a company's products are especially important to any company. The cooperation of the middleman is essential to successful sales. Most companies have spent years and a great deal of money in building the special relationship they have with wholesalers and retailers. If you go to any trade show or convention, you will see company representatives renewing and cementing old friendships, often with a lavish entertainment hand. Many manufacturers have built their close relationships with their middlemen over several generations.

6. *Customers.* Here we are talking not about the general public, but about a company's most precious possession—its "loyal users." Marketing today is a constant war of attention. Through price changes, product improvement, and promotions, manufacturers seek to wean customers away from competitors. It is often the job of public relations to help keep customers loyal and happy. Sometimes this is done through the subtle building of an image that engenders a fierce and stubborn loyalty. Try telling your friend that "his" beer is an inferior brand. I'll bet you'll find him defending his choice to the death.

Although many retail stores build a warm, friendly image by going out of their way to see that "the customer is always right," certain exclusive shops do just the opposite. They do not want to deal with anyone who does not quite meet their standards of "class" and income.[1]

Why Publics Behave the Way They Do

For all of us in public relations, life would be a lot easier if people would behave in simple, predictable ways. But they do not. Often their behavior is unexpected; frequently their reactions to our messages are quite unpredictable. So for the past 30 years or so, we have been trying to gain a better understanding of why people act the way they do. What makes them tick? Why was it that Joe folded his arms across his chest and stared at you coldly when you began to talk to him about your notes? Was it fear, anger, embarrassment, chagrin? What was it *inside* him that made him act the way he did instead of some other way?

It is extremely important for all of us in every form of communication to understand something about human behavior. We need to know not only *how* people react to certain messages, but *why* they react that way. It is important to know not only *who* hears us (our publics), but *what* they hear us saying (the way they interpret our messages). Marketers have long recognized that within the narrowest market segment there is often a wide variety of perceptions of the message they are trying to get across. The car that is

---

[1]A young New York actress was once treated badly by an exclusive leather goods shop. She decided on revenge. With different clothes and makeup, and with an upper-class English accent, she returned to the store. The manager and all the help fawned over her. The actress kept them leaping about for an hour, trying to please her. She finally stalked from the shop majestically, informing them that, in her opinion, they might better return their merchandise to the Thrift Shop, where they seemed to have obtained it.

a status symbol to one person may be seen as a convenient way of getting to the office by someone else.

We have a long way to go in understanding human behavior and personality. However, reseachers in the behavioral sciences have discovered some interesting facts that are very helpful to us in the public relations field. Anthropologists, sociologists, and psychologists are all concerned with various aspects of human behavior. Let us look briefly at some of the ways they can help us understand the various publics to which we must appeal.

The Way We Live

Anthropologists are interested in the way people live—how they behave in relation to one another, their customs, beliefs, myths, and traditions. Together, these characteristics of the way we live are known as our *culture.*

One of the interesting things about the United States is that, because of the many different immigrant groups, American culture is made up of a number of subcultures. In some places, these subcultures are quite evident: Scandinavians in Minnesota, Chinese and Japanese in San Francisco, Spanish-speaking people in Miami, and Germans in St. Louis. In other cases, within single large cities, for example, several subcultures may exist side by side. The point the public relations person has to keep in mind is that the cultural background of each one of these groups still plays an important role in its beliefs, attitudes, and life styles. If we violate a group's cultural standards, we can get ourselves in trouble. This is particularly true when we are attempting to communicate with a public made up of a particular subculture.

If you are directing your efforts toward a Latin American group, it is to your advantage to have at least a speaking acquaintance with the Latin mind and the Latin life style. Japanese culture is so different that it poses even greater challenges for most Westerners. For years, English-dominated firms in Canada had difficulty in reaching the French-Canadian market: The language and culture gap was wide and deep.

Earlier, we spoke of public relations' role in changing perceptions. One of the public relations expert's problems is that the subculture's perception may already be quite different from what we assume it to be. Other cultures have perceptions of such things as wealth, youth, and time that differ widely from our own. Fortunately, there are ways to overcome the difficulties encountered in dealing with various cultures. In most large cities there are marketing research firms that specialize in dealing with major subcultural groups, such as the Spanish-speaking market. If such a firm is not available, then your message should be reviewed by a member of the subculture. If you are addressing a foreign-language group, for example, be sure what you have to say is written in the original by a person fluent in that language and is not simply a translation from the English. In all likelihood, the English translation will not ring true.

This holds for any aspect of culture. If your public is young people, you had better know what you are doing and saying. The generation culture gap is a wide one, as you may have noticed. A thorough understanding of any important factors that might affect how your public receives the intended message is essential.

Social Class

In America, we do not think of ourselves as being particularly class conscious. Indeed, class lines are not drawn nearly so sharply here as they are in certain European countries. Yet sociologists maintain that Americans can be subdivided into recognizable social classes on a number of criteria: age and social prominence of the family, wealth and accomplishments, profession or type of work, education, preference in food and clothing, reading and recreation.

According to social scientists, the upper-upper class and the lower-upper class are only 3 percent of the population. The upper-uppers might be characterized as those of wealth, accomplishment, and social position over at least three generations. The lower-uppers are those new to great wealth and social position. Upper-middle—about 10 percent of us—would be the professionals and top-level executives; lower middle would be white-collar workers—about 30 percent of the population. Upper-lowers are blue-collar workers (35 percent), and the remainder are those at the lowest level of employment or unemployment, those without education or skills.

It is important for public relations people to recognize these class distributions, for frequently we will be called upon to address distinct social groups. Researchers have shown that these groups are likely to have very distinct traditions of their own. Their life styles, attitudes, perceptions, values, and standards may differ quite widely from those of the class adjacent to them. Blue-collar workers, for example, are more likely to purchase heavy, massive furniture and accessories for their homes. They are also likely to take pride in the manner in which they care for and maintain their homes and farms.[2] Upper-class people, on the other hand, are likely to be less conservative in their home decorating. Interior furnishings are often chosen for "smartness" rather than durability. Another line of research has pointed out the great social gap that seems to exist between blue-collar and white-collar workers. Recognizable differences not only exist in the woman's role as wife and partner, but those differences are strongly felt. Crossing social class lines can often be like crossing the borders into a foreign country.[3]

Not only do life styles vary, but it has been demonstrated that this feeling

[2]James F. Engel, David T. Kollat, and Roger D. Blackwell, *Consumer Behavior* (New York: Holt, Rinehart and Winston, 1968), p. 42.

[3]Pierre Martineau, *Motivation in Advertising* (New York: McGraw-Hill, 1957).

of "social gap" between the classes has its roots in definite psychological differences. Martineau[4] has identified some of them: Middle-class people are oriented toward the future, whereas lower-class people are more likely to live for today. As a result, lower-class individuals tend to think in very short time spaces. Furthermore, middle-class people, partly because of being better educated, tend to be much more willing to take risks. Security is a major concern for members of the lower class.

All these factors must be considered by public relations people. To ignore them is risky, but knowledge of them can present great opportunities. In the presidential election campaign of 1980, the Republican party made great inroads in traditionally Democratic working-class areas. They did a brilliant job of capitalizing on the terrible sense of insecurity brought by high rates of unemployment.

The People around Us

Our friends, neighbors, and families have a great deal to do with the way we behave. Our attitudes and perceptions are often the attitudes and perceptions of our particular group. These *reference groups* have been defined as "a group with which an individual wants to be associated, and whose beliefs, attitudes, values, and behavior the person will seek to emulate." Since we in public relations are in the business of influencing beliefs, attitudes, values, and behavior, knowledge of these reference groups is important to us.

Reference groups have a strong influence over their members. To agree with the group in its beliefs and attitudes is one way for the individual to earn acceptance. The acceptance of group standards is known as *identification*. We identify with a certain group by behaving the way its members do. Going against the group opens one to the risk of rejection.

Opinion Leaders

Public relations people have learned that one way of overcoming resistance to changing attitudes or ideas is through the use of *opinion leaders* or *trendsetters*. You may have met some of them already—the person who seems to be into the latest style before anyone else, the person who introduces a new fad, hobby, or sport. These people, because they are leaders, can often guide a group in a new direction very quickly.

In public relations, we use these opinion leaders in a variety of ways. In the last chapter we noted the importance of thought leaders in communication. They are the first cousins of opinion leaders and can be regarded

[4]Martineau, *Motivation in Advertising.*

in much the same way. If I am exploiting a new style, I am going to see that it is first worn by just the right person. "Keeping up with the Joneses" seems to be a national obsession. So, in promoting a product or an idea, it seems logical to look for Mr. and Mrs. Jones.

How We Get "Turned On"

As a public relations person, I'm very much interested in getting you to be enthusiastic about something. I want people to be excited—and talk—about my political candidate, my new can opener, my wind surfer. As far as public relations people are concerned, indifference is the worst possible outcome. So it is important for us to understand what happens when people get "turned on"—when someone turns the key in our ignition and we become *motivated.*

We know a lot more about motivation today than we did just a generation ago. Psychologists have been able to identify our major needs, and they believe it is often the satisfaction of these needs that leads us to behave in certain ways. A pain in the stomach at noon indicates that we are hungry. We have a need for food. Our need motivates us to go down to the cafeteria to get a sandwich. But be careful; a person might also be motivated to eat by something other than hunger—the chance to break bread with an attractive companion, for example.

A prominent psychologist, Abraham Maslow,[5] has recognized that our needs fall into a hierarchy, or ranking. His "hierarchy of needs" is widely accepted by management, marketing, and communications people. From low to high, these needs must be satisfied in order according to Maslow. And, he says, the lower-order needs are more powerful motivations than the higher-order needs when they are unsatisfied. The basic needs Maslow identified are these:

1. *Physiological:* Food, shelter, bodily needs.
2. *Security:* Both physical and mental or emotional.
3. *Love, affection:* The need to feel people like us.
4. *Regard and respect:* The need to feel we are well regarded by others. We need to feel good about ourselves, too.
5. *Self-actualization:* Making it: accomplishing our own goals, putting our talents to work.

At first glance, these needs might be hard to match up with various kinds of behavior. But remember, most psychologists feel that *all* our behavior is motivated, geared to accomplishing some goal. Therefore, there has to be

---

[5]Abraham H. Maslow, *Motivation and Personality* (New York: Harper & Row, 1954), pp. 80–106.

FIGURE 3-3   In community relations, the company's participation in charitable activities offers many opportunities for building goodwill and image improvement. In this ad, United Way makes a nice gesture in thanking all those companies and their employees who have participated in fund-raising efforts. Notice that no one is omitted, from top corporate executives who have contributed their management skills to the "newest mailroom clerk who swallows his shyness and asks his fellow workers for a last-minute contribution." It is important to note, too, that this ad, produced as a service by the Advertising Council (an industry public service organization) is a public "thank you" that enhances the public relations value of the efforts made by American business.

THANKS FOR HELPING TO KEEP UNITED WAY IN BUSINESS.

Every year, United Way successfully continues to support local human service agencies in communities all across the United States.

A lot of the credit for this success goes to the dedicated efforts of people in business—to top corporate leaders who volunteer their organizational skills and financial expertise, to middle-management people who work lunch-hours and evenings to help organize local campaigns and collect money, to the newest mailroom clerk who swallows his shyness and asks his fellow workers for a last-minute contribution.

And by operating like any other modern, well-run business enterprise, United Way succeeds in delivering the maximum in human services for the dollars that are collected.

Thanks again for *your* help.

 A Public Service of This Newspaper & The Advertising Council

Thanks to you, it works. For all of us. **United Way**

A

Credit: United Way of America.

a need behind it. You are in this classroom because you were motivated to go to college. What motivated you? Perhaps it was the sense of inner security preparation for the future might give you. You might be trying to better your position in life so you will have the regard and respect of others. And certainly, once you have tasted an "A," you know the reward of the wonderful sense of inner satisfaction that comes from "making it on your own."

Similarly, in "selling" the public on our products, beliefs, and ideas, we first identify the need that may be satisfied by whatever it is we have to sell. Marketing people today seem to do this almost by second nature. In many cases, when your public relations efforts are directed toward a product, the need will be quite clear to you. Customers do not "need" a new and improved furniture polish. What they do need is the bundle of satisfactions that comes from the complimentary remarks of their friends (respect), and the knowledge that they are good homemakers (self-actualization).

The needs associated with products—whether they are clothes, cars, or a particular brand of beer—are not hard to identify. But what if you are the public relations director of a charitable or cultural organization? Can you reward your supporters by satisfying their needs? You certainly can. For "doing good" with support and money often carries with it a rich reward of love and respect—and self-love and self-respect. This is the source of that "feeling good about yourself" that happens when you put your check in the mail. As a public relations person you can never let your public lose sight of the reward that awaits them as they answer their needs.

How We Began

Public relations people are also in the business of teaching. All of us are constantly "learning" about things. We learn about a new style from a friend, from a store window, from an article in a fashion magazine. We learn about political candidates before we vote for them, we learn how lumber companies feel about conservation and how the PTA feels about busing. Sometimes this teaching aims at immediate results. We receive letters from organizations that ask us to act right now—by return mail—on this belief. Others teach their lessons steadily over a long period of time. Oil companies, for example, wish us to understand that they are very much concerned about both the environment and the energy crisis, and that they are working hard to do something about both. Since our success as public relations practitioners often depends on how well our publics learn their "lessons," we should be familiar with some of the theories dealing with how learning takes place.

1. *Stimulus-response theory* is most frequently associated with the Russian physiologist Pavlov. In his famous experiment, he caused a dog to salivate by presenting it with food in association with the sound of a buzzer. He found that after a while, the dog salivated as a result of the buzzer alone. An association between the food and the buzzer had been established.

Two important principles were derived from this experiment: (1) Repetition. The more often buzzer and food were associated, the quicker learning took place. (2) Contiguity. The closer buzzer and food came together, the quicker learning took place.

2. Operant, or *stimulus-response theory,* is usually associated with the psychologist, B.F. Skinner. This theory suggests that we learn primarily as a result of *trial* and *error.* A *need* motivates us to act in a certain way. We have a need to have people like us. We discover that if we are polite and kind and loving, people *do* like us; that if we are cold and unkind, people *don't* like us. The more often we find we make new friends by being kind and pleasant, the more it reinforces our learning that such behavior is the best way to act if we are to gain the affection we need. Skinner demonstrated that the more closely reinforcements followed behavior, the more quickly people learned. Horse players are said to be victims of reinforcement theory. They usually get a winner (reinforcement) just often enough to keep them betting—and losing.

One of the best-known experiments illustrating cognitive learning involved an ape in a cage, a bunch of bananas, and a box. The bananas were placed high in the cage just out of the ape's reach. The ape made a few tentative jumps at the bananas, missed, and sat down to consider the situation. After a moment, his eye lit on the box, which had also been placed in his cage. He stared at it for a long moment. Then light dawned. He ambled over to the box, picked it up, placed it under the fruit, and jumped from it—and got his bananas.

3. *Cognitive learning* theory can be illustrated by the work of Wolfgang Kohler. It is quite different from stimulus-response or operant behavior theory. Cognitive learning theory holds that we do not just react to certain stimuli or situations. We are capable of gaining understanding by perceiving the relationships between certain elements. We have goals or problems we want to solve. We thrash our way through to the achievement of our goals.

Learning Theory Applied to Public Relations

Those of us who practice public relations owe a great deal to those who have investigated the learning process. Some of what takes place in this process I am sure you recognize. Other aspects may not be so familiar. Below is a summary of some of the research findings and how they can be applied in public relations:

1. *Repetition.* In public relations, we cannot be satisfied with delivering our message once. Whenever possible, we deliver it again and again. But note: Though we may be delivering the same message an attempt must be made to state it in a number of different ways in order to maintain interest.

2. *Contiguity.* The farther we get from the event, the less effective our message is likely to be. The story about the college's experiments with off-campus classrooms and "twilight" class time should appear close to registration time.

3. *Reinforcement.* You will recall that in operant learning reinforcement takes

place when we are rewarded as a result of our actions. This is an important concept in the marketing of products and ideas. Today's marketer seeks to reward us by satisfying our needs. We seek to tell you not how good we are, but how much good we are going to do you by making you more successful, or happier, or more respected. Note almost any television commercial today. Whether for deodorant, coffee, or automobile tires, the user is always rewarded in the end.

4. *Sources.* Teachers, as you have discovered, vary greatly in quality. The better and more authoritative the source, the more likely the lesson is to be learned. This is why corporations will often employ a well-known or highly popular spokesperson to express their point of view. Thought leaders are generally highly regarded people.

5. *Mediums.* Teachers use a number of mediums in getting across their lessons—lectures, slide films, demonstrations, and so on. In public relations, the variety of mechanisms you use will affect your success rate. News stories, film, radio and television, and speeches are all ways of expressing your message and reaching your public.

Learning is absolutely essential to the public relations function. It is one of the pillars that supports the entire structure:

1. *A message is created and communicated.*

2. *A definite public receives our message.*

3. *A learning process takes place within that public.*

4. *The learning results in a pattern of behavior or thought on the part of that public.*

SUMMARY

Public relations addresses itself to many kinds of people called "publics." These include *employees, stockholders, suppliers, neighbors, middlemen,* and *customers.*

As members of the publics we all act differently and have different personalities. We call it *human behavior,* and it is important for the public relations person to understand what shapes this behavior: our *background;* our *social class, friends,* and *neighbors;* and our *psychological make-up.*

All of these factors result in *needs,* and having needs, we are *motivated* to fulfill those needs.

In addition, the public relations person who is trying to get across to his or her publics must understand how *learning* takes place—*operant* or *cognitive*—through *repetition, contiguity,* and *reinforcement.*

KEY TERMS

Culture	Maslow's hierarchy of needs
Social class	Stimulus-response theory
Life style	Repetition
Reference group	Contiguity
Identification	Reinforcement
Opinion leader	Operant learning theory
Trendsetter	Cognitive learning theory
Motivation	

THE WAY IT HAPPENED

I suppose most of your students are familiar with the fact that marketing principles as developed out of the needs of profit organizations are applicable to nonprofit organizations as well.

But when you remove the profit motive from an organization, don't you remove most of the "push"? Isn't it like trying to run a four-cylinder car on two cylinders? Fortunately, the answer seems to be "No, it's *not* like that—because there are a lot of potent motivators in addition to money."

My firm was asked to advise for an organizational ticket drive for a big annual athletic event. The club conducting the drive had many of the top marketing and sales executives in the city as members. How do you motivate highly paid executives like those to go out and peddle tickets?

We divided our salespeople into teams and named them for different colleges—Texas, Princeton, Syracuse, etc. Each week we had a sales report in a room decorated with college banners, and with a band playing college songs. We also had a cash bar. The winner each week was widely acclaimed and cheered. The final results we announced at a dinner at which all the brass were present, and the "top producer" was announced and cheered.

The "team" concept is very common in fund raising, of course. What is important for your students to remember, I think, is the motivational factor involved—*peer acceptance and recognition.* Performing in the presence of their peers and performing well drove these experienced sales executives to their utmost efforts.

> Jim Lansing
> Lansing Associates
> Del Monte, California

A PERSONAL PROJECT

One of the strongest problems in public relations is trying to change an attitude *when the person involved is afraid to let go of that attitude.* To them, their attitude represents security. Your suggested change frightens them.

How do you overcome this fear? One way is to demonstrate that the change is not quite so frightening or threatening as the person imagines. Try this: Select a number of your classmates who are devoted consumers of one particular soft drink. They prefer it above all others, and they would not dream of switching. To them, its superiority to similar drinks is obvious.

Ask them to take a taste test, blindfolded. Let them try their drink and two others. Ask them to identify theirs. I think you may be astonished at the results. I know your friends will be. If only one out of three can identify the favorite drink, maybe their rigid attitude is not as important as they thought it was.

READING TO BROADEN UNDERSTANDING

BERKMAN, HAROLD W., AND CHRISTOPHER C. GILSON. *Consumer Behavior* (Encino, Calif.: Dickenson, 1978), HF 5415.3, B 42. Chapters 4 to 8 are very complete on cultures, subcultures, groups, social class, the family.

BRITT, STEUART HENDERSON (ED.). *Consumer Behavior and the Behavioral Sciences* (New York: Wiley, 1968), HF 5415.3, B 7. Articles by leading people in the field. Read "Attitude Change," p. 450, and "Propaganda," p. 454.

DARROW, RICHARD W., DAN J. FORRESTAL, AND AUBREY O. COOKMAN. *The Dartnell Public Relations Handbook* (Chicago: The Dartnell Corporation, 1967), HD 59, D 28. See Part 2, "Internal Communications," p. 226, and Part 3, "External Public Relations—Stockholder, Community, Government," p. 348.

DICHTER, ERNEST. *Handbook of Consumer Motivations* (New York: McGraw-Hill, 1964), HF 5415.3, D 5. Subtitled "The Psychology of the World of Objects." This well-known book opened the eyes of a lot of marketers as to why we buy every "object," from toothpaste to automobiles. You'll enjoy reading it.

RUNYON, KENNETH E. *Consumer Behavior,* 2d ed. (Columbus, Ohio: Charles E. Merrill, 1980). A very clearly written text on the subject. See particularly the chapters on motivation (p. 192) and learning (p. 216). Highly recommended as a permanent part of your library.

4

THE PLACE
OF PUBLIC RELATIONS
IN THE MARKETING
ENVIRONMENT

OVERVIEW AND GOALS

In this chapter we will see where public relations fits into the marketing plan, which is the activities carried out in transferring goods and services from supplier to consumer. You will learn how marketing, and thus public relations, covers not only goods and services, but also nonprofit organizations, special interest groups, and individuals as well. In "selling" these, public relations plays a definite part. When you have completed this chapter, you should be able to

> **Define** what is meant by the marketing mix.
>
> **Understand** the role played by public relations in sales promotion.
>
> **Understand** the different aspects of promotion.
>
> **Carry out** the methods used to evaluate the impact of promotional public relations.

So far public relations has been defined as a process of communicating with people so that they learn and gain better perceptions and attitudes about us. Public relations seeks to get different kinds of people, different publics, to "feel better" about us. When we do establish good public relations with people, it is much easier to do business with them. They like us; they feel comfortable with us; they trust us; they have high regard for our company and our product or service. Therefore, it becomes much easier for us to gain and keep them as customers.

That seems simple enough, doesn't it? And for many people it is. Public relations has fulfilled its function when it gets a picture in the paper, causes a favorable article to appear, or gets a product free exposure to millions of people. The fact that these things have occurred may be enough. But not for you, as a student of business. There is a far more special place for public relations than pictures in the paper or free publicity. To understand the public relations function, you must understand exactly what this place is.

The Marketing Mix

After the marketing department has done its homework and discovered, via marketing research, that there is indeed a "need" for its product or service, after it has identified the target market at which it will direct its efforts, a *marketing plan* must be created. This marketing plan is the outline of the overall *strategy* for selling the product. It consists of the *marketing mix,* a choice of *tactics*[1] in five identifiable fields of marketing activity:[2] product features and quality, the manner of its distribution, how it is to be priced, the design and function of its packaging, and the way it is to be promoted.

Since many tactical decisions are possible within each of the five fields, you can see that there is a great variety of possible mixes. In fact, from industry to industry and product to product, there is hardly one tactical mix that is exactly the same as any other. For example, Coca-Cola spends millions in advertising each year (promotion), whereas King Edward Cigars, a best seller, spends next to nothing. Brooks Brothers carries an excellent line of men's wear (product), but it has only 12 stores (distributors) located across the country.

Promotion

The term *promotion* sometimes gives marketing students a little trouble. The trouble stems from the fact that the word has different meanings which are often used interchangeably. In order to avoid confusion, let us look at some of the ways the word is used.

---

[1]*Tactics* are "the adjustments required in a plan or strategy as the actual event unfolds." W.S.E. Crissy, William H. Cunningham, and Isabella C.M. Cunningham, *Selling* (Santa Barbara: Wiley, 1977), p. 485.

[2]*Strategic planning* "relies on developing a clear company mission, objectives and goals...." Philip Kotler, *Principles of Marketing* (Englewood Cliffs, N.J.: Prentice-Hall, 1983), p. 74.

1. Sales promotion. *This is usually regarded as any activity that encourages sales movement.*
2. Special promotions. *These are generally events—sales or fashion shows or "moonlight madness" nights.*
3. Promotional specialty items. *These are items such as calendars and pens.*
4. Point-of-purchase promotion. *These are the displays in selling areas; this kind of promotion is usually called POP.*
5. To "promote." *In the retail trade, promotion is often synonomous with merchandising: "We are planning to promote women's medium-priced dresses this spring."*
6. A promoter. *This use of the term usually refers to an entrepreneur who puts together an entertainment event of some kind—a boxing bout or rock concert, for example.*

Now let us see what the marketer means when he or she refers to "promotion" as part of the marketing mix.

In marketing texts, we find most authors agree that four activities fall within the marketer's concept of promotion:

1. Personal selling. *The traditional buyer-seller confrontation.*
2. Mass selling. *As in advertising, when the selling message is brought to hundreds and thousands of people at the same time.*
3. Sales promotion. *Any activity that encourages sales movement.*
4. Public relations. *The generating of product publicity.*

So we are part of the overall marketing plan. We are part of the tactics available to the marketing manager when he or she plans a campaign for the successful growth of the company's product or service. Product publicity is the most direct and immediate of these tactics. But it is not the only public relations activity contributing to sales success. Remember, we said very early that public relations involves getting people to "feel good about us." From used car dealer to multinational oil company, there is not an organization whose sales cannot flower under the warm sun of public goodwill.

How Wide and Deep Is Selling?

If we in public relations are a part of marketing, with a role to play in promotional or selling tactics, then perhaps we had better understand the dimensions of selling. They may be bigger than you think.

We all accept the fact that beer, razor blades, and breakfast foods are "sold" in the marketplace. But what about ballet companies and art museums? Politicians and Heisman Trophy candidates? Colleges and children's homes?

LIBRARY
FORSYTH TECHNICAL COMMUNITY COLLEGE
2100 SILAS CREEK PARKWAY
WINSTON-SALEM, NC 27103-5197

Beliefs and aspirations and dreams? All of them are sold. All of them are subject to promotion, and therefore subject to the tactics of public relations.[3]

Sales Promotion and Public Relations

Let us go back now to the important issue of *sales promotion.* It is here that public relations has its most intimate relationship with the marketing process.

Perhaps you have heard of the push-pull effect in sales promotion. This simply means that promotional devices and events are used both to *push* the products onto the dealer's shelves and to help them be *pulled* off by the consumer. Here are some examples of both actions at work. When the sales representative for a food manufacturer meets with the buyer for a food chain, she may say, in part: "Here is our schedule of advertising that will appear in your market during the next six months, and here are the promotions we plan to carry out at no cost to you. These promotional events are certain to increase store traffic for you and to increase the sales of our products. I would suggest your order be big enough to meet the anticipated increase in demand." That's the *pushing* effect—getting the products into the store. The *pulling* effect begins when the promotions take place and, as promised, increase store traffic and product sales.

Dealer Promotions and Supplier Promotions

Retailers recognize the push-pull effect of sales promotion; they also recognize that what they do on their own in the way of promotion can contribute to the movement of products off their shelves. Thus we have two distinct categories of sales promotion: those that originate with the retailer, and those that are supplier- or manufacturer-sponsored.

You have encountered these many times. It is almost impossible to walk through a store without noticing both of them. The manager of kitchenware in a department store decides to put on a "Beautiful Kitchen" promotion. He redecorates his department, gets the use of a store window for three days, and is given an advertising appropriation. Both the idea and the money for the promotion come from the store. A manufacturer of kitchen utensils doing business with the store may have said to the manager: "We have a very successful promotion we are going to make available to you next September 12th, 13th, and 14th. Mrs. Bixby-Jones is an expert at omelet making, and her demonstrations are always well-attended. We will supply you with displays, the eggs, Mrs. Bixby-Jones, and of course, a stock of free omelet pans. Your

---

[3]See Philip Kotler, *Marketing For Nonprofit Organizations,* (Englewood Cliffs, N.J.: Prentice-Hall, 1975), in which he points out that all the principles applicable to the promotion of profit-making goods and services are equally applicable to the "marketing" of a wide variety of nonprofit institutions.

FIGURE 4-1   **The answer to a publicist's prayer: The local press turns out to shoot a picture of the promotion in action.**

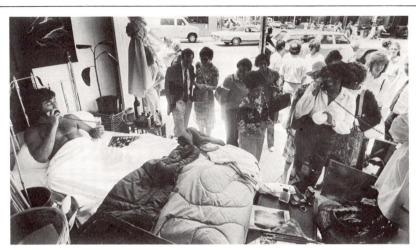

— John Pemberton/Staff

Jorge Berrio reclines in a Jacksonville store's window display during a promotion for a men's cologne.

Athlete gets bed (not bored) in window

By Don Meitin
Times-Union Staff Writer

A naked man on a street corner in downtown Jacksonville would normally draw the police.

But Jorge Berrio, who was not entirely naked, drew rave reviews from Jacksonville women yesterday as he reclined, hairy chest bared, in a window of a downtown department store.

"My God, he's absolooooootely gorgeous!" said Nan Brata when she spotted the supine Argentine.

Berrio is accustomed to being in the public eye, but he is usually seen from a distance, clothed in soccer togs. He is a professional soccer player with the Jacksonville Tea Men.

Yesterday he was in bed, reclining on a pillow under rumpled sheets in Furchgott's downtown store window and talking by telephone to the hundreds of women who admired him through the glass. It was a promotion for a men's cologne and duplicated

the scent's sexy magazine ad in which a man is having a phone conversation with a woman who obviously knows him *very* well.

Berrio was impossible not to notice. Lying in bed for all the lunch-hour passers-by to see was a handsome, 30-year-old man with sparkling teeth, a straight smile, curly hair and an accent that was an elegant pastiche of Fernando Lamas, Ricardo Montalban and Desi Arnaz.

The most popular question came as no surprise: "What are you wearing under that sheet?"

His answer varied, but usually he was matter-of-fact and not particularly sexy: "Soccer shorts."

Julie Wampler, a bank employee who came by on her lunch hour, had a difficult time giving up the phone to others who stood waiting outside the store.

"He's got a beautiful smile," she

said. Berrio thought she did, too. After a few others had their turn, Miss Wampler was back.

"How about a couple of soccer tickets?" she asked. Berrio wouldn't commit himself; instead he extolled the virtues of the cologne.

Many women proposed joining Berrio in bed. But the soccer player was diplomatic.

"I think this bed is a little small for two," he would say.

"I think it would be cozy," argued Miss Wampler.

Occasionally, a man would stop by. Arnold Frankel, blue blazer correct, tie just right, briefcase in hand, watched for 20 minutes. He was not envious at all.

"I think it is just great, great," said Frankel. That was magnanimous, because Frankel, who is from Fort Lauderdale, is in the perfume and cologne business and sells a rival brand.

"It probably wouldn't go in the window of Saks Fifth Avenue in New York, but I think it's not bad for Jacksonville," he said.

Not all the women were stunned by Berrio.

"I talk to my husband at least three times a day. Why do I need to him?" said Laverne Brooks.

A youngster took the phone and actually wanted to talk about soccer. Berrio was gracious and, sizing up the youngster, figured he was not ready for the cologne pitch — not yet, anyway.

Berrio, who is married and has two children, took in stride the questions and innuendos tossed him by women.

"I am having a good time," he admitted.

The promotion runs through next Friday, and a different man will be in bed each day from 11:30 a.m. to 2 p.m.

Credit: Copyright 1982, Florida Times-Union.

customers, incidentally, will eat the omelets free." I am sure you understand that Mrs. Bixby-Jones is not going to arrive quietly and depart the same way, for a great deal of the success of this promotion will depend on *advance publicity*—the public relations function.

So, in addition to manufacturer-prepared posters, newspaper ads, and mailings, something else has happened. A few days before the omelet demonstration, a person from the company's public relations department or public relations counseling firm will contact the editor of the local newspaper's food

FIGURE 4-2   Sports and games of all kinds offer an excellent public relations opportunity. Here is a release from Piedmont Airlines about its sponsorship of an auto race team. That this makes good public relations sense is spelled right out in the press release by William G. McGee, senior vice-president of marketing: "When you look at the NASCAR/Winston Cup schedule, you are largely looking at a Piedmont Airlines route map." As the release points out, Piedmont's home town of Winston-Salem, North Carolina, can lay a partial claim to being the cradle of stock car racing.

SMITH REYNOLDS AIRPORT
P.O. BOX 2720
WINSTON-SALEM, N.C. 27156
PHONE 919/767-5697

01 (fE) 82   FOR IMMEDIATE RELEASE

DAYTONA BEACH, Fla. -- There will be 6,600 people with a new reason to cheer for Ricky Rudd as the Busch Clash provides a "preview" of the 1982 NASCAR/Winston Cup series. And many of these people are accustomed to far faster speeds than Ricky will hope to reach on the fast Daytona Beach track.

These are the 6,600 people of Piedmont Airlines, new sponsor of the Richard Childress-Ricky Rudd team in Grand National Auto Racing, and Piedmont's people should have ample chance to see their team in action.

"When you look at the NASCAR/Winston Cup schedule, you are largely looking at a Piedmont Airlines route map," William G. McGee, senior vice president-marketing, said.

"From Daytona Beach, where Piedmont began service in 1981, to Atlanta, to Charlotte, to the Tri-Cities area of Tennessee, to Richmond - almost anywhere you look to find racing you'll find a strong Piedmont presence."

Indeed, Piedmont's home town of Winston-Salem, N. C., can lay a partial claim to being the cradle of stock car racing.

Bill France, owner of the Daytona Beach Speedway, got his start at promoting racing in the Carolinas, much of it at the venerable Bowman Gray Stadium in Winston-Salem. His success since then has been legendary.

The senior member of the Childress/Rudd team, Richard Childress, also claims Winston-Salem for his home town. Childress' facilities are located near Piedmont's headquarters, and Childress' pit crew will be made up of Winston-Salem people.

Piedmont's ties to the NASCAR/Winston Cup circuit have been strong, even before its Childress/Rudd sponsorship.

FIGURE 4-2   *continued*

- 2 -

The airline provides eight or more charter flights a year to racing events and believes that figure has the potential to double or triple in the near future.

The General Aviation Division of Piedmont has equally close ties. With facilities located in Roanoke, Richmond, Norfolk, Greensboro, and Winston-Salem, and serving as a distributor for Beechcraft and Piper airplanes, Piedmont's General Aviation Division has long counted the racing industry among its outstanding customers.

"We expect a great deal of enthusiasm among our people," McGee said. "Ricky Rudd is very popular with Piedmont employees already. He lives in the Norfolk region where Piedmont has more flights than any other carrier and the most employees, including its personnel at the airport, the General Aviation Division, and our pilots and flight attendants based in Norfolk."

Of course, those pilots are accustomed to speeds in excess of those the Childress/Rudd team will reach at Daytona Beach.

#####

FIGURE 4-2   continued

FOR IMMEDIATE RELEASE   For Further Information Contact:
Piedmont Aviation, Inc. Photo   Don McGuire
                                   Staff Vice President
                                   Public Affairs
                                   Phone: (office) 919 767-5697
                                          (home)   919 765-1327

PIEDMONT AIRLINES UNVEILED ITS RACING colors for the NASCAR/
Winston Cup circuit with the racing team of Ricky Rudd (left)
and Richard Childress at the airline's corporate headquarters
in Winston-Salem, N.C. Rudd will be driving Pontiac Number
Three, built by Childress at his facilities in Winston-Salem.
Rudd and Childress recently signed to represent Piedmont on the
NASCAR circuit beginning February 14 with the Daytona 500. The
aircraft in the background, incidentally, is a Piedmont B-737,
equally brand new.

FIGURE 4-2   continued

Credit: Piedmont Airlines, a division of Piedmont Aviation, Inc.

page. She may even have Mrs. Bixby-Jones with her. Two days later, a delightful and amusing story, complete with pictures and recipes, appears in the food section of the paper. The headline reads:

OMELET EXPERT ONCE COACHED MAHARAJAH:
MRS. BIXBY-JONES, MASTER OF 1000 OMELET
RECIPES, HAS TAUGHT HER ART TO PRINCES AND
PRESIDENTS

"Omelet-making is a high art," says Mrs. Bixby-Jones, of London, England. She should know, for this world-acclaimed expert is aware of just the exact temperatures and the perfect twist of the wrist to flip over the golden beauty at its peak of perfection.

Mrs. Bixby-Jones will be demonstrating her art in the kitchen wares department of Wilson's Department Store beginning at 9 A.M., September 12th and continuing through the next two days. Admission is free. . . .

Do you get the idea? Of course. Without that story in the food section, which caught the eyes of several thousand dedicated homemakers that morning, the omelet-cooking promotion could not possibly have been the smashing success it was.

Planning Public Relations

If public relations is an integral part of the marketing mix, and the marketing mix is the backbone of a marketing plan, then it follows that public relations, too, must be the subject of careful planning.[4] Or, to put it another way, public relations cannot simply be left to chance. We cannot wait for "targets of opportunity" to present themselves. Those of you who have had courses in management are already quite familiar with the anatomy of a plan.[5] Generally speaking, we follow these steps:

1. *Establish a goal.*
2. *Survey the surrounding circumstances.*
3. *Determine a method—and alternative methods.*
4. *Establish a means of measuring results.*
5. *Get feedback to evaluate results.*

This, in effect, is what a marketing director does to create and put into operation a marketing plan. He or she

1. *Establishes goals in terms of dollars, sales, or market share.*[6]
2. *Gets a good fix on the current political, legal, economic, and competitive environment.*
3. *Perfects the marketing plan, with contingency plans, from the tactics available.*
4. *Arranges to receive regular sales and share-of-market reports.*
5. *Evaluates these results as they come in and amends the plan if necessary.*

The company director of public relations, or the organization's counseling firm, goes through much the same thing.

1. *With full knowledge of the overall marketing objectives, public relations creates its own objectives and goals. These are not created in a vacuum, but are closely coordinated with the marketing goals.*
2. *The public relations department or counsel decides on the tactics and techniques to be employed in reaching its goals.*[7]
3. *Measurement methods are set up to evaluate results.*
4. *Evaluations, both during the marketing campaign and at the end, take place.*

[4]In Chapter Six, we will examine planning in depth.

[5]For a diagram of a plan, see Carlisle, *Management Essentials,* SRA 1979 p. 105.

[6]The important subject of product and market testing will be taken up in the next chapter.

[7]Aside from the case of the omelet demonstration, we have not discussed public relations techniques and tactics as yet. You will begin to learn them shortly—many of them, for many different circumstances.

FIGURE 4-3   There are associations of all kinds dedicated to supporting the interests of their members. A great deal of their work is in public relations. This press release from the California Fruit Tree Agreement (a great name!) is interesting. The California growers of Bartlett pears, plums, peaches, and nectarines might not have been able to get far individually, but by joining forces, they are making their united voice heard.

California Tree Fruit Agreement

Bartlett Pears, Plums, Peaches, Nectarines

Mailing address: P.O. Box 255383 ☐ Sacramento, CA 95865 ■ (916) 483-9261 ☐ 701 Fulton Ave., Sacramento

March 1982

Dear Food Editor:

We like to maintain our newspaper food editor mailing lists with as much accuracy as possible.

As the California Summer Fruits season will soon be here, would you please take a moment of your time to respond to the enclosed self-addressed, stamped postcard? Thank you.

We look forward to working with you in 1982. Please let us know if there's anything further we can do to assist you.

Sincerely,

Robyn Wilk

ROBYN WILK
Director, Consumer Services

RW:sa
Encl.

Credit: *California Fruit Tree Agreement.*

Evaluating Public Relations

Those of you who have studied marketing have a good understanding of the difficulties involved in measuring results. More exactly, we have difficulty determining the *relative effects* of the components of the marketing mix.

Let us say we have completed the first 12 months of a successful marketing effort for our brand of club soda. How should the credit for the sales success be fairly distributed? Did the product succeed because of its excellent quality? Did the price prove irresistible? Did the nicely designed plastic bottle catch the eyes of customers? And if all of this may be true to some extent, what was, for example, packaging's share of the glory?

I think you can see the marketer's problem. He or she is faced with solving an equation containing at least five factors of unknown value. Of course, you know what happens. If the product is a marketing success, everyone involved is quick to claim a share of the credit for her or his department's particular contribution. There is not a competent public relations person who is not convinced that a public relations coup that put the company's product on the front pages of 100 major city newspapers was worth every cent as much as the $10 million advertising campaign.[8]

Measuring Communications Effectiveness

The problem of measuring, in terms of sales, the effectiveness of the various elements in the "mix" continues to plague marketers. Fortunately, we in public relations have a far easier problem. Our problem was made simpler for us by a member of the advertising profession. About twenty years ago the Association of National Advertisers sponsored a study entitled *Defining Advertising Goals, Measuring Advertising Results* (DAGMAR).[9]

The study pointed to a very important principle: Advertising's job, purely and simply, is to *communicate* to a defined audience information and a frame of mind that stimulates action. Advertising succeeds or fails depending on how well it communicates the desired information and frame of mind to the right people at the right time and at the right cost. Note the twice-repeated phrase "information and a frame of mind." Isn't this just what we are trying to do in the practice of public relations—to provide information and create a frame of mind; to change attitudes, perceptions, and ideas? The ANA study went on to point out that although it might be difficult to measure advertising's impact in terms of sales results (due to all those marketing unknowns), com-

---

[8]For a nice, sincere expression of this idea see Arthur M. Merinis, "Marketing's Stepchild: Product Publicity," *Harvard Business Review,* November–December 1972, pp. 111–12, in which a publicist points out, "If this time and space had been purchased at advertising rates, it would have amounted to $1,047,000."

[9]The work was edited by Russell H. Calley and published by the ANA in 1961; see reading suggestions at the end of the chapter.

FIGURE 4-4   **As you can see by reading the names on the border of this broadside, the use of resorts such as the Ponte Vedra Club plays an important role in corporate internal relations. Often a resort's major source of income will be from booking these corporations. Note the emphasis, last sentence, second paragraph, on activities for "off hours." It is important in these corporate conferences that at least half the time be set aside for amusement and recreation such as golf, tennis, swimming, and fishing.**

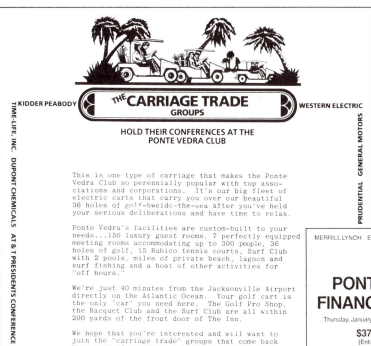

Credit: Ponte Vedra Club.

munications effectiveness was something that *could* be measured—and the study went on to show how.

Using Research to Evaluate Public Relations

If, as the ANA study pointed out, one can measure the effectiveness of communication "information and a frame of mind," then it matters little whether the source of that communication is advertising or public relations, a TV commercial or a feature story in a magazine.

This is the very excellent position we are in when we set out to draw up a public relations plan that is going to be part of the overall marketing plan:

1. *We set up our goals and objectives taking cognizance of our environment.*
2. *We plan our techniques and tactics.*
3. *We provide the measuring devices that will evaluate our progress toward our goals.*
4. *We evaluate our performance.*

The measuring devices that will evaluate our progress are called *research,* the subject of our next chapter. Let's see how we put it to work for us.

Let us say your client, the Fairmont National Bank, has a new management. It has decided to launch a major marketing effort to increase the number of depositors. You, as public relations counsel, understand the importance of the public's attitude. You know, from past experience, that an image of "warm friendliness" is important to a bank. You know that many people tend to feel uncomfortable and intimidated on entering a bank and that for many years bankers themselves had an image (inherited, perhaps, from the Depression years) of sternness. Therefore, one of your public relations goals is to have people look on your client as a bank that is as comfortable as an old shoe, one in which everyone on the staff is friendly, understanding, and anxious to please. Your bank is to be regarded as one in which even the smallest depositor is treated as a friendly nextdoor neighbor.

The first step in the evaluation process is to find out how people perceive *all* the banks in your community in terms of friendliness. You set up a research project (you will see how this is done in the next chapter) and measure the exact degree of friendliness attributed by the public to all 15 banks in your community. Let us say the survey reveals your bank to rate ninth on the friendliness scale. You are now able to establish a logical goal: to bring the Fairmont National Bank to third place or better in the public's perception of its "friendliness" within the next 12 months. You now have everything in place for an evaluation: a starting point (sometimes called benchmark after the mark on work tables used by tailors in measuring goods), a time frame, a goal, and a mechanism (the research survey) for measuring results at regular intervals.

You launch your public relations campaign. At intervals of 3, 6, 9, and 12 months, you repeat your original survey. To your delight, you discover that Fairmont moves up steadily on the friendliness scale until, at the twelfth month, it is in second place. If your clients at the Fairmont National Bank wonder exactly what they got for the fees they paid you (and being bankers, they probably will), you can show them—exactly.

SUMMARY

Public relations does not exist in an independent state, but is an integral part of the overall function of marketing. Specifically, it is part of the marketing mix—that combination of tactics available in the fields of product development, pricing, distribution, packaging, and promotion. It is within promotion that public relations finds its place.

Today we realize that selling has far broader implications than was once thought. Motorcycles and jeans are sold—as are political candidates, contributions to charities, seats at the opera, places in classrooms, and a great variety of attitudes and perceptions. In selling, public relations often finds itself closely associated with product promotions—the events that help pull the products off the store shelves. Public relations can do much to enhance a sales promotion's effectiveness.

Like the overall marketing plan, there is also a public relations plan. We set up benchmarks and goals, decide on tactics, and prepare the devices by which we will evaluate performance. Fortunately, evaluation of performance is far easier to carry out in public relations than it is in marketing itself. Marketing has too many variables. Thanks to work done by the Association of National Advertisers, it has been shown how success in communicating can be measured through research. Research is essential to the practice of public relations, and we discuss it in the next chapter.

KEY TERMS

Marketing plan	Marketing mix
Marketing strategy	Sales promotion
Marketing tactics	Special promotions
Promotion	Promotional specialty items

POP   Dealer promotions
Promoter   Supplier promotions
To "promote"   Public relations plan
Personal selling   Evaluation
Mass selling (advertising)   DAGMAR

THE WAY IT HAPPENED

In few fields of business will you find a closer relationship between the merchandising of a product and publicity.

How many times have you found yourself watching a program and saying, "I just read about that in the paper!"

The popular CBS program "60 Minutes" is particularly adept at creating these relationships. We have to say "creating" because it all can't be attributed to good luck.

For example, in 1982 a leading manufacturer of electric steam irons suddenly closed his plant on the West Coast and moved his manufacturing process to a foreign country. Two hundred and fifty people were thrown out of work and the economy of the town was shattered. The story was featured in newspapers across the country *almost simultaneously* with its coverage in a segment of "60 Minutes."

In the same year, "60 Minutes" ran a story about the revelation that the CIA had lured notorious Nazi war criminals and given them asylum and citizenship in this country in return for spy services. This feature ran on the Sunday night *before* the story made the front pages of hundreds of newspapers.

Considering the amount of time it takes to write and film one of the television segments, the CBS and "60 Minutes" performance can only be admired.

A PERSONAL PROJECT

Early in this chapter you were introduced to the marketing mix, which you learned consists of five factors: product, distribution, promotion, packaging, and price.

Every nationally distributed product has its own individual mix, carefully designed by a marketing department to help it achieve sales success. Each one is different from the other.

For example, King Edward Cigars, a highly successful brand, spends very little on promotion. Coke, on the other hand, spends millions. You can see that the packaging of one is terrible, while that of the other (Coke) is pretty good. The distribution of both is fantastic. But as a product, King Edward doesn't claim to have the quality of a Havana cigar and is priced accordingly.

Pick out two nationally advertised brands and see if you can tell, through observation, how their marketing mixes compare. Where observational methods don't suffice, use other sources—including the companies themselves—to determine their policies in the five mix categories.

READING TO BROADEN UNDERSTANDING

Your college library has many good books on marketing. I suggest you glance through a basic one, such as Boone and Kurtz.

Journal of Marketing. High-level stuff. This is the Bible of the industry.

Advertising Age. More lively than the above, with lots of current marketing information.

CALLEY, RUSSELL H., ED. *Defining Advertising Goals* (New York: Association of National Advertising, Inc., 1961). This is the little book that started marketers on a new way of measuring the effectiveness of their persuasive messages.

KOTLER, PHILIP. *Marketing For Non-Profit Organizations* (Englewood Cliffs, N.J.: Prentice-Hall, 1975). An important book showing how marketing principles also apply to foundations, charitable institutions, and schools.

There are several important marketing statements you should be familiar with, among them T. Levitt, "Marketing Myopia," *Harvard Business Review*, July–August 1960, pp. 1–15ff, and Pierre D. Martineau, "Social Class and Spending Behavior," *Journal of Marketing*, October 1958, pp. 121–30.

5

THE ROLE OF RESEARCH
IN PUBLIC RELATIONS

OVERVIEW AND GOALS

The most essential aspect of the practice of public relations is the possession of facts.

In this chapter, you will learn how public relations people gain possession of the facts through various forms of research. You will see that a great many facts are already collected; we need only know how to find them. Other facts are not known and must be discovered. This requires the use of the survey method—a structured research procedure of considerable value to every public relations professional. When you have completed this chapter, you should be able to

> **Differentiate** between primary and secondary information.
>
> **Understand and carry out** the steps in a survey research project.
>
> **Appreciate** the part played in public relations by public opinion research.

Trying to carry out a public relations project without having all the relevant facts in hand is like jumping into a swimming pool without being sure there is water in it. In marketing itself, there is a long and well-known list of major tragedies that occurred because someone forgot to do the necessary homework. And it is impossible to create a public relations plan without a benchmark or starting point. Determining where you are—the starting point—depends on research or information gathering. One of the first steps in creating any plan is to gather all the relevant information possible.

Gathering Secondary Information

Your college library contains vast amounts of information on a great variety of subjects. The investigative work has already been done; it is up to you to dig it out. This kind of information is known as *secondary information.* It comes in many different forms and originates in many different sources.[1] The list below gives some of these sources.

1. Census reports. *These contain basic statistical information on the population of the United States and the characteristics of its people. Published every 10 years.*
2. Libraries. *The reference section of a library contains a very large amount of easily retrievable information in the form of indexes, lists, statistical material, handbooks, encyclopedias, atlases, multi-volume sets, and so forth.*
3. State and municipal records. *These include tax rolls, real estate holdings, and licenses.*
4. Chambers of commerce. *Most chambers of commerce have a research department that compiles facts about local business and industry.*
5. The media. *Newspapers, magazines, and the broadcast media do constant research in their own markets and in particular about their own audiences.*
6. Trade associations. *Almost every kind of business has an organization set up to serve the interests of the industry (the Cotton Council or the Florida Citrus Commission, for example). These are usually excellent sources of information regarding the industry.*
7. Trade publications. *Few industries do not have at least one publication (usually a magazine, such as* Fishing Gazette *or* Paint and Hardware Review*) devoted to industry interests. Their back files contain a great deal of specialized information.*
8. Office records. *The files, records, and computer data banks of business are rich sources of information concerning the business and its customers.*

---

[1] For a comprehensive list of information sources, see William W. Cook, "Fact-Finding for Public Relations" in Philip Lesly (ed.), *Public Relations Handbook,* 2d ed. (Englewood Cliffs, N.J.: Prentice-Hall, 1978).

FIGURE 5-1   One of our greatest sources of secondary demographic information is the census. This page is a breakdown of labor statistics by population centers. Census publications are available by state.

Table 104.   **Employment Characteristics for Places of 10,000 to 50,000: 1970**

[Data based on sample, see text. For minimum base for derived figures (percent, median, etc.) and meaning of symbols, see text]

Places	Bartow	Belle Glade	Boca Raton	Boynton Beach	Bradenton	Brandon (U)	Browardale (U)	Browns Village (U)	Cape Coral (U)	Coral City (U)	Cedar Hammock-Bradenton South (U)
EMPLOYMENT STATUS											
Male, 16 years old and over	**4 263**	**4 945**	**10 786**	**6 319**	**7 039**	**3 958**	**4 637**	**6 152**	**4 010**	**7 831**	**4 279**
Labor force	3 060	3 995	6 151	3 616	3 805	3 187	3 890	4 736	2 086	6 474	1 538
Percent of total	71.8	80.8	57.0	57.2	54.1	80.5	83.9	77.0	52.0	82.7	35.9
Civilian labor force	3 053	3 990	6 141	3 606	3 802	3 140	3 871	4 707	2 075	6 434	1 538
Employed	2 904	3 900	5 996	3 461	3 726	3 104	3 750	4 526	1 998	6 308	1 459
Unemployed	149	90	145	145	76	36	121	181	77	126	79
Percent of civilian labor force	4.9	2.3	2.4	4.1	2.0	1.1	3.1	3.8	3.7	2.0	5.1
Not in labor force	1 203	950	4 635	2 703	3 234	771	747	1 416	1 924	1 357	2 741
Inmate of institution	388	46	27	46	156	—	—	—	—	296	—
Enrolled in school	276	270	754	235	272	197	237	439	114	447	108
Other: Under 65 years	246	405	1 074	543	745	208	369	578	666	355	406
65 years and over	293	229	2 780	1 879	2 061	366	141	399	1 144	259	2 227
Female, 16 years old and over	**4 575**	**4 998**	**11 676**	**7 353**	**9 351**	**4 397**	**5 152**	**7 598**	**4 400**	**8 452**	**5 228**
Labor force	1 901	2 734	3 436	2 483	3 199	1 688	3 114	4 005	1 199	3 854	989
Percent of total	41.6	54.7	29.4	33.8	34.2	38.4	60.4	52.7	27.3	45.6	18.9
Civilian labor force	1 901	2 734	3 436	2 483	3 199	1 688	3 114	4 005	1 199	3 854	989
Employed	1 751	2 622	3 358	2 380	3 082	1 647	3 038	3 723	1 149	3 680	961
Unemployed	150	112	78	103	117	41	76	282	50	174	28
Percent of civilian labor force	7.9	4.1	2.3	4.1	3.7	2.4	2.4	7.0	4.2	4.5	2.8
Not in labor force	2 674	2 264	8 240	4 870	6 152	2 709	2 038	3 593	3 201	4 598	4 239
Inmate of institution	48	8	45	43	393	—	—	—	—	175	—
Enrolled in school	295	312	634	301	431	284	341	627	121	521	119
Other: Under 65 years	745	1 626	4 470	2 429	2 228	1 938	1 497	2 518	989	3 434	1 623
65 years and over	586	318	3 091	2 097	3 100	487	200	448	1 091	468	2 497
Male, 16 to 21 years old	**653**	**791**	**1 214**	**554**	**764**	**512**	**790**	**1 154**	**307**	**1 241**	**250**
Not enrolled in school	274	406	279	186	331	112	393	581	114	509	115
Not high school graduate	150	291	75	105	224	40	208	382	45	273	63
Unemployed or not in labor force	93	56	17	26	81	20	78	205	19	191	18
MARITAL STATUS AND PRESENCE OF OWN CHILDREN											
Women, 16 years old and over	**4 575**	**4 998**	**11 676**	**7 353**	**9 351**	**4 397**	**5 152**	**7 598**	**4 400**	**8 452**	**5 228**
With own children under 6 years	762	1 279	1 202	941	988	969	1 500	1 646	336	2 311	363
In labor force	329	631	303	413	415	271	963	877	96	952	127
With own children 6 to 17 years only	1 162	1 068	1 761	1 009	1 184	1 261	1 238	1 811	578	2 246	353
In labor force	594	730	732	612	753	631	904	1 225	282	1 185	193
Married women, husband present	**2 768**	**2 967**	**7 815**	**4 744**	**4 720**	**3 177**	**3 017**	**3 393**	**3 260**	**5 622**	**3 463**
In labor force	1 204	643	1 899	1 457	1 631	1 105	1 859	1 095	865	2 480	593
With own children under 6 years	611	970	1 111	794	742	901	1 223	684	296	2 142	344
In labor force	239	447	241	281	267	233	749	515	82	826	114
With own children 6 to 17 years only	985	841	1 518	835	850	1 111	948	1 043	500	2 010	306
In labor force	453	566	564	463	514	512	652	611	236	996	162

PERCENT IN LABOR FORCE

	(1)	(2)	(3)	(4)	(5)	(6)	(7)	(8)	(9)	(10)	(11)
Male:											
14 and 15 years	7.2	10.9	18.6	21.3	18.8	12.5	18.2	9.8	10.4	11.6	6.7
16 and 17 years	27.1	41.6	49.0	37.4	44.8	48.9	47.0	26.5	46.1	33.0	33.9
18 and 19 years	50.8	54.7	62.8	81.5	58.2	65.6	73.6	67.4	74.8	62.1	30.0
20 and 21 years	50.3	84.5	47.3	81.5	78.2	62.8	78.8	85.6	89.4	61.3	89.5
22 to 24 years	71.0	93.5	72.4	90.5	81.7	89.1	89.2	85.9	74.1	79.7	61.3
25 to 34 years	83.0	96.7	92.2	93.6	90.9	100.0	93.6	93.9	94.1	92.7	100.0
35 to 44 years	89.3	95.2	96.6	95.1	89.7	96.3	93.9	93.1	90.2	96.1	89.5
45 to 64 years	84.4	81.8	69.2	74.5	71.7	88.8	83.9	84.3	63.4	92.1	97.4
65 years and over	32.4	32.8	14.5	11.6	12.2	15.1	37.9	29.2	13.2	29.6	63.4
Female:											
14 and 15 years	7.4	13.9	9.2	4.9	17.9	8.7	14.1	6.3	—	1.7	20.0
16 and 17 years	9.8	24.4	32.8	42.5	17.0	26.3	20.5	10.9	27.9	19.7	20.2
18 and 19 years	32.0	52.4	63.9	61.8	43.0	63.7	42.7	37.6	54.4	62.2	49.5
20 and 21 years	63.7	65.5	52.1	57.3	54.2	71.5	66.6	52.9	48.5	54.8	58.6
22 to 24 years	48.6	64.3	61.2	51.0	50.4	36.7	61.6	54.9	60.6	64.8	55.5
25 to 34 years	47.5	62.2	36.9	55.0	58.7	35.8	73.3	69.0	64.8	46.0	41.8
35 to 44 years	58.1	60.7	43.3	47.8	63.8	47.2	68.1	61.7	44.2	51.3	55.8
45 to 64 years	46.6	58.8	32.1	41.5	53.0	42.9	60.3	55.3	31.6	46.3	25.9
65 years and over	12.1	16.3	5.1	5.6	6.8	5.3	15.2	19.6	4.2	8.2	3.1

WORKERS IN 1969 BY WEEKS WORKED

	(1)	(2)	(3)	(4)	(5)	(6)	(7)	(8)	(9)	(10)	(11)
Male, 16 years old and over	3 433	4 202	7 197	4 021	4 183	3 426	3 940	5 041	2 423	6 775	1 797
50 to 52 weeks	2 336	2 112	4 008	2 310	2 797	2 441	2 161	2 575	1 331	4 738	1 104
27 to 49 weeks	620	598	1 850	1 142	871	577	1 449	813	671	601	372
26 weeks or less	477	492	1 339	569	515	408	330	653	421	421	321
Female, 16 years old and over	2 445	3 304	4 339	3 039	3 738	2 010	3 427	4 581	2 549	4 468	1 378
50 to 52 weeks	1 132	686	1 433	1 059	1 749	779	1 125	1 799	603	898	514
27 to 49 weeks	676	460	1 511	1 014	1 035	609	1 528	695	466	378	474
26 weeks or less	637	1 158	1 395	966	954	622	774	1 087	480	1 192	390

CLASS OF WORKER, 16 YEARS OLD AND OVER

	(1)	(2)	(3)	(4)	(5)	(6)	(7)	(8)	(9)	(10)	(11)
Male employed	2 904	3 900	5 996	3 461	3 726	3 104	3 750	4 526	1 998	6 308	1 459
Private wage or salary workers	2 239	3 282	4 525	2 550	2 892	2 597	3 016	3 609	1 584	5 341	1 066
Government workers	407	391	843	394	379	281	381	658	135	671	157
Local government workers	246	251	308	266	253	189	299	419	75	461	94
Self-employed workers	258	227	619	511	450	226	353	247	279	292	236
Unpaid family workers			9	6	5			12		4	
Female employed	1 751	2 622	3 358	2 380	3 082	1 647	3 038	3 723	1 149	3 680	961
Private wage or salary workers	1 062	2 081	2 615	849	2 350	1 124	2 351	2 878	774	3 027	729
Government workers	622	384	567	301	549	416	613	719	243	606	169
Local government workers	521	316	251	201	390	334	435	554	223	375	111
Self-employed workers	63	113	147	189	77	77	70	97	83	42	55
Unpaid family workers	4	44	29	41	16	30	4	29	49	5	8
Male employed, in agriculture	228	1 606	120	318	221	96	271	200	84	82	50
Wage or salary workers	207	576	90	228	191	70	110	141	43	64	36
Self-employed workers	21	30	30	90	30	26	161	59	41	18	14
Unpaid family workers											
Female employed, in agriculture	38	1 012	24	187	85	33	44	24	—	6	15
Wage or salary workers	38	1 007	8	177	79	17	34	12	—	6	15
Self-employed workers	—	5	16	10	—	11	6	12	—	—	—
Unpaid family workers	—	—	—	—	6	5	4	—	—	—	—

LABOR MOBILITY FOR MALES[1]

	(1)	(2)	(3)	(4)	(5)	(6)	(7)	(8)	(9)	(10)	(11)
Male, 30 to 49 years old in 1970	1 658	1 977	2 616	1 581	1 653	1 911	2 043	2 227	792	3 786	651
Nonworker in 1965, nonworker in 1970	147	69	77	84	139	6	119	93	51	104	44
Nonworker in 1965, worker in 1970	116	190	186	87	223	77	373	360	27	248	72
Worker in 1965, nonworker in 1970	98	63	88	61	81	42	80	46	44	120	33

[1] The concept "worker" includes the employed plus members of the Armed Forces.

Credit: Bureau of the Census, U.S. Department of Labor.

Management Information Systems (MIS)

Basically, the information system is a formally structured method of obtaining, recording, and storing useful information on a regular basis.[2] Once put in place, the MIS operates automatically. For example, a sales manager may set up a system by which he or she is assured of receiving regional sales reports by 10 A.M. every Monday. A public relations department may arrange a monthly opinion poll on a particular company policy. MIS-generated information is stored for easy retrieval in files and data banks.

Gathering Primary Information

Primary information is the term used to describe information that is not already in existence, but must be mined from the source. Sometimes this "mining" is easy, and good luck plays a major role. This happens quite frequently. Suppose your history teacher assigns a paper on the Battle of Gettysburg. You would quickly discover that there is a tremendous amount of written material on this battle, most of it known to your teacher. But suppose you should discover in your attic an old shoebox containing some ancient letters by a relative of yours who actually fought with Lee's Army of Northern Virginia at Gettysburg. Now you would have primary information of a most exciting kind. You would be in position to write a paper of considerable interest.

"Stumbling" on useful and interesting information often happens, but in business usually we have to dig for it. There are four major methods for doing so:

1. *Observation.* Just keeping your eyes and ears open often results in valuable primary information. In fact, many companies train their salespeople to do just that. Is a competitor testing a new product? Is a fad beginning to sweep the West Coast? Are the rumors heard in buyers' offices so persistent that they bear looking into? Counting is one of the simplest methods of gathering information by observation. How many cars pass a given intersection between 5 and 6 P.M.? How many working mothers live within a 1-mile radius of your take-out food store?

2. *Experiment.* Any case in which a product or idea is actually tried out can be regarded as a research experiment. In marketing and in public relations, we have many examples of this. You have seen many products—soft drinks, beers, cigarettes—whose superiority has been demonstrated by "taste tests." But you can be sure that long before the product reached the market, tests were carried out to determine which taste would be more acceptable. Certainly the gasoline mileage figures that accompany all car advertising today

[2]For a more formal definition, see Richard H. Brien and James E. Stafford, "Marketing Information Systems: A New Dimension for Marketing Research," *Journal of Marketing,* July 1968, p. 21.

were derived from experiments. Manufacturers will often experiment with prices until they discover the one that produces the highest return.[3] The ultimate test in marketing is the "test city." In this test, we use a "laboratory" city and re-create the national marketing plan within that one city. A typical public relations experiment was the one you encountered in Chapter Four when we measured the change in attitude toward the Fairmont Bank, using our benchmark as a constant.

3. *Panels and independent experts.* Many companies, particularly in the food and homemaking field, retain panels of judges to whom research questions are referred. A company may be experimenting with a new cake mix. It will distribute the mix to its panel, and the members ask to bake with it and report in two weeks. At the meeting, the remarks of all members of the panel are carefully recorded and analyzed.

We often use the independent expert to determine how certain people are thinking or reacting. One of public relations' most important functions is to keep a close watch on changes in attitudes and opinions. Going out and talking to the right people can often give an early indication of changes in ideas, attitudes, and preferences. We will have a lot more to say about this when we discuss public relations' role in politics.

4. *The survey method.* This is probably the most widely used of all methods in gathering primary information. It is also the most difficult. Research has become a highly specialized task practiced by experts who are skilled and knowledgeable in their field. We will examine a research project carried out by the survey method and see why it demands the utmost in care and expertise.

The Survey Research Project

The project is usually seen as being done in four distinct steps:

1. *Selecting a sample.*
2. *Preparing a questionnaire.*
3. *Choosing a method for questioning respondents.*
4. *Evaluating the data.*

Each step requires the utmost care and carries pitfalls for the unwary. If you make a misstep in any of the four, the entire project may turn out to be worthless.

The Sample

A couple of cc's of your blood can provide everything needed for the laboratory to make an accurate count of the various factors in your blood. It isn't necessary to drain all your blood out of your system to get the job done.

[3]For a discussion of the relationship of demand, price, and cost on expected profit, see Martin L. Dell, *Marketing Concepts and Strategy*, 2nd ed. (Boston: Houghton Mifflin, 1972), pp. 871-2.

It would also be much too expensive and time-consuming to question *all* the people in a city or market. So we try to take a sample from a particular group, which is known to researchers as a *universe* or *population.* If we can make our sample as accurate a representation of our universe as a drop of blood is of your arterial supply, we will be in good shape. Unfortunately, researchers cannot be quite that accurate. But they can come close, and with remarkably small samples. Research people recognize two basic kinds of samples: non-probability and probability.

Let's take nonprobability *samples* first. In this kind of sampling, we ask our questions of whomever happens to be handy. Sometimes quota controls are applied to these samples. We predetermine the characteristics of our sample and apply quotas: "50 percent men and 50 percent women," "only people with incomes over $12,000 per year."

The best-known type of *probability sampling* is the *random sample.* Everyone in the universe starts with an equal chance of being included in the sample. We might decide to select every third person in the class. But "every third" will depend on where we start our count of "one." We could take every twentieth name in every third column in every twentieth page of the phone book. Instead of a random sample from the entire universe, *stratified sampling* first groups the universe according to certain characteristics, then selects from each group randomly. If you were doing an attitudinal study (a common form of public relations research) involving a racial question, you would want to be sure your sample was stratified according to the racial makeup of your community.

Our sample is subject to two kinds of errors. The most pervasive is the *sampling error.* Because it is almost impossible to select a sample that truly reflects our universe, some error is always present. This error is a result of chance in random choice. It can be calculated statistically, and this is why in election years you hear the forecasters say that their figures are "subject to 6 percent plus or minus error." *Nonsampling errors* occur when we make an error in selecting the sample. For example, researchers must be careful about using the telephone to carry out interviews in Great Britain, because many working-class families do not own telephones. The results, then, become *skewed,* or distorted, by this error.

Questionnaires

One of the lowest forms of life, according to many researchers, is the person who uses the research study to promote a certain point of view. It is possible to write a questionnaire that proves almost anything. This is the second cousin to "lying with statistics," another fine art.

A questionnaire should be designed to reveal the facts. This is not easy to do, for the following reasons:

1. *Many people have a tendency to lie, exaggerate, or otherwise distort the truth.*

2. *We often say what we think we should say: "Yes, I like apple pie with vanilla ice cream. Doesn't everyone?"*

3. *Our egos get in the way: "I will minimize my age and maximize my income."*

4. *We would rather agree than disagree; it's easier.*

5. *We will not say anything that might make us look bad. Saying "I don't know" is terribly hard for some people.*

One general rule for questionnaire writing is to do it so that the respondent *reveals* the truth rather than simply states it. Sometimes a person will answer more correctly when asked if he or she is "between 21 and 24," rather than "state your age."

There are six common techniques by which information is obtained from respondents. Each has its advantages and disadvantages.

1. *Telephone.* A tremendous amount of limited information can be gained via the telephone. Batteries of operators can be employed to ask one or two quick questions, resulting in thousands of answers. But both question and answer must be brief; the respondent cannot be expected to stay on the phone long.

2. *Mail questionnaires.* Because they may be answered at leisure, they permit far more detail than the telephone interview. But printing and mailing charges raise the cost per answer, and many questionnaires may go unanswered. Some researchers may provide the respondent with a gift to increase the number of returns.

3. *Personal interviews.* These often provide an astonishing amount of information in depth. But the interviewer must be skilled and therefore well-paid.

4. *Personal dropoff.* This technique combines the advantages of personal and mail interviews. It is not, however, inexpensive. The interviewer "drops off" the questionnaire and collects it, thereby increasing the rate of return.

5. *Panels.* Panels are valuable to the public relations researcher because they are made up of the same people for a period of time, so small and subtle shifts in attitudes or opinions can be detected.

6. *Psychological techniques.* The field of psychology has provided researchers with several means of getting at the truth. Among the techniques borrowed from psychology are word association; projective techniques, which ask for the interpretation of a picture or finishing a sentence such as "I like Blinkies because . . ."; and the depth interview, which is much like the psychiatrist's interview in which the respondent is encourged to express whatever thoughts come into his or her head.

Evaluation

Public relations research studies are often evaluated on the basis of their outcomes. Did the study produce something useful? Are we going after significant and useful information? Or are people likely to say, "Very interesting, I'm sure—but how do we use it?"

We may encounter far more difficulties after we have gathered our facts. Sometimes we do not hear what the facts are trying to tell us. We get a message, but it is the wrong one. There are several interesting reasons for this. Sometimes we *hear what we want to hear.* This is not an unknown psychological phenomenon. We hope the survey will disclose that a certain style of dress is popular. To us, that is what the respondents seem to be saying, though the implications may have been quite different. Often our *expectations* lead us astray. Results that run counter to what we expect are hard to accept. In 1948, despite polling indications to the contrary, several newspapers went to print early and trumpeted the victory of Dewey over Truman in the presidential race. Sometimes we just plain *misinterpret* the message our data has brought. A study was once done on chain supermarkets in a city. Among other facts, the study disclosed that in one particular chain the average age of the customers was higher than in any of the other chain stores. The researchers drew the conclusion that this particular chain must offer, in its policies and products, much more that was appealing to the older customer. They reported this to the client.

But one researcher questioned this conclusion. All the stores carried the same national brands and were laid out just about the same way. Where was the significant factor that set the one chain apart? The variable turned out to be an intensive course in human relations, given to every store manager in the chain. Managers had learned how to become masters at ingratiating themselves with their customers. But would that make customers *older?* A further survey concerning customer attitudes was necessary before the simple truth emerged. Personal treatment in the store fostered loyalty. Unlike many younger customers who shopped for bargains from store to store, the customers who shopped in this particular chain of stores stayed—and in doing so became older.

Data Processing and Statistical Analysis

The small computer terminal has brought data processing and control within the reach of even small business concerns. It would be surprising if your college admissions or student affairs office did not have one. *Data processing's* job is to "convert crude fragments of observations and responses into orderly statistics for interpretation."[4] When you answer a questionnaire by

⁴Hugh G. Wales, David J. Luck, and Donald A. Taylor Rubin, *Marketing Research,* 5th ed. (Englewood Cliffs, N.J.: Prentice-Hall, 1978), p. 304.

marking squares with a soft pencil, from which the information is transferred to punch cards, your answers are being data processed.

Statistical analysis requires the command of a special body of knowledge. It is defined as "the refinement and manipulation of data that prepares them for the application of logical inference."[5] Various statistical methods provide averages, dispersions, correlations, and tests of significance. A simple statistical test, for example, can give you the limits of acceptability when two samples differ.

Public Opinion Research

As we have seen, primary and secondary research is a source of facts. The *kinds* of facts are almost limitless. Almost anything is grist for the mill as far as the public relations person is concerned—how many dentists in Luzerne County, Pennsylvania, or the price of hogs in Iowa.

One of public relations' most important areas of inquiry is *public opinion*—what people are thinking at any given moment about any particular subject. As you will see later, knowledge of public opinion is absolutely vital in politics. The Gallup organization, among others, regularly releases figures on the public's shifting attitudes on taxes, gun control, the ERA, and other subjects of public interest. During presidential primary campaigns, we can follow the candidates' fortunes almost daily as the polls reveal their ratings. But the public has a great many opinions on subjects other than politics. How your particular "public" is thinking is a research fact that is essential to your performance as public relations advisor.

SUMMARY

Research is absolutely essential to the work of public relations. Research involves two basic kinds of facts: secondary information, which already exists and is recorded and stored, and primary information, which is developed from a research project.

Management information systems are *structured* methods by which information is gathered, recorded, and stored. The MIS is a fruitful source of secondary information.

Research facts may be gathered by observation, by experiment, from panels and experts, and by the survey method. It is the latter we usually think of as a research project.

[5]Ibid., p. 321.

The survey research project has a very definite form: the sample, the questionnaire, the method of collecting information, and the evaluation. Each has advantages and disadvantages, as well as opportunities for error.

One of the most important kinds of research-produced information for the public relations practitioner is the status of and changes in public opinion.

KEY TERMS

Primary information   Questionnaire
Secondary information   Questioning techniques
MIS   Personal dropoff
Observation method   Panel
Experimental method   Psychological techniques
Panels and independent experts   Evaluation
Survey methods   Statistical analysis
Sample   Public opinion research

THE WAY IT HAPPENED

As you may have noticed, it is not unusual for politicians to change their positions and opinions.

In mid-1982, the administration in Washington, within a period of weeks, let its support be known for several issues dear to the hearts of its most conservative supporters—school prayer, gun control, abortion. At about the same time, a noticeable cooling off in the administration's belligerent "hard line" attitude was taking place, and an invitation to discuss armament reduction was extended to the Russians. Were there reasons behind these moves? Of course.

In the case of the President's more conservative supporters, we know there was considerable interest and dissatisfaction. They felt there had been far less enthusiastic support for certain issues than they had been led to expect. Another event had also taken place: a surprising popular groundswell against nuclear weapons. All over the country, protests were taking place.

In both cases, the people in the administration were probably aware of what was going on before the general public. How? Because they pay people to tell them these things. Pollsters are not active just at election time; they are busy every day of the year doing "attitudinal surveys," advising politicians which way the wind is blowing even while it is still a zephyr.

A PERSONAL PROJECT

What do you think of your college? What do others think of it? Who are the different people whose perceptions of your alma mater are important to its well-being? And just what is it, specifically, that your college would like people to think?

You would be surprised how many colleges do not have the answers to these questions. It might be interesting to jot down some ideal attitudes toward your college. Then, using the techniques explained in this chapter, make a survey of a sample of students and find out what they actually *do* think.

Now you will have a "here" and a "there." You may find that there is a long journey to be made by public relations.

READING TO BROADEN UNDERSTANDING

Almost all college marketing texts contain a good chapter on basic research techniques. Try J.C. Evans and Louis Berman, *Marketing* (New York: Macmillan, 1982), chap. 3, p. 51, or Ben M. Enis, *Marketing Principles*, 3rd ed. (Santa Monica, Calif.: Goodyear, 1980), chap. 4, p. 86. See James S. Norris, *Advertising*, 2d ed. (Reston, Va.: Reston, 1982), chap. 5, p. 105. For a look at high-level research in action, see the *Journal of Marketing Research* and the *Journal of Advertising Research*.

6

THE ROLE OF PLANNING IN PUBLIC RELATIONS

OVERVIEW AND GOALS

In every enterprise, whether commercial or personal, success depends on sound and careful planning. In this chapter, you will learn about different kinds of plans, their characteristics, and how they are created. You will see the steps the public relations person must take, including the final steps of creating the tactics by which the plan will be carried out. Finally, we will see how the plan itself is evaluated. When you have completed this chapter, you will be able to

>**Understand** *the part played by planning in public relations.*
>
>**Understand** *the use of premising and forecasting.*
>
>**Distinguish** *among various kinds of plans.*
>
>**Apply** *the four basic steps in planning.*

Of all the management functions, planning is recognized as being the most important.[1] Planning must come before anything else. Events simply cannot flow logically or efficiently without it.

[1]James A. F. Stoner, *Management,* 2d ed. (Englewood Cliffs, N.J.: Prentice-Hall, 1982), p. 99.

Planning is universal in its application. General Motors is busy planning its new models of three years from now. Someone in your class is planning to get married. Fighters have a "fight plan," and coaches have a "game plan." Perhaps some of you landed in college by chance, but most of you planned to enroll. As a result, you came up with a plan. You could put it on paper: "Here's where I am now, here's where I want to go, and here's how I plan to get there."

If you will refer back to Chapter Four and the job we did for the Fairmont Bank, you will see that our public relations program was a plan. We had a starting point, a goal, and a way to measure progress. These three steps are basic to planning.

Premising

Premises are assumptions about factors that may affect our plan, but over which we may have little control. Premises are the "everything else being equal" element in planning. Often they are stated in the negative. "Our plan ought to work if the price of gasoline does not double." Or, "I think we can assume that the public won't lose its taste for hamburgers." Premising helps us develop contingency plans too. "What will we do if the public *does* lose its taste for hamburgers?"

Forecasting

Forecasting is related to premising. Forecasting does not use crystal balls or tea leaves. Like the weather expert, we make our forecasts on the basis of facts (a low is developing over the Des Moines area) and figures (the temperature is 90° in Miami).

Public relations people, as you know, are very much interested in detecting trends. We are not only interested in their direction and intensity, but we would also like to be able to forecast where those trends will take us, and this is frequently possible. We are helped by related fads, too. When we press a certain emotional button, does the same thing happen each time?

Often, however, we do not have hard facts and figures to guide us. Then we must rely on "expert opinion." True, experts in some fields have gotten a bad name because they tend to differ so widely in their forecasts. But the "voices of experience," such as salespeople and sales managers, editors, research directors, and political figures, are often valuable in helping us make a forecast.

Kinds of Plans

Plans come in a number of different shapes and sizes. Some are distinguished by the amount of time they take. They can be short-, intermediate-, or long-range. Our plan for the Fairmont Bank, which ran for 12 months, would probably be regarded as intermediate. A great many public relations plans are very long-range, indeed—practically open-ended. We may never quite reach that goal of achieving 100 percent public acclaim for our client, but we keep trying.

Many public relations plans are *single-use plans*. That is, they are designed for a specific task and remain in effect only as long as it takes to complete the plan. *Standing plans* are just the opposite. They are prepared plans that are ready to be put in place when needed. Public relations may have a standing plan regarding fires or accidents at the plant—"Here's how we'll go about getting the facts and releasing them." The latter situation involves two kinds of standing plans: a *procedure* (Here's how we will go about getting the facts), and *policy* (In case of fire or other kinds of accidents, company policy is to get the full facts to the press and public just as speedily as possible).

Programs and Projects

A public relations firm or department will often submit a program that is, in effect, a detailed, long-term plan. This plan usually consists of a number of *projects*.

Let us say your public relations firm had been asked to submit a plan to increase attendance at the games of the local professional soccer team. Your program would probably include such separate projects as these:

1. *Creation of a business community "booster's club."*
1. *"Give-away" nights in which free tote bags or jerseys would be given to the first 1,000 ticketholders.*
3. *A "parents' night" in which a parent would be admitted free when accompanied by a child.*
4. *"Pee-Wee League" clinics at which the pro players would provide instruction for the youngsters.*

Strategy versus Tactics

We can also distinguish between plans that are strategic in nature and those that are tactical. *Strategic planning* involves broad, overall objectives; *tactical planning* involves lesser plans that contribute to the overall strategic plan.

A major public relations strategy at a store might be to establish it as a gracious and pleasant place to shop. One of our tactics to achieve this strategic goal would be to institute a policy of accepting all returned merchandise without question and with immediate full refund.

Implementing the Public Relations Plan

In public relations, or in any other enterprise, one always proceeds with a definite destination in mind—that is, one always has a plan. Plans can be classified in certain ways, and the time element plays a part in all types. Now let us see what happens when we get down to the actual making of a public relations plan.

Basic planning involves four distinct steps:

1. *Establishing definite goals or objectives.*[2]
2. *Assessing the present position in relation to the goal and the availability of resources to gain the goal.*
3. *Weighing, by prediction, estimation, or forecast, the factors that could affect the process of reaching the goal.*
4. *Creating the tactics, devices, or techniques by which the plan will be implemented. This includes the creation or provision of alternative tactics.*

Let us now examine each of these steps from the point of view of the public relations practitioner.

Getting Goals in Focus

The first job in planning a public relations program is to make sure that all the goals are in focus, that they are the proper goals, and that they fit into the organization's overall policy framework.

The public relations department, as a functioning part of an organization, must never lose sight of its organization's broad objectives and goals, and the policies that have been set up to achieve them. Interestingly enough, many organizations are not too clear about their overall goals. They themselves may have been aiming at the wrong targets—or worse, targets that help to distort the true target until it is too late. This fact alone can render all public relations efforts diffuse or meaningless. This is one of the reasons why, in many corporations, public relations directors play an important role in counseling management on policy within the changing environment of their operations.

The wrong answer to the question, "What business are we in?" has led many a company into bankruptcy. The subject is one of growing interest to both management and marketing people.[3] Motorcycle manufacturers discov-

---

[2]For a discussion on the interchangeability of the terms "goal" and "objective," see James A. F. Stoner, *Management*, 2d ed. (Englewood Cliffs, N.J.: Prentice-Hall, 1982), p. 98. See also Boone and Kurtz, *Principles of Management*, p. 65, for definitions.

[3]The discussion of the question was given great impetus by Theodore Levitt's article, "Marketing Myopia," in the *Harvard Business Review*, July–August 1960, pp. 45–46.

FIGURE 6-1   This is part of a brochure produced by Sawgrass featuring its Players Club course. Other pages contain publicity on the First Annual Food Extravaganza, new building plans for the Cabana Club, and special facilities for business meetings. Public relations departments are often called upon to prepare material used in mailings to prospective customers.

Golf Pros Prepare to Meet the Challenge of the Players Club

The 1982 Tournament Players Championship (TPC) returns to Jacksonville at the new Players Club course at Sawgrass March 15-21 with the greatest field of leading money winners on the TPA Tour (formerly the PGA Tour). One hundred forty four golfers will compete for an increased purse of $500,000 as they test their golfing proficiencies for the first time on the challenging Tournament Players Club course.

Representing a bold step into the future for golf and the TPA Tour, the new Players Club course will serve as the permanent site of the TPC, previously played on the oceanside course at Sawgrass for the past five years.

The new course is a spectacular "stadium" course designed to give spectators a birds eye view of the action. "Stadium golf" is the term most frequently used to describe the Players Club course, having been designed and constructed with the concept that golf in the 80's will thrive not only as a participant's game, but as a spectator sport as well. Huge natural amphitheaters and spectator mounds have been built along the course providing a clear view for as many as 40,000 tournament viewers.

The 6,950-yard (from the back tees) course was designed by renowned golf architect Pete Dye. The course offers a balance between left-to-right angled holes. Water is placed equally on the left and right sides of the fairways and greens, and the entire course is surrounded by a moat. Dye's creative and imaginative sculpting of the almost jungle-like terrain has resulted in a challenging golfing experience for pros and weekend duffers alike.

For information regarding TPC tickets, badges and/or package plans contact the TPC Office at (904) 399-5950.

Credit: Sawgrass—An Arvida Resort Community.

ered long ago that they were not in the economical transportation business, but in the "fun, frolic, and freedom" business. Others have not been so fortunate. American car makers clung to a bigger-is-better philosophy for years—and gave up 25 percent of their market to imports.

Frequently companies cling to images (and the policies that create these images) that are not only wrong, but potentially destructive. Here again, public relations has a job to do. It took decades to convince bankers that they were not in the banking business, but in the "serving and helping people take care of their money business." Once the idea had sunk in, banking images and policies changed. The bank became as pleasant a place to deal as the corner grocery store.[4]

Some organizations simply run out of goals and have to seek new ones. The March of Dimes saw its goal, overcoming infantile paralysis, almost completely achieved. Today the funds it raises are devoted to aiding handicapped children.

One of the public relations person's greatest enemies is *inertia*. Resistance to change is endemic in many organizations, and the larger ones seem particularly prone to it. "Sticking your neck out" is not highly recommended in some executive suites. "Daring innovators" are sometimes looked upon as being as unstable as the person on the flying trapeze. It becomes safer and easier to let things slide—why tamper with success?[5] But if there is one theory people in public relations understand, it is that change is inevitable, and that change sometimes happens with frightening speed. The history of American business is full of those who, while they admired their models, did not notice that the parade had gone marching by.

One of public relations' brightest contributions has been its performance in the airline industry. Uniforms, flight attendant selection, plane insignia and decoration, menus, reservations, baggage handling—all disclose the deft touch of alert public relations practitioners. (Had America's railroads paid a little heed, maybe there would be fewer weeds growing between the tracks!) But railroad men kept on being railroad men, just as they had always been: brakemen and conductors, engineers and passenger agents. As someone pointed out years ago, a hog could travel from Chicago to Los Angeles more conveniently than a person. The conductors got older and sterner, the food got worse, the cars got colder, and the highways got easier. After a while, all those beautiful, romantic names we used to read on the sides of boxcars— the Frisco, the Santa Fe, the L. & N. and the Burlington—began to disappear.

---

[4]There was a wonderful dream sequence in the motion picture, "Pennies From Heaven" (1981) in which a hard-hearted banker becomes the nicest and most accommodating of men.

[5]Listerine Antiseptic is a notable exception to this rule. The disagreeable stuff in its unadorned package has been the despair of its more sophisticated competitors for years.

Characteristics of Goals

There are certain other criteria against which we can measure goals. They should meet these tests:

1. Are they specific? *They should leave no doubt in anyone's mind just where you are going. After all, how can you know when you get there if you do not know where you are going?*

2. Can you measure them? *Goals should be stated in measurable, precise terms—dollars, days, coupons, opinions, attitudes.*

3. Do they have time limits? *A specific date for reaching your goal is crucial, for often costs are involved.*

4. Are the goals realities or dreams? *Goals should be set within the limits of good sense. It does not hurt to accept modest results as long as the results are in the right direction.*

5. Are the goal setters the "doers"? *Public relations goals should be set by public relations people after consultation with appropriate other people in the company.*

Assessing Present Position or Environment

No organization functions in a vacuum; it works in an "environment" of factors that impinge on it and affect its actions. These are often outside forces over which management has little control. But although management may have little immediate control over many of these factors, it does not mean that they are not subject to change—and that public relations cannot play an important part in helping to bring these changes about. Let us look at some of the environmental factors that must be taken into consideration when plans are made.

1. *The position and condition of the organization itself in relation to its publics.* This is similar to the second planning step mentioned earlier. What is our present popular image? What share of the market do we command? What are our present resources in capital, staff, and manufacturing ability?

2. *The economic weather.* The condition of the economy is certainly going to affect corporate planning and thus public relations planning. From college to corporation to charitable organization, cycles of inflation and deflation may alter our goals.

3. *Legal and ethical considerations.* Every enterprise operates within a body of law guiding its activities. Some, such as the antitrust laws, directly affect the conduct of business. Others, such as the pure food and drug laws, are intended to protect the consumer. Some of these laws are hard to interpret, and there is a steady stream of cases passing through the courts.[6]

[6]The *Journal of Marketing,* published monthly, carries a feature, "Legal Developments," which summarizes important business-related cases adjudged or presently before the courts.

Questions of business ethics continually appear in the press and are a point of concern for public relations people. International companies doing business in the Orient often run afoul of ethical standards different from their own. The mere acceptance of "presents" often raises ethical questions. Foundations, associations, trade publications, and ethics committees all keep a close watch on the behavior of their associates.

4. *Social standards and life styles.* Life as we live it keeps changing, often dramatically. If you have anything to do with public relations, you had better pay close attention. Our social standards and life styles take many forms, every one of them with an effect on public relations planning. There has been a "sexual revolution" and great changes in the status of women and minorities. The whole "face" of our population is changing—it is getting older and it is living in different places. About 50 percent of all married women work, and the two-income family is becoming commonplace. We no longer "shock" as easily as we once did; we see things and hear words in our theaters that would have closed them down a generation ago. New interests and facts sweep over us. The kid who is playing an electronic game today will probably be operating a giant computer tomorrow.

5. *The political atmosphere.* Politics plays a big part in the social environment. Which way the "wind is going to blow" is certain to affect public relations plans in a most definite fashion. The Reagan administration, for example, after it was in power for less than two years, significantly altered many of the ground rules under which business operates.

Weighing Significant Factors

In addition to environmental factors that affect plans, there are other factors that must be taken into consideration.

1. *Do we know our public?* The marketing people call this a *market profile.* In many cases, particularly in marketing public relations, these audiences may be identical. In any case, it would be your job as a public relations specialist to know them like a brother or sister. Profiles are often drawn in terms of age, sex, income, occupation, education. In addition, you may want to know *how* your target group thinks and *why* its members think that way. As we saw earlier, social class will be very important. There are vast differences in life styles, tastes, and standards among classes. Certainly the message you use to address university graduates will be different from the one you choose in making a presentation to an organization of agricultural workers,[7] even though both messages may deal with the same topic.

2. *Who are our opponents?* Frequently, public relations takes place in an adversary situation. We may be "for or against" a union organizing committee, an organization of environmentalists, or the Society for the Preservation of Barbershop Harmony. How strong are these people? What are their public relations tactics? What are their weaknesses and strengths?

---

[7]See Pierre Martineau, *Motivation in Advertising,* (New York: McGraw-Hill, 1957), p. 164, for buying habits by social class.

3. *What are our friends doing?* Have others faced a similar situation, and what has been their experience in dealing with it? What are their current activities with which you must coordinate your own?

4. *Is there a target of opportunity?* The world keeps changing. A few years ago, only a few "society figures" or famous people appeared as spokespeople for commercial products. The growth in the popularity of professional sports— and the television audience they command—has changed all that. Today, stars in a dozen sports are associated with every imaginable kind of product. The "sports figure," regardless of age, has become a standard feature in public relations promotional events.

5. *Have you been thinking "down the road"?* Much planning in public relations is of the long-term variety, as you have learned. But how far into the future have we peered? How proficient can we be at *anticipating* events, rather than waiting for them to hit us on the head? Can we get out in front of the parade, instead of joining it when it is already past the reviewing stand?

   For many years, schools and colleges regarded themselves as far above the hurly-burly of politics and commerce. It has taken some of them a long time to understand that relations with legislators, alumni, and the public are vital to their existence. Only now have many schools begun to understand that they are in competition with many others "selling" the same "product and service." In many universities, as you will see in a later chapter, the public relations department simply "gets publicity" rather than being part of an overall marketing program.

Creating the Tactics

We have now come to the point where we have our plan well in hand. We can see our goals clearly; we understand the constraints and conditions under which we must operate. Now it is up to us to implement our plan. We must create the tactics by which the strategy will be carried out.

The word "create" is an important one. The facts and figures on which we had based the first three steps of our planning process are obtainable through research. Our fourth step involves *ideas.* Ideas are the children of imagination and spirit and excitement and daring. Many public relations tactics are "standards"—they've been used for years. In this book you are going to become familiar with many of these tactics, which are used by a variety of people and organizations in a variety of ways. But at one time, those "standard" tactics were someone's brilliant idea.

People have attempted to harness the creative process with such devices as "brainstorming"[8] and "attribute listing." But creativity is essentially a lonely process. Great ideas are often born in odd circumstances and at odd times.

[8]The technique of getting people together and discussing ideas in an uninhibited fashion (brainstorming) is often credited to Alex Osborn of the famous advertising firm of Batten, Barton, Durstine, and Osborn. See Alex F. Osborn, *Applied Imagination,* 3rd ed. (New York: Charles Scribner's, 1979). See also John E. Arnold, "Useful Creative Techniques," in *Source Book for Creative Thinking,* (New York: Scribner's, 1962), p. 255.

I would love to know how someone came up with the idea of selling pantyhose in supermarkets packaged in egg-shaped containers.

I once created a facetious rule called Norris's Third Law—"Never laugh at anyone with a crazy idea." I was half joking, but now I am not so sure. Many a million-dollar idea has probably died because someone hooted it into oblivion. Ideas are sometimes very fragile things and have to be handled carefully.

Let us see where this tactic-creating function fits into a real-life situation. You are going to open your own restaurant. You have decorated the room, hired the chef, decided on the type of food you will serve and the prices you will charge. You also know what your competition is and have a general idea of conditions in the restaurant business. In particular, you have a clear picture of the kind of customer you hope to attract. Now, what are you going to do, aside from print and broadcast advertising, that will make you known and bring in the right people? Whatever reviews you can get from food editors, whatever stories you can generate and get published, whatever "happenings" occur at your place, whatever people can be induced to say about you, and to whom they say it are all part of your public relations tactics. *And somebody has to think them up.*

Moreover, you are going to want to have quite a few of these tactics up your sleeve, because some work better than others, and you never know when the opportunity for a new one is going to arise. Are your plans in place for the Christmas party for the kids from the Children's Home? Have you designed the jerseys for the softball team that will represent you next summer? With what sort of fanfare will you greet the new pastry chef who is coming straight from Vienna?

Evaluation

No self-respecting plan is complete without some means of evaluating its outcomes. As we have seen, a research technique, regularly applied, can measure attitudes and perceptions. We get important feedback from the research results. A management tool that is often used is MBO—management by objectives. Here the objectives are set by agreement, and regular reviews are made of progress toward the objectives.

Some evaluations turn out to be less specific than those gained in scientific research. Often we simply want the answer to the question, "Did it work?" In the case of our restaurant, if that great idea you had for a story fell on every editor's deaf ears, you know it did not work. But if your guests kept mentioning that Christmas party for the kids, and how much they admire you for doing it, then you know something is working.

Sometimes results must be evaluated in terms of dollars. This is often the most difficult evaluation to make. Did we get our money's worth? Was It "cost effective"? It is often hard to know. So much of relations with people is played out in terms of images, attitudes, and perceptions; so much of it works gradually, with change far in the future. Perceptions of our presidents, for example, become firm only after their performances in office have been examined—and written about—by many people. Not too many years ago, jazz was regarded by many as something no "respectable" person would listen to.

SUMMARY

Planning is basic and essential to all enterprises. Often, plans require a look into the future by means of premising and forecasting.

There are a number of kinds of plans: short-term and long-term; temporary and standing plans; programs, projects, and procedures. Plans always involve strategies (the broad, overall methods) and tactics (the detailed activities within the strategy).

Plans have definable steps: establishing goals, assessing present position and circumstances, estimating obstacles, aids, and outside influences, creating tactical methods, and establishing methods for evaluating progress.

Goals are not always easy to determine. They should have certain characteristics. They should be specific, measurable, have time limits, be realistic, and be carried out by the people who form them.

The environments in which plans are carried out are legal, economic, social, political, and internal. In addition, other important facts can affect plans: the nature of our publics, competitors, opportunities, and the future.

Creativity is much more difficult to define than the facts revealed by research. But creativity is essential if we are to create an outstanding public relations plan. Fortunately, many of the tactics used in public relations are "standards" that can be applied in a variety of cases.

KEY TERMS

Premising   Project
Forecasting   Strategy
Long- and short-term plans   Tactic
Standing plans   Planning steps
Program   Goals

Assessing position

Economic, legal, political, and social considerations

Environment

Creativity

Evaluation

Feedback

THE WAY IT HAPPENED: "PLANNING BEGINS AT HOME"

You probably sat down with a counselor and planned your curriculum when you began college. I hope you sat down and had a good long talk with yourself, too. Because planning your college career is one of the trickiest assignments you'll ever face.

Today relatively few students enjoy the luxury of a preset, inflexible curriculum. Many, many students, particularly in community colleges, find themselves juggling time, course requirements, and employment demands. Some of them get their plans all wrong and suffer for it. I've met quite a few of them.

If you work, you have to plan your courses around your work hours. How many courses can you handle? If it's a nice leisurely quarter with classes meeting two or three times a week, you should be able to find the proper amount of time for homework. But what if it is one of those short quarters with classes every day? Three courses under that system can kill you.

I hope you have planned your college work schedule sensibly. The proper plan is going to make a tremendous difference in your performance as a student. And don't worry too much about the long-term goals at this point. It's the short term "As" that are important to you right now.

A PERSONAL PROJECT

Ask yourself and three of your friends, "What are you going to do this summer?" In a surprising number of cases, you will find the answers rather vague: "Oh, I don't know—the usual thing, I suppose. Look for a part-time job, get a good tan, maybe visit some relatives."

Now ask the question in a slightly different form: *What are we going to do this summer that will improve our chances of future long- or short-term success?*

This, obviously, is going to involve planning. You have established a goal—your success. Now, what specific steps are you going to take to help you toward your goal?

These are specific, so write them down. A summer school class on Mondays, Wednesdays, and Fridays. A job in a specific office. A certain number of books to be read, with definite titles. Certain definite people to seek out and talk to about your future.

Make this list, pursue it, and at the end of summer see how many items you were able to accomplish. What did planning do for you?

READING TO BROADEN YOUR UNDERSTANDING

Stoner, James A. F. *Management*, 2d ed. (Englewood Cliffs, N.J.: Prentice-Hall, 1982). See p. 131 for concise explanation of the four basic steps in planning. Chapter 4 contains an explanation of the somewhat more involved strategic planning process.

Terry, George, and Stephen G. Franklin. *Principles of Management*, 8th ed. (Homewood, Ill.: Irwin, 1982). On p. 176 of this book you will find six common reasons why plans go wrong; avoid them!

Hayes, J. L. "Making Time to Plan," *Restaurant Business*, September 1, 1981. Yessir, you have to plan menus, too.

Conarroe, R. R. "Climbing the Corporate Success Ladder: A Self-Marketing Program for Executives," *Management Review*, February 1981. Careers have to be planned, too. The better your plan, the faster you climb the ladder.

Johnson, H. "Softselling Your Ambitions," *Black Enterprise*, February 1981. Another way to get there.

Runde, R. "PLanning Now for Your Longer Life," *Money*, March 1981.

Nowling, Jack K. "How to Write the PR Program," *Public Relations Journal*, July 1976. The planning process applied to the real thing.

GETTING THE STORY TO THE PUBLIC: MEDIA

OVERVIEW AND GOALS

Not having outlets for our stories is like being all dressed up with nowhere to go. In this chapter, we are going to examine the places our stories appear (the media) and how they get there. You will see that we must not only know the right people to contact, we must also have a strong sense of what is and is not newsworthy.

When you have completed this chapter, you should be able to:

> *Recognize* the quality of newsworthiness.
>
> *Understand* how newsworthy events are arranged.
>
> *Recognize* the people who are your contacts in the media.
>
> *Be familiar with* the variety of mediums that might carry your message.

Relating to a public occurs through the eyes and ears: the pictures and words we see, and the sounds and words we hear. These stories and pictures about ourselves, our product, or our cause are generally known as *publicity*—

the device by which we literally *relate* to the public ideas and facts we wish them to have. It is publicity's task to be written or portrayed and delivered in such a manner that it will be seen, read, and remembered by as many of its particular audience as possible.

For example: If I am a manufacturer of bass plugs, I will want to write a story so startling, eye-catching, and memorable that it will hold the interest of all. Moreover, I will want my story to come to the attention of the greatest number possible of a special group of people—those who fish for bass.

Newsworthiness

"News," whether it is printed or broadcast, consists of those things that happen each day. These events can be expected to have varying degrees of general interest—a blizzard in Chicago, a big fire in Boston, a speech by an important diplomat, and all the latest sports scores. There is also far more specialized news, of interest to limited groups of people, but news nevertheless: a new development in beekeeping, or a breakthrough in the treatment of the common cold. The public relations person must be careful to distinguish between news and newsworthiness. *Newsworthiness* is that quality of news which endows it with excitement, interest, and memorability.

The Philadelphia *Inquirer* slid downhill for years although it provided its readers with plenty of news. The slide did not stop until it acquired an editor who required newsworthiness of his reporters in the stories they reported. New readers were attracted to the paper. Advertising increased, and its old rival, the *Bulletin,* was left far behind and eventually died.

You have probably heard the old chestnut about its being news when "man bites dog." I suppose if the letter carrier bit someone's pet poodle it would be good for a few lines, especially if the owner had him arrested. But suppose the persistent reporter was not satisfied with "man bites dog." Suppose she dug a little deeper and discovered that the letter carrier, a veteran of twenty years of dealing with neighborhood dogs, had developed a method of sending his attackers into a hypnotic trance? And suppose the "bite" was a symbolic one, reminding the dog when he emerged from his trance that he would never, *never* nip at anybody again? Editors, as you are about to see, love news. Even more, they love news with a high degree of newsworthiness.

Let us say that you, as a public relations person, send out a press release that the board of directors has elected Henry J. Simpson president of Acme Shipbuilding. The release contains the usual biographical material and will certainly be good for two or three inches in the business section. But what if you discovered, on inquiry, that Mr. Simpson, in his devotion to perfection, had once turned down an opportunity to become a junior executive in the company. His reason? He did not feel his performance as a welder was as good as it should be. He refused to move until it was up to what he called "Acme standards."

FIGURE 7-1   **The writer of this news release, aimed at food page editors, has taken a relatively dull statistic (35% increase in consumption over an 18-year period, nothing very world-shaking) and used it as a springboard for publicizing the many advantages of the banana. This release contains many facts a food editor can use and, in fact, might be an excellent source of a feature story. Note that the release form is captioned not with a company name, as is usual, but with "News From Chiquita"—a trick you might pick up for your company.**

 CHIQUITA
BRANDS, INC.

1271 AVENUE OF THE AMERICAS
NEW YORK, NEW YORK 10020
212/397-4917

CONTACT: John P. Bishop

"YES, WE DO HAVE BANANAS", SAYS CHIQUITA

Take another look Eddie Cantor, because "Yes, we do have bananas"; plenty of 'em! The fact is in 1981 Americans consumed more than five billion pounds of bananas, bringing per capita consumption up to the 26.1 pounds per year level -- an increase of almost 35 percent from 1964's consumption figures.

If we analyze the banana's attributes, we see there are many reasons for this dramatic increase in the fruit's popularity. Part of the reason is that bananas, unlike many other fresh fruits, are available year round. Pound for pound, they are also one of the best buys in your produce department. But the folks at Chiquita Brands -- the best known name in the banana business -- feel there is much more to it than that.

Over the past two decades, we have witnessed a tremendous surge in the number of people concerned with nutrition, health and weight. In the search for diets that are health and nutrition oriented, as well as calorie conscious, it seems as though everyone is turning to the banana. People everywhere and in every age group are finding that bananas, with their distinctive

-more-

Credit: Chiquita Brands, Inc.

This release crosses the business editor's desk the next day and she studies it for a moment. She gets up slowly and walks over to the managing editor. "Maybe there's a story here," she says. The managing editor reads it and calls for a rewrite person and a photographer. The next morning, there it is—right in the middle of the front page:

NEW SHIPYARD PREXY CHOSE
PERFECTION OVER PROMOTION

"Our Customers Pay For The Best," Says H.J. Simpson.

"So I Worked Hard Till I Was."

The copy is the kind of rags-to-riches, devotion-to-the-job story that thrills all those who believe in the free enterprise system. And the picture? There's the new president, out on a girder, welding torch in hand and face mask pushed back, about to show his staff that he hasn't lost his touch. *Newsworthiness* did it.

The People Who Receive Us

The publicity person must keep in mind that the media—print and broadcast—offer a wide variety of audiences, both in character and number. It is up to you to know who and what they are. A story, or *press release,* cannot be sowed at random, hoping it will fall on fertile ground. (You will be shocked when you discover how many wind up in the wastepaper basket.)

You may have a story you wish to be read by the widest audience possible. You may send it to the editors of every major newspaper in the United States. You may attempt to get it on the wires—and thus to the clients of one of the general news services: Associated Press, United Press International, Reuters.

But your story may be of interest to a limited number of people, or in a limited geographical area. Your job then becomes one of zeroing in on these people or that area. This involves knowing audiences and how to reach them. If you are promoting a new high-performance car, *Road and Track* or *Car and Driver* readers are the ones you want to reach. On the other hand, a release about a new ski wax can hardly be expected to do you much good in the Miami *Herald.*

If your story is of particular interest to black women, then certainly you are going to want to have the editor of *Ebony* or *Essence* magazines on your

FIGURE 7-2   How to make life easier for the editor, and thus increase the likelihood of parts of your story being used. Note the box at top of the release, giving the editor a quick scan of usable contents. Compare this with the release on p. 25.

NEWS RELEASE

**The
Sun Belt
Conference**

Suite 1010
1408 N. Westshore Blvd.
Tampa, Florida 33607
(813) 872-1511

Tampa, Wednesday, March 3, 1982
No. 6-24
FOR IMMEDIATE RELEASE

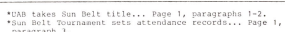

*UAB takes Sun Belt title... Page 1, paragraphs 1-2.
*Sun Belt Tournament sets attendance records... Page 1,
 paragraph 3.
*Sun Belt All-Tournament Team... Page 1, paragraphs 5-7.

UAB BLAZERS CAPTURES FIRST SUN BELT CHAMPIONSHIP

The Sun Belt Conference completed its most successful post-
season basketball tournament ever this past weekend in
Birmingham, as UAB won its first championship in the six
years of the Sun Belt Conference.

It was the third consecutive matchup between UAB and
Virginia Commonwealth for the championship, the only two
teams to compete in the final game since the Blazers and the
Rams entered the league three years ago. UAB completed the
season with a 23-5 mark and now will advance automatically
to the NCAA tournament. Virginia Commonwealth finished with
a 17-11 record and will wait for post-season opportunities.

The tournament set several attendance records. Saturday
night's crowd of 11,658 was the highest single session
attendance in the six years of the Sun Belt Conference
Tournament. The total attendance, which was 29,079, set a
three-session tournament mark, and also eclipsed the total
attendance mark for tournaments including four sessions.

This year's tournament was also the hardest fought tournament in Sun Belt Conference history. All games were close
with the largest margin being the championship game which
was 94-83. Jacksonville and South Alabama played to
overtime in the first round. It was the fourth overtime
game in tournament history.

SUN BELT ALL-TOURNAMENT TEAM

Oliver Robinson, who has dominated every honor category in
the Sun Belt Conference this season, was honored as the
tournament's Most Valuable Player. UAB's Robinson was the
unanimous choice for the tournament's MVP as he led the
Blazers to a perfect 2-0 mark in this year's tournament. He
also was honored last Thursday as the Sun Belt Conference
Player-of-the-Year.

In addition to Robinson, other members of the All-Tournament
team included UAB's Craig Lane, who came off the bench to
spark the Blazers' underneath board game and was a big
factor in the resurgence of UAB's inside game. Lane and
Robinson shared All-Tournament honors with teammate Chris
Giles, who had 21 points, 19 rebounds and 14 assists versus
South Florida and Virginia Commonwealth.

UNIVERSITY OF
ALABAMA IN
BIRMINGHAM

JACKSONVILLE
UNIVERSITY

UNIVERSITY OF
NORTH CAROLINA AT
CHARLOTTE

UNIVERSITY OF
SOUTH ALABAMA

UNIVERSITY OF
SOUTH FLORIDA

VIRGINIA
COMMONWEALTH
UNIVERSITY

Other All-Tournament honorees included South Florida's
Willie Redden, who led the Bulls to the semifinals and
dominated UNCC and UAB's inside game with 41 points and 26
rebounds. In addition, Monty Knight of Virginia Commonwealth, who single-handedly kept the Rams alive during their
games with his great outside shooting, received the All-
Tournament honor, as did Rory White of South Alabama.
White, former Sun Belt Player-of-the-Year and three-time
All-Sun Belt Conference, led the Jaguars past Jacksonville
in the opening round with his great inside and outside play,
and scored 30 points in South Alabama's two-point loss to
Virginia Commonwealth in the semifinal round.

-more-

Credit: The Sun Belt Conference.

FIGURE 7-3   **The sports tournament is a natural for most resorts and community developments. Probably none has gone so far or so fast, as Sawgrass with the Tournament Players Championship. The site of Sawgrass was scrub pine and swamp on the North Florida coast just a few years ago. Today the name is known worldwide through its famous tournament—the Tournament Players Championship. All this, of course, offers tremendous opportunities for the publicist. In this release, Sawgrass seeks to add to its prestige with a world-class tennis tournament. Note that Lipton, Volvo, and *Tennis Magazine* get a share of the publicity.**

An Arvida Resort Community
Ponte Vedra Beach, Florida 32082
Telephone (904) 285-2261

FOR IMMEDIATE RELEASE

CONTACT: Ruth Ann Kleinsteuber
            Director
            Public Relations
            Sawgrass
            P.O. Box 600
            Ponte Vedra Beach, FL 32082
            (904) 285-2261

(SAWGRASS ATTRACTS TOP TENNIS, TOO)

PONTE VEDRA BEACH,FL.--Say Sawgrass to a sports writer, and chances are he'll respond with "One of the toughest courses on the golf tour." Site of the prestigious Tournament Players Championship, the rolling, wind-swept links has brought a measure of fame to this oceanside resort community half an hour's drive south of Jacksonville. But the image is changing and tennis has taken its place alongside golf as one of the major sports amenities at Sawgrass.

Each September, world-class tennis comes to Sawgrass when they host the exciting Lipton World of Doubles tennis tournament. Thirty-two of the world's best men's doubles teams like Smith and Lutz, Stewart and Riessen and defending champions Gottfried and Ramirez battle it out for $175,000 in prize money and points on the year-long Volvo Grand Prix circuit.

With the playing of the Lipton World of Doubles and the signing of Dick Stockton as Touring Professional, the word has gotten out that Sawgrass is now one of the finest tennis resorts. TENNIS Magazine has named Sawgrass one of the Greatest Tennis Resorts in the United States.

(more)

Credit: *Sawgrass—An Arvida Resort Community.*

mailing list. Farm families are reached by the weekly newspaper *Grit,* as well as many other farm publications. A report on a successful experiment in store layout will be of considerable interest to the editors of *Progressive Grocer,* as well as to their readers.

If you are the public relations representative for a particular industry or enterprise, you will know your customers and competitors. Since you are one of the group, you will have little trouble in deciding what is interesting or exciting. If your company has recently perfected a new snorkle, certainly the editors and readers of *Diving Industry News* will be enthusiastic about getting all the details.

Making News Happen

Sometimes newsworthiness occurs only when it is made to occur. The news is in the *event,* and the event must be made to come about. Therefore, the public relations person is often responsible for writing the publicity generated by the event, as well as setting up the event itself. In many cases, the newsworthiness of the event will generate reams of publicity and pictures, from writers and cinema photographers all over the country. This situation, of course, finds the public relations person knee-deep in clover.

Sometimes the "events" are simple one-shot affairs and are well known to all of us in the public relations business. They are easy to arrange, take little time, and if planned correctly, generate some nice publicity "breaks." Others are far more time-consuming and complicated. An army of people may be engaged in a year-round effort to insure the success of some campaigns. Their impact and publicity-generating effect may be tremendous.

The Press Luncheon

A lunch, to which certain interested members of the press are invited, is an "event" that will usually generate a respectable story in the press—and thus publicity for your client.

Recently, a well-known figure in the boxing business wrote a book about the people and events he had known in a lifetime of promoting and match-making. Much of it was hilarious, and some of it was pretty racy, with some "now it can be told" stories. The public relations people for the publisher of the book sent out the customary releases to book editors and "trade press." Then they did something more. They arranged a luncheon at a midtown restaurant to which they invited sports writers from the city's papers. Many of them had known the author for years; his name had appeared in the sports pages a thousand times.

They also invited a list of old-time boxers, some of whom had been mentioned in the book. Out of the mists of the half-forgotten past they came. What stories they had to tell! The sports writers sat there enthralled, and

FIGURE 7-4   A professional little news release all the way. The "to, from, placement, time frame" helps the editor in making the placement decision. The one paragraph of copy is factual and has no excess wording.

STOKES & COMPANY

February 2, 1982

TO: FLORIDA TIMES UNION
                Business News Department

FROM: Judith Sisler
                Advertising Director

PLACEMENT: What's New - Appointments and Promotions

TIMEFRAME: For immediate use

STOKES AND COMPANY has promoted Roger O'Steen to head the Condominium Division and Coordinate the development of Sugar Mill in Mandarin; Sugar Creek in Tallahassee; The Oceans of Amelia, Fernandina; St. Augustine Ocean & Racquet Club and Southpoint at Daytona.

4319 SALISBURY ROAD • JACKSONVILLE, FLORIDA 32216 • TELEPHONE (904) 731-8170

Credit: Stokes and Company.

then hurried back to their typewriters and wrote their stories. Of course, they mentioned the book, the author, and the publisher, too.

The Macy's Thanksgiving Parade in New York City is more than an event. It is a tradition. From the city and its boroughs and suburbs come spectators by the thousands. Taking kids to the parade has become as traditional as taking them to see Santa Claus. No matter how bad the weather, people line the streets for blocks as the bands and clowns and giant balloons go by. The parade ends in Herald Square in front of Macy's—and the official Christmas shopping season is open.

Other Events

Many other events not only provide the opportunity to generate publicity, but themselves need publicity if they are to achieve their full effectiveness.

A *sale*, such as a "moonlight madness" event at a shopping center, must be publicized as widely as possible. Simply bringing the elephants from the railway yards to the circus grounds is a grand event full of pictures and story possibilities. In the spring, when the "blessed events" begin at the zoo, everyone is delighted. One baby chimpanzee is worth a thousand words. Most cities of any size have an exhibition hall or a fairground. Almost every industry you can imagine has some sort of *convention* or *trade show* each year. The "county fair" is a fixture in American rural life. All of them need, and have, the ability to generate publicity. A traveling *fashion show* is welcomed by local retailers. It is a perfect event for generating publicity of interest to the style-conscious of the community. What about *jazz festivals?* Newport is no longer a little Rhode Island town where the rich folks used to spend their summers; it is the place where Dizzy blew and Della sang and Big Joe Turner used to shout the blues. It must have generated a ton of publicity stories and pictures. On graduation day, are there plenty of reporters and photographers present? Your college's public relations department has made every effort to see that there are. You can be sure the program chair has made sure to select a speaker who will not only be inspirational, but newsworthy as well.

Media—The Personal Touch

A *contact* might be described as "the right person to talk to." Public relations people value their contacts. They treat them with tender loving care and attention. The loss of a contact can sometimes be more grievous than the loss of a friend. Knowing the right person to see or talk to is often the key to an effective publicity effort. Let us meet some of these people.

As we discuss these people, keep in mind what the relationship means. It means that you will never lie to or mislead them. If you promise one of them an "exclusive," then that is what you deliver. Your publicity releases

FIGURE 7-5   Nationally known brands and companies do a great deal of public relations work, but the many small, local institutions must get themselves before the public, too. Often, the local enterprise crams more information into a release than is necessary or can be handled by the editor. Here we have an example of a press release that tried to accomplish too much at once. The opening paragraph is a likely item for the "What's Going On Around Town" column. With the addition of the dance director's name and phone number, it is almost sure to make it. The story on the guest auditioner would be an interesting item for the entertainment page if accompanied by a photo and if the story were built up to contain more human interest material on the dancer and her accomplishments. Here, a *real* newsworthy event might have been discovered—she once danced a command performance before an Indian prince and his retinue at 3 in the morning. As for the "Specifications," the paper can hardly be expected to provide space for what is actually the responsibility of the director to provide to applicants.

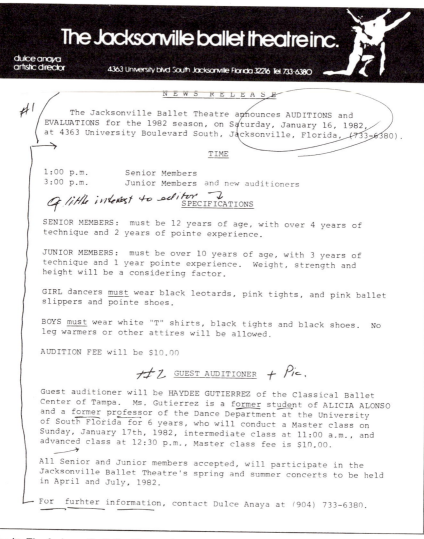

The Jacksonville ballet theatre inc.

dulce anaya
artistic director
4363 University blvd South Jacksonville Florida 32216 Tel 733-6380

N E W S   R E L E A S E

#1

The Jacksonville Ballet Theatre announces AUDITIONS and EVALUATIONS for the 1982 season, on Saturday, January 16, 1982, at 4363 University Boulevard South, Jacksonville, Florida, (733-6380).

TIME

1:00 p.m.   Senior Members
3:00 p.m.   Junior Members and new auditioners

Of little interest to editor

SPECIFICATIONS

SENIOR MEMBERS: must be 12 years of age, with over 4 years of technique and 2 years of pointe experience.

JUNIOR MEMBERS: must be over 10 years of age, with 3 years of technique and 1 year pointe experience. Weight, strength and height will be a considering factor.

GIRL dancers must wear black leotards, pink tights, and pink ballet slippers and pointe shoes.

BOYS must wear white "T" shirts, black tights and black shoes. No leg warmers or other attires will be allowed.

AUDITION FEE will be $10.00

#2 GUEST AUDITIONER + Pic.

Guest auditioner will be HAYDEE GUTIERREZ of the Classical Ballet Center of Tampa. Ms. Gutierrez is a former student of ALICIA ALONSO and a former professor of the Dance Department at the University of South Florida for 6 years, who will conduct a Master class on Sunday, January 17th, 1982, intermediate class at 11:00 a.m., and advanced class at 12:30 p.m., Master class fee is $10.00.

All Senior and Junior members accepted, will participate in the Jacksonville Ballet Theatre's spring and summer concerts to be held in April and July, 1982.

For furhter information, contact Dulce Anaya at (904) 733-6380.

Credit: The Jacksonville Ballet Theatre, Inc.

will be factual and newsworthy. You will never be guilty of crying "wolf" when there was only a mouse. You will never leak a phony or misleading story that, once printed or broadcast, could embarrass both reporter and medium. In short, you will treat your contacts as valued allies. But who are they?

1. *Editors and Reporters.* Keep in mind that there are department editors and reporters. There is a sports editor, and there are sports reporters. There will be an editor for the women's page (called by various names such as "Life Style" these days), and there will be reporters who cover the food and restaurant beat.

   There may be a Sunday edition in your city, with a complete staff of its own. If your community is big enough, there will certainly be a business page with an editor and writers. In the general news department, reporters are often assigned to different "beats"—City Hall, police, science, churches. As you have noticed, newspapers often are published in identifiable *sections*—real estate, entertainment, home and garden, and so on. Newspapers also publish special editions such as the year-end business review. The editors of these editions will often welcome a story tailored to their special needs.

2. *Television News Teams.* The faces of your TV news team are as familiar as old friends. But if you read the credits at the end of the show, you will discover that many others are involved—writers, editors, and cameramen.

3. *Photographers.* Newspapers have their own sports and news photographers who are sent out on assignment. Magazines will purchase photographs from freelance professional photographers or request that the author supply photographic illustrations. Your community probably has several professional photographers and studios. It is well to know all of them, if possible, as their abilities and prices will vary considerably.

Working with Media Representatives

There are a number of well-known techniques used in working with the press. They range from the simple to the complex.

1. *Telephone queries.* In most cases the press will regard you as the primary source of information regarding your company. The caller may need some kind of specialized information, or he or she may be calling to confirm a rumor. You must be as helpful as possible and as frank and open as circumstances permit. You are expected to have all the facts at your fingertips.

   Press relations are often severely tested when events occur with a large potential for damaging reputations: fires, accidents, malfunctioning products. "Papering over" the problem is the worst thing you can do. This is the time for you to be as honest and direct as possible. You have every right, however, to ask that judgment be withheld until all the facts are in and the full story is known.[1]

2. *Press conferences.* When your organization has an announcement of some importance to make, it is customary to arrange a meeting for the members

---

[1]The motion picture *Absence of Malice* (1982) concerned the problem of conclusion jumping in the press and the damage it can cause.

FIGURE 7-6 This contents page is from a popular car magazine. It demonstrates the public relations possibilities of trade and specialized publications. Every article covers a commercial product in great detail, and a great deal of it is "news" to the reader.

ILLUSTRATION BY RICHARD CORSON

JULY 1982   VOLUME 33, NUMBER 11

Road & Track (ISSN 0035-7189) is published monthly by CBS Publications, the Consumer Publishing Division of CBS Inc., 1515 Broadway, New York, N.Y. 10036. *Road & Track* is a registered trademark of CBS Inc. **Editorial and Production offices** located at 1499 Monrovia Ave, Newport Beach, Calif. 92663, phone 714 646-4451; Robert J. Krefting, President; Thomas O. Ryder, Vice President, General Manager; George H. Allen, Senior Vice President/Magazines; Michael Brennan, Vice President; Richard A. Bartkus, Vice President. CBS Publications is the Consumer Publishing Division of CBS Inc. Second class postage paid at New York, N.Y. 10001 and at additional mailing offices. Printed in U.S.A. **POSTMASTER: Please send change of address to ROAD & TRACK, PO Box 5331, 1255 Portland Pl, Boulder, Colo. 80322,** © 1982, CBS PUBLICATIONS, the Consumer Publishing Division of CBS Inc. All Rights Reserved.

FIGURE 7-6 continued   **This page is an excellent example of the kind of valuable publicity that can be provided by the trade or specialty press. This detailed story on the Saab 900 Turbo was worth considerably more than its weight in gold. Imagine— a highly authoritative story, published in a highly respected publication, read by an audience that is knowledgable and enthusiastic. You can't do much better than that!**

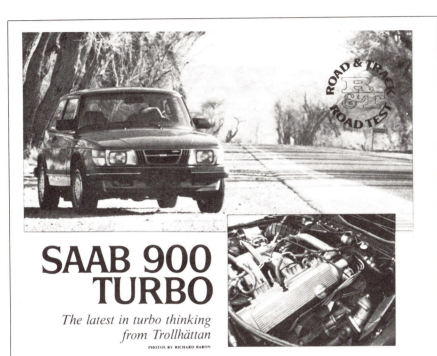

SAAB 900 TURBO

The latest in turbo thinking from Trollhättan

PHOTOS BY RICHARD BARON

SAAB IMAGINE AN ENGINE that assesses the quality of its fuel and, what's more, optimizes its operation based on what this fuel has to offer. Better yet, imagine such an engine in production, not simply in some research lab. Best of all, imagine it in a car we've found distinctly pleasurable in previous versions. Having performed all these feats of imagination, you can appreciate our reasons for this road test of the APC-equipped Saab 900 Turbo.

APC stands for Automatic Performance Control, Saab's name for the detonation-sensed boost modulation of its Turbo models. Back in June 1980, when we had our first look at a prototype APC system, we called it "Saab's Turbo Boost with a Brain." After more extensive driving in admittedly less extraordinary settings (our Engineering Editor went to the French Riviera for the prototype intro), we're prepared to argue that APC is the most elegant—though subtle—innovation in turbo engineering in quite some time.

First, let's discuss how it works; then we'll share our road test impressions. Throughout, we'll be probing your technoid quotient (the higher your sense of technical esthetics, the more likely you are to be turned on by APC).

For technical openers, appreciate that any properly optimized engine occasionally tiptoes near detonation. For a given quality of fuel, as measured by its octane, a particular engine will be most efficient at some optimal compression ratio and ignition timing. Lower its c.r. or retard ignition, and efficiency suffers. Raise the c.r. or advance the ignition, and you do more than tiptoe near detonation—you positively stumble into it.

Enter the turbo: Its increased charge density on boost makes the engine believe it has a higher c.r. than indicated by its combustion chamber geometry. Increased temperature of the

compressed air encourages detonation as well. Thus, with all else equal, a turbo powerplant will have a higher octane appetite than its normally aspirated brethren. Now automakers are understandably reluctant to see their turbo beauties detonating themselves to death, so various engineering responses have evolved.

The most common is to lower a turbo version's c.r., but this pays dues in an off-boost loss of efficiency. Another approach is to retard ignition timing as well, either in response to boost level or (more to the point) in response to incipient detonation sensed by a knock sensor. Notice, though, retarded ignition is hardly a freebie either.

Saab's approach with APC is clearly more elegant. It retains the c.r. and ignition timing of its normally aspirated counterpart, but senses detonation and varies the boost accordingly. APC intelligence requires relatively few components: the detonation sensor, a pressure transducer, an rpm-sensing gizmo, a solenoid linked to wastegate plumbing and the inevitable black box. The knock sensor is on the engine block and of the usual piezoelectric crystal type, generating minute voltages when it gets knocked about. The pressure transducer measures boost in the intake manifold. The reason for the engine speed sensor is that detonation is rpm-sensitive as well as octane-related. These three signals, rpm, boost level and any knock, go to the black box (it's gray, actually) controlling the solenoid. If all systems are go, the solenoid tricks the wastegate into thinking there's less boost being generated and this in turn causes the wastegate to stay closed longer, allowing boost to increase. If the detonation sensor's message is a no-go, the solenoid, wastegate and its attendant plumbing bring about a reduction of boost until detonation ceases. All this cleverness occurs at a rate of 12 times per second, giving a continuous, though subtle control of boost in ➡➡➡

46   ROAD & TRACK

Credit: Road and Track, CBS Publications.

of the press. The place of the meeting may be in the offices of the company, or in the meeting rooms of a convenient hotel or restaurant. A carefully selected list of guests is invited, according to the interests of their editors and publications. Refreshments are sometimes served. A release or press kit containing pertinent information may be provided.

3. *Plant tours* and *new product stories.* These events have many of the characteristics of the press conference. A *briefing* is more general in nature than the press conference. It is held for the purpose of providing the press with background material. "Picture day" at the beginning of college football practice is a kind of press conference for photographers.

Getting News to Publications

In photo sessions, plant tours, and press conferences, we bring the press to us. Far more frequently, we must go to them. Probably the simplest way to do this is to pick up the phone, call a reporter, and ask if you can come over to the news room. This is all right when you have something of immediate local interest. But often we want our stories to reach a far wider audience. Then we turn to the *syndicates.*

1. *News syndicates.* These are the famous Associated Press, United Press International, and Reuters. Time after time, in your newspaper, you have seen stories from the "wire" of one of these services—and so labeled just beneath the headline. In addition to these general news services, there are other syndicates of a more specialized nature in the religious, financial, and labor fields.

2. *Feature syndicates.* A great many syndicates distribute features such as comic strips, cartoons, and columns. Cartoons, in particular, are excellent publicity vehicles. They make their point quickly, graphically, and often with considerable impact. No one should underestimate the power of a cartoon. They have changed the course of history.[2] Among the best-known feature syndicates are King Features Syndicate and McNaught Syndicate, Inc.

3. *Photo syndicates.* Every public relations staff should have its skilled photographer—or access to one. Obtaining a photo worthy of notice by the syndicates is not easy. The picture must have professional quality plus a clever, creative idea behind it. Associated Press News Photo, Wide World Photos, and Black Star are among the better union syndicates offering photos to the news media.

[2]One of the most famous is Thomas Nast's "Tweed King," published in the 1890s, depicting graft in New York.

FIGURE 7-7   Publications often produce their own brochures for the use of those who may be seeking publicity through their pages. This is particularly important when many people and organizations in the community are nonprofessionals. This publicity handbook, issued by the Florida *Times-Union,* is practically a short course in public relations. Note the section on ideas and their importance.

HOW NEWS GETS INTO THE PAPER:

All news — or feature — stories start with an idea. That idea may be from the reporter, or his or her editor. In this case, the idea comes from within the newspaper.

But ideas come from elsewhere, and this is where you come in.

Ideas come from letters to the newspaper, telephone calls, casual conversations — and from publicity chairpersons and public relations specialists.

You stand a better chance of expanded coverage if you can offer an idea for a story that is different from the ordinary. We call this an "angle" or "news peg."

For example, a story of a woman giving birth on Valetine's Day is not especially unusual.

But the story that a passenger train had to make an unscheduled stop so that she could be taken to the hospital is. And that is a story we would not have known had it not been for the public relations person at the hospital.

WHY:

Individuals — or clubs or corporations — usually seek to reach people en masse through the news media for one of seven reasons. Consider the purpose of your release, and some of the possible repercussions, before submitting it.

1.) To build an image. You wish to build a favorable image of your organization. That image must be based on reality. If your aim is to portray your organization as totally altruistic and devoted to charitable acts, the acts must exist for the publicity to be credible.

2.) Promotion. You may wish to gain general public support of an idea, person or product. Your cause must be worthy of public support because in seeking mass support, you also expose it to mass criticism.

3.) To provide information. This, from the newspaper point of view, is the most valid reasion for a press release since it represents the things the newspaper stands for — to provide people with information they seek, need or are entitled to.

4.) To seek a specific public action. You may wish to rally people to a specific cause, such as approval or disapproval of a zoning variance or the building of a new bridge. Your audience in this case is more narrow than in point 2 above.

5.) To seek a specific response by individuals. You may wish them to attend a meeting or lecture, vote for or against a specific candidate or donate money to your cause.

2

104

FIGURE 7-7 continued

6.) To defend against public attack. You may be defending your organization against criticism by opposing groups, individuals, unfavorable news stories or criticism by governmental bodies.

7.) To sell something. If sales are the primary purpose of your release, forget it. Editors consider strictly commercial releases a waste of their time and try to separate the news and advertising functions so that one does not affect the other.

WHO IS THE AUDIENCE FOR YOUR NEWS RELEASE?

Ultimately it is the audience of the newspaper, but the immediate audience is editors and reporters. The interest of the two coincide because the first concern of a good editor is his/her audience.

You first should offer your idea to the reporter in charge of the type of news you are submitting. If you don't know who that reporter is, call the editor in charge of that particular section of the newspaper — City Desk, Style, Business, etc. A complete list of editors and their phone numbers is included in the pull-out section of this booklet.

Editors prefer that you deal with only one section of the newspaper, but you may want to hedge your bets. If your organization can be covered under sports, style and local, contact all three departments. It's up to us to see that your story gets in only once. But you should note on your release each department it has gone to.

To know to whom to submit your release, you have to know . . .

WHERE TO FIND THEM

At this point, let's take a a quick stroll through the various departments of the newspaper, acquainting you with their various functions and the type news they handle.

THE CITY DESK

The City Desk at The Florida Times-Union is responsible for coverage of news in Jacksonville, Atlantic, Neptune and Jacksonville Beaches and Clay County.

By definition, the City Desk is the primary operation to deal with what is called "breaking" or "hard" news. The city reporters are assigned to a variety of "beats" — areas of continuing coverage — including:

- City Hall
- Police
- Energy
- Environment
- Politics
- Religion
- Medicine
- Minority Affairs

3

Credit: Florida Publishing Company.

FIGURE 7-8 **How to write a theme. The author of this release does not simply talk about Ramada's new refurbishing program, he dramatizes it by using the "bucking the trend" theme. This device not only takes the story out of the announcement class, it makes the release much more newsworthy in an editor's eyes.**

RAMADA NEWS Ramada Inns, Inc., 3838 East Van Buren Street, Phoenix, Arizona 85008

FOR IMMEDIATE RELEASE   Contact: Kenneth G. Jensen
                                                   (602) 273-4604

                    RAMADA GAINS AGAINST INDUSTRY TRENDS;
                       SHOWS INCREASED OCCUPANCY

        PHOENIX, Ariz. -- October 9, 1981 -- Ramada Inns, Inc., which over the

past three years has spent more than $100 million to refurbish its owned hotels

in the U.S., is bucking industry trends by posting occupancy gains in what can

be best described as a "soft" market.

        For the first seven months of 1981, Ramada's domestic company-owned

hotels are up in occupancy 3.9 percentage points over the same period last

year. At the same time, the hotel industry as a whole is down in occupancy

nearly two full percentage points, according to industry analysts.

        "We are swimming upstream in a very soft market," said Juergen

Bartels, president of Ramada's Hospitality Group. "Hotels and the travel

industry in general, are off this year."

        "We are convinced that our refurbishing program and our improved

customer services have created the kind of lodging experience that our guests

have wanted," Bartels said. "We are ahead of our own forecasts for occupancy

in a period that most analysts saw as flat or down."

        In addition to the money spent by Ramada on its owned hotels, its

licensees have spent more than $125 million to renovate their hotels.

                        More . . . .

FIGURE 7-8   continued

Page 2 -- Ramada Inns, Inc.

"The expenditure of this kind of money during the sagging economy that we have been through is indicative of a real commitment to product improvement," Bartels said. "The gains that we have seen in occupancy are proof that we have a product that appeals to customers."

So far, Ramada has refurbished about 12,000 of its 17,000 domestic company-owned hotel rooms. It also has done extensive work on lobbies, restaurants, corridors, lounges and exteriors of almost all of its 100 domestic Ramada hotels and inns.

"I believe we have some of the finest rooms in the mid-priced hotel industry. It has been money well spent," Bartels said. "We will continue to improve our product wherever possible."

Ramada licensees, who operate about 500 hotels within the United States, have refurbished about half of the 68,000 rooms under their control. They also have improved lobbies, corridors, restaurants, lounges and meeting rooms.

"We are spending just over a million dollars per property and our licensees are nearly matching that," Bartels said.

With more than 93,000 rooms in about 630 hotels worldwide, Ramada is one of the world's largest international hotel chains.

###

Credit: Ramada Inns, Inc.

4. *Distribution services.* There are firms that distribute publicity material for a fee. They are particularly good at getting material to thousands of smaller newspapers. Rather than "releases," they send out the material already cast in plates. A feature, column, or entire page may arrive at the newspaper office ready to "drop in." The small, short-handed newspapers love this. There are also wire services especially set up for public relations people. For a fee, they transmit by teletype direct from the public relations office to the publication. *Clipsheets* are another great favorite of the small-town newspaper editor. Stories arrive from the service in various sizes and can be clipped out for use. Those jokes you see at the end of a column to fill it are usually from a clipsheet.

5. *Specialized newspapers.* Just as there is a magazine for every category of trade or industry, there are many newspapers directed to special groups. *Grit* is a famous paper directed to farm families. *Wall Street Journal* and *Barron's* appeal to the financial community. There are black newspapers such as the Chicago *Defender* and the Pittsburgh *Courier.* There are at least 75 foreign-language newspapers devoted to the interests of various ethnic groups in the United States. Lists and descriptions of newspapers can be found in *Ayer's Directory* and in *Standard Rate and Data.*

Magazines

Much of what has been said about newspaper publicity holds for magazines, but there are some important differences. A magazine carries a limited number of stories and articles—far fewer than most newspapers. A magazine usually has but one editor and a few staff writers or assistant editors. General magazines rely on outside writers; specialized publications often write their own material.

The magazine editor may often be difficult to reach. A great deal of unsolicited material crosses the editor's desk, including unsolicited publicity material. Most editors know what they want and who can write it for them. They know writer's agents and most "name" writers in the business. The unsolicited freelance article seldom has much chance. One way you can help a magazine editor is to supply subjects or ideas. Included with this can be pictures and background information. A member of the staff, a freelance, or you may be asked to prepare the article. Remember that most editors are pressed for time. A phone call or inquiry by mail will be appreciated. Personal interviews should be businesslike and to the point. Particular magazine editors are, of course, on the invitation lists for the press conferences, luncheons, and tours mentioned above.

As with newspapers, there is a great variety of magazines. There are general news magazines such as *Time* and *Newsweek.* There are those known as "shelter magazines," which are devoted to the interests of the homemaker. Look at the magazine rack in any store, and you will see that there is at least one publication dedicated to almost any special interest you might name— fishing, sailing, skiing, travel, and even getting married *(Bride's Magazine).* In addition to the magazines on the store rack, there are hundreds of others

FIGURE 7-9 Fact sheets such as this are an important tool. Every public relations department has an up-dated file of these for all media. Note that the sheet contains all relevant information needed when a release is to be sent out.

```
                                              REVISED_____/_____
                              PRESS FACT SHEET
Newspaper:___THE BEACHES LEADER
Mailing Address:___P. O. Box 50129, Jacksonville Beach, FL. 32250
Street Address:___712 North Third Street, Jacksonville Beach, FL. 32250
Telephone:___249-9033_____(X) Weekly ( ) Daily ( )_____
Managing Editor___Bill Dryden, Publisher___City Editor___Fred Desapio
Mail Prepared Releases to:___Fred Desapio, P. O. Box 50129, Jax., Bch., FL. 32250
Hours to Phone or Visit:___9:00 - 6:00 Monday & Tuesday - 9:00 - Noon Thurs. & Fri.
Copy Deadline:___Monday, 12:00 noon_____Pictures:___same
Use Glossy Prints: (x) Yes ( ) No / Mats: (X) Yes ( ) No
Preferred Size: ( ) 4x5 ( ) 5x7 ( ) 8x10 ( ) Other:___x___
Use Color: ( ) Yes (x) No / Format: ( ) 35MM ( ) 2-1/4
Special Editors/Writers:_____

Editorial Contact:___Fred Desapio
-------------------------------------------------------------------
Newspaper:___Clay County Crescent
Mailing Address:___P. O. Box 578, Green Cove Springs, FL. 32043
Street Address:___806 Walnut Street, Green Cove Springs, FL. 32043
Telephone:___284-3166_____(x) Weekly ( ) Daily ( )_____
Managing Editor:___Elaine Williamson___City Editor___none
Mail Prepared Releases to:___P. O. Box 578, Green Cove Springs, FL. 32043
Hours to Phone or Visit:___Monday & Tuesday
Copy Deadline:___Tuesday, 12:00 noon_____Pictures:___same
Use Glossy Prints: (x) Yes ( ) No / Mats: ( ) Yes (X) No
Preferred Size: ( ) 4x5 ( ) 5x7 ( ) 8x10 (X) Other_any size
Use Color: (x) Yes ( ) No / Format: ( ) 35MM ( ) 2-1/4
Special Editors/Writers:_____

Editorial Contact:___Elaine Williamson
```

Credit: Florida Publishing Company.

you never see. These are the ones devoted to the special interests of those in trade and industry. Generally, they are known as the *trade press.* You may never have heard of *Electrical Contractor.* But if anyone you know is in the business of wiring houses, he or she certainly has. And he or she reads each issue with interest. A comparable publication exists, literally, for any trade, enterprise, or interest you can imagine.

Magazine editors may be hard to see, and your story chances few and far between. But when your story *does* break, you usually get your money's worth. This is particularly true of the trade press. Almost every story in a trade or industrial magazine is a great publicity break for someone. The very nature of the trade press makes this so. Most of the editorial material is about people and developments in a particular business.

Take, for instance, a magazine called *Iron Age.* In one issue, there is a story about a big steel company and the new manager it hired for one of its divisions. It is a straight success story of the division's success and its plans for the future, with pictures of the new manager. Following this is an article about a Midwest manufacturing company and how its new management techniques have increased production. *Somebody* had to supply the facts for those articles.

Books

Books can be long-lasting and effective public relations tools. Sometimes they are sponsored directly, but often the connection is indirect.

If an author is writing a book about a particular industry, company, or official, he or she will undoubtedly come to the public relations department for aid and information. Unless he or she has in mind a "smear" or exposé, the public relations people will give the writer all the help and encouragement they can.[3] Sometimes a company will arrange to sponsor a book. In this case, author, subject, publisher, and costs are all arranged beforehand. Or the company may arrange to prepare and produce the book itself. Many companies produce "help" or "usage" books, such as Shell Oil's book on safe driving.

Some of the most beautiful books are those sponsored by state and government tourist bureaus. Often in the form of tourist guides, they are enticing invitations to visitors. In France, the Michelin Tire Company produces the *Guides Bleu,* containing routes, local descriptions, hotels, and restaurants. One of the most famous of company-produced books is the *Guinness Book of World Records,* published by the Guinness Brewing Company of Dublin, Ireland. It has become so well known that it generates its own publicity. People are continually attempting to swallow more goldfish or stay in a tel-

---

[3]For example, *An American Dynasty: The Story of the McCormacks, Medills, and Patter-sons*—a dynasty of newspaper publication.

ephone booth longer in order to get their names in the book. Incidentally, the *Guinness Book of World Records* was first published to aid bartenders in settling arguments.

Sometimes books have public relations benefits quite by chance. Certainly the manufacturers of Mazola Corn Oil, a cooking oil low in unsaturated fats, must have been delighted with the American Heart Association Cookbook, which recommends nothing but unsaturated fat to prevent cholesterol buildup.

Brochures and Pamphlets

It often falls to the public relations department to produce a variety of "literature." These may vary in size and elaborateness from the expensive annual report to simple employee booklets.

Your college may produce booklets giving course descriptions. The department of student services contains dozens of booklets describing various careers. In many cases, these are products of individual companies or trade associations. One very important booklet, as far as company employee public relations is concerned, is the orientation booklet. This publication, often amusingly illustrated and written, welcomes the new employee to the corporate family. It contains information about company policy, history, rules, and procedures. The comic strip, ideal for telling a story simply and graphically, is often put in booklet form. Comic strips are particularly effective in getting across a story that otherwise might be ignored by a youthful or unsophisticated audience.

Broadcast Media: TV, Radio, Films

Just as the requirements for magazines differ from those for newspapers, so we must recognize certain differences in other media.

TV news and entertainment programs are watched by millions, but the public relations opportunities are far fewer than those in the print media. However, the impact can be far stronger. Given the right personality and the right circumstances, a blow heard 'round the world can be struck. It only took a few matinee idols, topcoats thrown over shoulders and carefully combed locks waving in the breeze, to almost destroy the hat business. And why do you think certain American dress designers "loaned" the First Lady the gowns that would be seen in every home by those watching the evening news? The opportunities may be rarer, but everything from a fad to a revolution has been started with a TV broadcast.

One of the publicist's problems with TV is the fact that so much of its entertainment format has been produced and filmed well ahead of time. Perhaps if one knew the writers and producers something might be done, but this is rare.

Some kinds of programming, however, offer great opportunities. Panels, talk shows, debates, and interviews all offer chances to project ideas forcefully, and at length. Authors talk about their latest book, entertainers their performances; industry experts of all kinds are called upon to express opinions. The producers of these shows are delighted to get the people, and the people are delighted to talk about what they like or do best. One thing to be careful of: Not all of us come off well under the unsparing eye of the camera. It is not enough to be an expert. A vibrant personality, good makeup, and diligent rehearsal help, too.

One of the most common types of commercial publicity on film seems to happen almost by chance. It began in Hollywood years ago when some entrepreneur decided that, if the kid was to be shown eating breakfast cereal, it might as well be *your* breakfast cereal. So began the business of "spotting" products where they could be seen by millions of viewers. Some directors conceal labels and products. Some fake them. Others are much more concerned with realism. I saw a picture recently starring Paul Newman. He was forever reaching in the refrigerator and offering somebody a beer. There must have been something symbolic about it, but I missed it. Even in the last scene at the dock, when Sally Field walked away from him, he was drinking a beer from the can and she was carrying one. Like most of us, the character portrayed by Newman is brand-loyal—Bud all the way.

Another beautiful "free ride" occurs in broadcast sporting events. The manufacturers of boxing equipment always see to it that their names are prominently displayed on trunks and gloves. Scoreboards usually carry the names of sponsors. When the camera comes in close on a football player taking a refreshing drink on the bench, note that the cup he is holding prominently displays the name of a soft drink manufacturer.

TV coverage is of particular importance to political figures. President Eisenhower is said to have been the first to use commercials in an election campaign. To every politician, local or national, coverage is of vital importance if he or she is to establish both personality and program. Prominent people in government have little trouble getting television coverage; others must work for it.

Special interest groups of all kinds strive for "exposure." The effectiveness of a demonstration, march, or meeting is multiplied thousands of times when it gets footage on the news broadcast. It is interesting to wonder what might have happened had Lincoln gotten some time on the evening news with his Gettysburg Address. Martin Luther King's "I have a dream . . ." speech lives forever on film.

Public Broadcasting Service (PBS)

These stations (there are over 200 of them) are different from the commercial network stations. Their emphasis is on arts and discussion. Many programs are produced by local stations for the use of other PBS stations;

others may be purely local in nature. PBS is always squeezed for money. It does not sell commercial time, of course, but it does allow an announcement at the beginning and end of each show. These may be companies in the station's own community or corporations such as Mobil or Texaco. This is an excellent public relations device, for the intellectual level of the average PBS viewer is probably somewhat higher than that of commercial network viewers. When people are brought programs they might not otherwise see—operas, symphonies, great plays, science and exploration films—they naturally tend to feel grateful to those who made it possible.

PBS, in addition to interview shows, often does reviews of books and movies, resulting in nice publicity—particularly when the reviews are good. PBS also buys shows from independent producers. One such show, produced for the Audubon Society, carried a powerful pro-environment message and a devastating attack on current Department of the Interior policies, which have loosened regulations regarding the use of pesticides, offshore oil drilling, and the destruction of estuaries.

Company-Produced Films

Motion pictures and slide film presentations are popular public relations and promotional devices, especially when they are designed for educational purposes. After all, who can speak more authoritatively on auto engine repair than Ford or General Motors? Insurance companies are experts when it comes to the subject of safety. Schools and hospitals have found that films are excellent training aids. Frequently you will find that these are produced and distributed by a drug or surgical supply company. Transparencies designed for classroom projection also fall into this category. Automatic video-audio or still picture-audio are often seen in stores and are very effective at trade shows and conventions, where there is constant audience change.

SUMMARY

Newsworthiness is the quality in news that gives it excitement and interest—and gets a release printed or broadcast.

You meet people who make the decisions about newsworthiness in many ways: press luncheons, interviews, and "events" of various kinds. These media contacts are editors and reporters, television news teams, and photographers. Sometimes the media come to us—by telephone, a press luncheon or conference, or plant tours and exhibitions.

There are a number of sources for disseminating a release: news syndicates, feature syndicates, photo syndicates, and distribution services, in addition to personal contacts. A great variety of specialized publications are available. These have "special interest" audiences whom you would particularly want to get your story. Books, brochures, and pamphlets are generally called "literature" and may be produced by your own office.

The broadcast media—TV and radio—present fewer opportunities to gain publicity than the print media, but their penetration may be far deeper. Broadcast media often reach millions of viewers at one time.

KEY TERMS

News

Newsworthiness

Press luncheon

News teams

Press conference

Plant tours

Syndicates

Distribution services

Specialized newspapers

Magazines

Books, brochures, pamphlets

Broadcast media

Slide films

Public broadcasting (PBS)

THE WAY IT HAPPENED

I had just completed my first book and was quite proud of my performance. It was a new text in advertising, and the people in our public relations department gave it a paragraph in the college employees' paper. I thought it deserved a little more than that.

So I called the newsroom of our local paper and asked to talk to someone in the business section. I told the reporter I had a story for him about an unusual advertising book and suggested that I come down and see him and bring my book. He agreed to see me.

When we sat down together I showed him my book and pointed out that all other advertising texts were about "Madison Avenue" and were illustrated by work for the giant national advertisers. My book, I pointed out, concentrates on "Main Street"—the people who do 90 percent of this country's advertising: local and regional agencies just like the ones in our town. All the illustrations of ads and commercials were work *they* had done.

The reporter took lots of notes and appeared interested. He had a photographer take a picture of the book, and photographed me walking toward the camera. Two days later—there I was on the front business page! A big picture showed me stepping out against a background of the book cover. The headline proclaimed:

MAIN STREET REPLACES MADISON AVE.

"The real world of advertising is not on high-powered Madison Avenue in New

York, but on Main Street, U.S.A.," says James S. Norris, Professor of Marketing. . . .

You see, I'd found my newsworthy angle.

A PERSONAL PROJECT

As you have seen, it is the "twist" in the story that often gives it its news-worthiness. Very often the interesting, newsworthy angle is hidden deep within the story and has to be extracted.

Let us see you take a very commonplace story—let's say, flower beds are being put in around the plant main entrance—and imagine the kind of buried twist that would change it from a release that might wind up in the wastebasket to one that might become a front-page feature.

READING TO BROADEN UNDERSTANDING

STEPHENSON, HOWARD, ED. *Handbook of Public Relations*, 2d ed. (New York: McGraw-Hill, 1971). Has good chapters on external publications, p. 615, company literature, p. 647, and newspapers, p. 671.

SCHOENFELD, CLARENCE A. *Publicity Media and Methods* (New York: Macmillan, 1963). See Chapter 6, "The Gatekeepers," on editors and broadcast media managers. Authors say we are like hitchhikers—we depend a lot on free rides.

DARROW, RICHARD W., DAN J. FORRESTAL, AUBRY O. COOKMAN. *The Dartnell Public Relations Handbook* (Chicago: The Dartnell Corporation, 1968). Part 4, p. 536, contains a tremendous amount of material on media. See Chapters 1, 2, and 3.

Standard Rates and Data (Skokie, Ill.: Standard Rate and Data Service). These volumes, which supply advertising rates and other information for all kinds of media, will give you a good idea on the breadth of the media field.

CUTLIP, SCOTT M., AND ALLEN H. CENTER. *Effective Public Relations,* 5th ed. (Englewood Cliffs, N.J.: Prentice-Hall, 1978). See Chapter 17, "Working with the Media, Particularly Rules for Good Press Relations," p. 384.

OTHER METHODS
OF REACHING
OUR PUBLICS

_____

OVERVIEW AND GOALS

We are now going to look at additional ways to reach our publics with the messages we design.

There are quite a few ways, as you might imagine—everything from rumors to all the devices commonly used in product advertising. The public relations person must understand *all* the media available for transmitting the message. When you have finished this chapter, you should be able to

> ***Understand*** *the use of each of the mediums covered in this chapter— rumors, bumper stickers, consultants, newsletters, demonstrators, and so on.*

Up to this point, we have considered what most people regard as the main vehicles of public relations: the print and broadcast media. Indeed, they do carry vast amounts of publicity covering a wide spectrum of subjects.

But all good public relations persons understand that there are many other vehicles for conveying messages to their publics. Each can be tailored to meet a particular need. In fact, one of these vehicles may be the perfect one for the job at hand. Let us look at some of them.

Rumors and Leaks: Word of Mouth

It is a fact of life that you, as a public relations person, are going to have to deal with. Rumors can spread with the speed of the common cold. This is especially true within your company itself.

Management is very conscious of rumor and the damage it can do to morale and productivity. The public relations department must be alert to detect these rumors and to correct them when necessary. When someone's secretary mentions that a management consultant firm has been retained, the event can be blown all out of proportion. Before long, the rumor has spread that the entire executive suite is about to be fired.

The proper way to handle rumor is to attempt to understand what motivates it and to deal with it quickly and accurately. The bulletin board notice, memo, or newsletter are all handy and quick means of setting the record straight. Often a face-to-face meeting with employees or the press can be used to handle the situation. A few years ago, a large company was shaken by rumors and innuendo when a particularly attractive young business school graduate was advanced over the heads of a number of more experienced executives into an important management position. The chairman of the board did not hesitate. He called press, stockholders, and employees together in a series of meetings, defended his position, denied the innuendos, and stated the reasons for his decision in a clear and forthright manner.

Rumors about products and product development go on in all industries. A few years ago a wild rumor shook Proctor and Gamble, the big soap manufacturer. A little sign they had been using for years on their products was said to be cabalistic, showed that P. and G. was in league with the devil, and that the use of their products would surely put a curse on you. Manufacturers take elaborate precautions to conceal their activities from competitors. The public relations department plays an important part in helping to keep next year's model under wraps until the unveiling.

A remarkable amount of "intelligence" work goes on in industry. Boardrooms have been "bugged." Advance information can be worth millions to some manufacturers. Small companies can often move much faster than larger rivals. "Beating 'em to the punch" can be a profitable tactic, as the office copier industry saw a few years ago. In all of this, the public relations department must act as "counterintelligence."

Wall Street and the stock market live on rumors. Some of these rumors are inadvertent, others are deliberately leaked. Someone is urged via "inside information" to buy options in an oil company stock. There are rumors of a takeover. They must have started last week, because the stock has gone up almost 7 points in the last few days. But is the rumor true? Or was it a deliberate leak so that a few insiders could grab their profits and run?

The day has long passed when companies would deliberately leak a rumor in order to harm competition, but it has been known to happen. Washington, D.C., is a happy hunting ground for leakers and leakees. Those leaked to are often members of the press, and the motives are varied. There were so many leaks concerning President Reagan's budget message in February 1982 that the date for delivery had to be advanced to avoid an anticlimax. So great was the leakage that the capital was said by one reporter to be "awash."

Bumper Stickers

There's nothing like giving your message a ride on someone else's rear bumper. At any stoplight, there it is—staring you in the face. As you have noticed, the range of subject matter is tremendous—everyone from the dogcatcher to Jesus, and every cause from your local police to preserve the whales. Bumper stickers can be very effective when well designed and clearly written. Most are not. It gets boring to read that surfers, nurses, fly fishermen, chiropractors, and electrical linemen "do it better." So? My favorites are people who "brake for unicorns" and the one that says what the world needs is more ambiguity—"or does it?" Some sweatshirts and jerseys fall into the same category.

Letters and Phone Calls

Salespeople have long understood the effectiveness of the thoughtful little note. A letter doesn't cost much in time or money, but done properly— what an impact it can have! Most sales texts list a number of ways a letter might be used: to congratulate someone on a new job or accomplishment, to call an article of interest to someone's attention, or simply just to let people know you are thinking of them. A letter is such a *personal* instrument that its impact is quite striking.

I recently sat in a meeting with a college director of admissions. He told how he had written to some students who had not registered for the new term. He said he missed them, and hoped they were okay and would be returning soon. He said that he had had many replies, and that some were "touching." The students could not get over the fact that someone cared enough to write them. Of course, the director of admissions struck a great public relations blow for the college, too.

For all kinds of "causes" mail is a perfect vehicle. It gives the sender a chance to state the organization's case in detail. It also provides the means of sending an appeal for money with enclosed pledge card and return envelope. *Mailing lists* make this form of public relations very effective. Through the purchase of lists of names and addresses, the organization can zero in

FIGURE 8-1 Company publications are often used to help management talk directly to employees in a personal kind of way. This editorial, "A Very Tough Test," signed by the chairman of the board, could very likely have been written by someone in the public relations department. As you can see, it is a little essay that used the school test analogy throughout. This is the kind of work you expect from a professional writer. It rallies the employees to meet a tough situation in terms each one of them can understand.

A
VERY
TOUGH
TEST

I think many of us can recall the discomfort and inconvenience that we experienced before sitting down to take a major test during our school years. There was the sacrifice of time in order to prepare adequately. There was the desire to achieve a high score — often triggering anxiety about one's own abilities. And, finally, there was the test itself which all too frequently included trick questions and pitfalls to separate those in the know from the guessers.

Florida Steel — and you and I — are in the midst of a very tough test of a different kind and like our classroom exams years ago there are some doubts and some feelings of insecurity.

Our task is to make the grade in seeing our Company through one of the most trying periods in its history. It is a test that is requiring no small measure of sacrifice. There is no doubt that the current recession has dealt us a blow. Closely monitored cost controls are here to stay, as are increased quality standards and the ability to meet customers' needs on tight, reliable schedules.

All of us have a stake in the successful outcome of the long- and short-term tests of our abilities and ingenuity. When the "grades" are passed out they'll be visible for all to see — on our production and our employment levels and in our "bottom line" results.

Edward L. Flom

Edward L. Flom
Chairman of the Board and
Chief Executive Officer

FLORIDA ▼ STEEL

TRIANGLE

Vol. 23   No. 3
Published monthly by Florida Steel Corporation
for employees and their families.

BOBBIE JUNE WILLIS
Public Relations Manager

RON WOERNER
Administrator, Creative Services

PATTY GLASNAP
Public Relations Coordinator

THE COVER
With construction down, delayed, or cancelled, Florida Steel like other companies is feeling the pinch. Read about some of the ways the Company is coping with the recession on Pages 3-5. (Cover photo is of a manufacturing facility on which the construction has been delayed.)

2

Corporate Offices	Fabricating Plants
1715 Cleveland Street	Fort Lauderdale, Florida
P.O. Box 23328	Fort Myers, Florida
Tampa, Florida 33623	Jacksonville, Florida (2)
Electric Steel Mills	Miami, Florida
Charlotte, North Carolina	New Orleans, Louisiana
Indiantown, Florida	Orlando, Florida
Jacksonville, Florida	Tampa, Florida (3)
Tampa, Florida	Atlanta, Georgia
Jackson, Tennessee	Charlotte, North Carolina
Steel Service Center	Raleigh, North Carolina
Tampa, Florida	Aiken, South Carolina

*Florida Steel is an Equal
Opportunity Employer*

Credit: Florida Steel Corporation.

on just exactly the kind of public it wants to talk to. Lists can be purchased through *list brokers* at about $35 per thousand, or they may be compiled from one's own sources. It is said that the Republican party, as well as the National Rifle Association, have perfected very sophisticated computerized mailing techniques.

Phone calls can be very effective in the hands of the right person. But be sure the message is brief and to the point. Remember that you are not "selling," as the phone soliciter is. Nor are you taking someone's valuable time to argue a particular point of view. The telephone has the advantage of intimacy (your voice) and immediacy. Registered lobbyists understand the use of the telephone very well. They know how a few confidential words, spoken to the right person at the right time, can work wonders.

Newsletters

Thousands of organizations have mailing lists of supporters—or potential supporters—whom they contact regularly via newsletters. Newsletters may be quite modest (a two-page mimeographed form, for example), but some are, in effect, magazines. Political and economic newsletters are particularly popular. Often their value is based on their ability to deliver "insider" information. Every major stock brokerage house mails its clients a weekly newsletter containing reviews, forecasts, and recommendations. For a few hundred dollars it is possible to subscribe to one of many "letters" giving expert opinion on stocks and bonds by private individuals (the only people, it is said, who regularly make money on the stock market).

Speakers, Demonstrators, and Consultants

Many organizations—insurance companies, trade associations, special interest groups—maintain bureaus of speakers. Their job is to carry the organization's message to selected audiences. The speakers are almost always practiced and skilled. The ANPA (American Newspaper Publishers Association), for example, sends a person on the road to speak to advertising and marketing executives on the advantages of newspaper advertising. Insurance companies provide speakers who lecture on safe driving. Brokerage firms hold seminars in which speakers lecture to selected audiences on the problems of money management.

These speakers can be very effective. Their audiences are carefully selected: people concerned with the decisions regarding advertising media, newly licensed drivers in high school, older people in affluent neighborhoods likely to be concerned about the returns and safety of their investments. Moreover, the speaker is giving *something of value.* As an expert, he or she is listened to carefully and respectfully. The fact that the speaker may also be delivering a "commercial" for a particular cause or product seldom bothers listeners—this is a small price to pay for needed information.

FIGURE 8-2 **If you will look in the job placement area of student services, you will find a number of brochures like this. Both companies and industries seek to tell their story to the student who may be a prospective employee.**

This booklet is produced by a personnel placement service for nurses. It is publicity for the personnel service, of course. But it is also designed to catch the eye of those who might be interested in a nursing career.

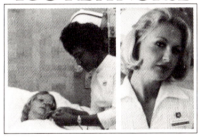

You're a nurse because you care about people...care about helping people that need help most. You're a nurse because you're an intelligent, compassionate, highly motivated individual. You're a nurse for many reasons, some obvious and some not so obvious, but all are special to you.

You probably made the decision to be a nurse many years ago. Maybe as far back as childhood when nursing won out over the flying trapeze and being a movie star. Then later on, when you really had to make the decision...it was easy. And that's about the last thing about being a nurse that was easy. Ahead of you were years of school and training...years of dedication to a goal and finally it all became a reality. Graduation...your first assignment...your first hospital.

Looking back now you probably wonder how you did it. How you worked so long and so hard. But you did and right now that's what is important. We know it's important and we understand why. We understand because throughout the United States, there are over 40,000 nurses working for Medical Personnel Pool who have shared some of your experiences.

Credit: Medical Personnel Pool.

Demonstrators and consultants are similar in several ways. They are experts in their particular fields, and they usually have something of value to offer. Often they are an attraction in and of themselves. A walk through a department store will usually reveal several "consultants" at work. In the cosmetics department there may be a person who offers advice on makeup and demonstrates the proper method of applying rouge. She is, of course, a representative of a cosmetic firm. Another person is tossing dirt on a rug and demonstrating how his vacuum cleaner sucks it up without a trace. The bride's department in almost any store has a consultant who can give advice on the fine points of putting on a wedding. Buyers of home furnishing often find they can get free advice from the store's interior decorator. A packaged fashion show is an elaborate demonstration complete with models, musicians, fashion expert announcer, and, of course, clothes. Manufacturers often provide demonstrator-consultants as part of a promotional package.

Sports Figures and Tournaments

Figures from the sports world make excellent workers in the public relations vineyard. Perhaps you may have noticed how many oldtimers wind up as "representatives" of one company or another. Some of them work freelance for several noncompetitive products. Others have close contractual ties with their companies.

The mere presence of a famous sports star often lends interest to an event. The expert fly or plug caster who puts on an exhibition at a sports equipment show makes a great representative for the company. Local professional teams often gain a great deal of goodwill for themselves by sending out players to conduct "clinics" for younger players. In fact, any athlete who is willing to demonstrate his or her skills can usually draw a crowd for you.

Probably the granddaddy of tournaments in sports exploitation is the prestigious Lipton's Cup, symbol of international yacht racing supremacy. It was contributed by Sir Thomas Lipton and is today as famous as his tea company.

The Lambert Trophy, awarded each year to the top Eastern college football team, is named for a jewelry company. The Kemper Open in golf and the Virginia Slims tennis tournament are other well-known commercially sponsored sporting events.

Advertising and Promotional Devices

Anything developed to carry a *commercial* message can also carry a *public relations* message. Let us look at a few examples.

Billboards, also known as 24-sheet posters, are an ideal way of getting across certain messages. But they must be used with care. Today's traffic speed is greater than it was just a few years ago. There are precious few seconds for reading and absorbing a billboard message. As a result, the illustration must be striking and the copy brief and to the point. Billboards are good for political candidates. At election time, candidates look for quick familiarization with name and face by as many people as possible. The short, snappy public service slogan is ideally suited to outdoor boards. Florida's "Arrive Alive" campaign lent itself perfectly to billboard use.

Billboards are flexible. They can be purchased in "showings" of various sizes, and sometimes singly. Special locations for your particular target market may become available. At a corner of a main thoroughfare near our campus, where most of our students pass each day, a rival educational institution has bought a board encouraging students to enroll at that school.

Transportation advertising, which includes posters in or on stations, cars, buses, and taxis, is relatively inexpensive and highly selective in its audience. For the public relations person, it offers a good opportunity to reach a lower-income, nonreading public that can be exposed to the message for lengthy periods of time. Charitable causes often use these cards. Gas, electric, and telephone companies frequently use them for image-building public service messages. The subway system in New York City did a great public relations job for itself a few years ago with the monthly selection of a "Miss Subways." The winner—a regular subway commuter—was announced and pictured on car cards.

Car cards are particularly effective when you can determine just where the riders are usually delivered and the routes they are accustomed to riding. The publicist for a trade show, for instance, might encourage attendance by stating that this particular bus or car will deliver the rider directly to the door of the auditorium where the trade show is being held. The limited space of a car card or somewhat larger end-of-car poster does not permit a lengthy message. But it does make it possible to say much more than can be said on a billboard. And people have longer to read the message.

In Paris, shelters at bus stops carry posters. New York City, after much political wrangling, is doing the same thing. In some airports, lighted displays beside moving staircases carry messages. Airport waiting rooms are an ideal place for posters and displays of various kinds. In some communities, bus benches have been utilized to carry messages. Litter containers in parks and other public places have been used for publicity purposes. These have been particularly effective in community public relations efforts to control littering. New York's "Every Litter Bit Helps" is one of several cleanup slogans, and what better place to display it than on the receptacle itself.

Direct Mail

We have already mentioned the use of letters in public relations efforts. But direct mail is something else again.

The terms direct mail and mail order are often confused. *Mail order* refers to the system of ordering items through the mail, no matter how the offer is made—advertising, catalog, or insert. *Direct mail* refers to offerings that are made directly to the consumer through the mail and ordered through the mail, usually via order blank and addressed envelope. The direct mail piece is called a *proposition* and it consists of identifiable parts:

1. *The envelope, carefully designed to encourage the recipient to open it and read.*

2. *A covering letter of some length (four pages is not unusual) which presents the basic appeal and argument.*

3. *An illustrated folder describing the product. This is often printed in four colors.*

5. *A warranty, guarantee, or "money back if not satisfied" offer.*

6. *An order blank and addressed, postage-paid envelope.*

Direct mail is a tricky medium and should be used only with the help of experts. It takes a true professional to compose the cover letter. Direct mail does not leave much margin for error. Printing and mailing become more expensive every day. The famous "breakeven point" (at which your proposition has returned its cost) is becoming as hard to attain as the 4-minute mile.

The soliciting of support for various causes via the mails has dropped off in recent years due to greatly increased costs. On the other hand, political figures are relying more and more on direct mail because of legal limitations on campaign contributions.

Public Service Broadcasting

Every TV and radio station is required, by the terms of its license, to broadcast a certain amount of public service programming. These usually consist of programs of support for causes of a simple or noncontroversial nature. The station is not only fulfilling federal licensing requirements, it is performing a public relations function of its own. Properly handled, the public service broadcast has the capacity of enhancing the station's image in the eyes of its public. Public service messages can be simple, brief announcements, backed with a design or poster. Or they may be longer, more elaborate programs.

One local CBS TV station is currently doing a magnificent job for the Big Brothers—an organization that provides companionship for fatherless children. The segments appear about once a week and last several minutes. They are spotted as part of the local news broadcast. The anchorman of the news team is shown with a different youngster each time, fishing, playing ball, and so on. They chat on camera, and the boy is given a chance to say how much he wishes he had a grown-up companion who could take his father's place occasionally. The kids are most appealing, and the program has done a great job bringing in recruits for Big Brothers. But what a wonderful public relations job for the station, too. So if you can point out to local radio or TV stations the public relations potential for them in supporting your cause, you may find yourself with a winner.

Advertising: Institutional and Advocacy

There is a point at which advertising and public relations seem to blend. As has been pointed out, any medium that can be used for advertising can be used for public relations. Generally, we think of advertising as a commercial message for a product or service. But advertising space or time can also be used to project a message about a company as well as its product. And it can also be used, as we will see, to project a concept or idea espoused by a company.

Both advertising and public relations are very much concerned with the image reflected by the company. In an earlier chapter, we pointed out that what you think of a company has a lot to do with what you buy from it. How you perceive an organization is very important. One of public relations' most important tasks, particularly for larger companies, is to make sure that the image projected by the organization itself, as well as its products, is a favorable one.

What we want people to think of us, and what we do not want people to think of us, is usually a policy decision made at a high corporate level. An integral part of marketing strategy is the corporate image the organization projects. An oil company does not want to be known for spilling oil all over the beaches. It does want to reflect an image of concern for conservation and commitment to relieving the energy crisis. Lumber companies remind us of how they plant as well as harvest trees to preserve our forests and provide a plentiful supply of wood products. Chemical companies point out how drinkable the water is right next door to their plants. Banks remind us that, through their efforts, backward countries are able to speed up their development. All of this, so often seen in magazines and newspapers and on TV, is called *institutional advertising*. But it is also public relations—corporate public relations.

Institutional advertising "advertises" the institution or company. *Advocacy advertising* does not advertise at all in the usual sense: It uses advertising space or time to advocate an idea. In effect, it is an editorial. It is a relatively new development, and not all organizations use it. Perhaps its first use was in labor disputes, when companies took paid space to state their position as opposed to the union's. Foreign countries have often taken full pages in such important papers as the *Wall Street Journal,* the *New York Times,* and the *Washington Post* to state their diplomatic or political positions. This often happens when the country feels it is not getting a good "press" and thinks it can state its own position better. Business organizations, too, may feel that they are not being treated adequately in the press—that their side of the story is not being made clear. Rather than write a "letter to the editor" for the correspondence column, they purchase space on the editorial page. They are thereby assured that the paper's politically aware readers will see their messages.

Most newspapers try to cover stories fairly and accurately. But on the editorial pages—in the writing of editorials and the selection of columnists—they are free to let their prejudices show. They are reflecting the "policy" of the paper as determined by management. TV and radio stations, being publicly licensed, do not have this freedom, theoretically. Particularly in their news broadcasts, it is almost impossible to convince all listeners that they are being treated fairly. TV and radio therefore offer *equal time* to those who wish to reply to editorials or comment on their treatment in a news item. Most stations are very good about this, and equal time may offer you a great chance to strike a free public relations blow. But be careful. The story must be written *for broadcast* and must be delivered by someone who "comes across" well. The amateur, stiff with fright and reading in a third-grade monotone, can do more harm than good.

Advocacy almost always involves controversy. Great care must be taken to recognize this. The cause, idea, or plan you are advocating may be quite different from what someone else might advocate. Often this is why you are advocating it. If you are the public relations department of the National Rifle Association, you are not going to advocate gun control legislation. Quite the opposite. You already have your friends and enemies, and you know who they are. But if you are a corporation, you must take care. The pleasure of "sounding off" can sometimes be quite costly. Your advocacy can unnecessarily offend a lot of people, including some of your own stockholders. There is another danger. By committing yourself to print, your words may return some day to haunt you. Somewhere there is someone (often a columnist) who is cutting out and filing your words. The day may come when you will be asked to eat them.

SUMMARY

In addition to the best-known methods of reaching the public, the so-called print and broadcast media, there are a number of others, and a good public relations person understands them. One is word-of-mouth rumors, whether or not deliberately started. Many are common vehicles for commercial messages, such as letters and phone calls, billboards, and transportation advertising. Others, such as consultants, demonstrators, and sports figures, are common to promotional activities. Institutional and advocacy advertising are special types that are of great concern to the public relations person.

KEY TERMS

The rumor mill	Sports representative
Word of mouth	Billboard
Bumper sticker	Transportation advertising
Mailing list	Direct mail
Newsletter	Insitutional advertising
Demonstrator	Advocacy advertising
Consultant	Equal time

THE WAY IT HAPPENED

How do you "reach out to" a public that can't be reached or touched by other means.

This was my problem. I was eastern sales manager for a big meat packer. We had just brought out a new brand of beef stew and it was going great—everywhere but in the Spanish-speaking areas of the Bronx, Brooklyn, and Queens. And that represents a *big* market.

We had one of the best advertising agencies in the world and they, too, were stumped, even though they had scheduled plenty of Spanish commercials on the cha-cha-cha radio stations.

A Spanish marketing expert straightened us out. "To reach them," he said, "you must appeal to what they really love, and all of them love taking chances—buying lottery tickets and numbers."

So on our Spanish-speaking stations we began talking—not about how "delicious" the stew was, but how there were special numbers on each can and if you bought a can with the winning number you would get it free.

Boy! Sales went through the roof in "El Barrio"—we really reached and touched them.

Gil Davis
Vero Beach, Florida

A PERSONAL PROJECT

A fortune awaits the person who can think up a new and efficient method for reaching the public with a message.

In fact, new ones are being conceived all the time. It was not long after light planes were perfected that someone got the idea of trailing commercial banners behind them.

Someone had to come up with the idea of painting the Bull Durham sign on barns, and I wonder who the genius was who first got the idea of putting messages on waste containers or bus stop benches?

There's always room for more. Why don't *you* think of a new medium? To start, here's you one free—the walls of laundromats.

READING TO BROADEN UNDERSTANDING

LESLY, PHILIP (ED.). *Lesly's Public Relations Handbook,* 2d ed. (Englewood Cliffs, N.J.: Prentice-Hall, 1978). This exhaustive volume carries two excellent articles on our subject in this chapter. Read "Using Advertising for Public Relations Communications" by Philip Lesly, p. 494, and "Direct Communications Methods," by Herbert M. Baus and Philip Lesly, p. 504.

GUBERMAN, RUBEN. *Handbook of Retail Promotion Ideas* (Reading, Mass.: Addison-Wesley, 1981). Though directed to the retail trade, almost every idea in the book can be adopted by the public relations person. A gold mine.

DUNN, S. W., AND A. M. BARBAN. *Advertising: Its Role in Modern Marketing,* 4th ed. (Hinsdale, Ill.: Dryden, 1978). See pp. 638–687 for a good discussion of public relations advertising.

THE PEOPLE
WHO CAN HELP YOU

OVERVIEW AND GOALS

In addition to direct contacts in the media, there are quite a few other people on whom the public relations person is dependent. In this chapter we meet some of them and learn how to use their services to advantage. When you have finished this chapter, you should be able to

>   ***Identify*** *correctly the major skills and services used by public relations people in carrying out their tasks.*

In addition to contacts in the media, there are a number of other people around town who will be important to you. This may not always hold true at the high corporate level or in the big public relations firm. But for the average public relations person in the average-size city, it is vital to know who can do what—and for how much.

Aside from producing public relations material and gaining publicity for clients, the average practitioner gets involved with people in many professions in carrying out tasks. Putting on a sports tournament or a trade show involves the services of a great variety of skilled and knowledgeable persons. One of the most valuable items in your office is a card file that tells you how you can find them at a moment's notice. It is, of course, a file that will grow and be brought up to date every year. Each new job you complete will probably bring you new "resource people." No one can list all of them—there is no telling what kind of information or service you may need next. When you are stuck, the Yellow Pages of the phone book are a great help. Here are some of the people and services you are going to want to know about.

Printers

Printers come in all shapes and sizes, and prices often vary dramatically. Some printers operate out of a single-room shop with an ancient offset press. Others have giant four-color presses that can reproduce art with beauty and accuracy. Your particular job should fit their capabilities. The little shop with the offset press can do a perfectly satisfactory job of printing such things as business cards, letterheads, and simple notices. You will probably find that prices are reasonable and competitive.

But if you are responsible for an annual report or other company literature that must reflect quality, you will want to take it to a major printing house. These houses not only have the four-color presses, they also employ skilled designers, artists, layout people, and sometimes copywriters. They are prepared to see that you get an absolutely first-rate job.

Because prices vary, it is wise to get at least three estimates on any job. Do not be afraid to go out of town for high-class printing. Not every small city has a print shop of the first rank. Where quality is of the utmost importance (as with an annual report), many companies ignore the cost factor. This is one place you will not want to cut corners. A chart that is slightly out of register (where one color impinges on another) can give an effect you hardly want. Delivery time is another factor to be taken into consideration. You will often find yourself faced with fast-approaching closing dates. You need to know the printers who can be depended upon to meet their commitments and deliver the job on time.

Art Services

A number of these services are listed under "Artist-Commercial" in the Yellow Pages. These are generally studios capable of producing almost any kind of graphic design you might need. Sometimes the "studio" is just one person; others may employ a dozen or more people.

Commercial artists are the people to go to when you need anything designed—whether it be a poster, a banquet menu, a brochure, or a letterhead. There is sometimes variation in price among them, but you would be well advised to ignore it. The difference is never that great. Since you are paying for that nebulous quality *creativity,* it will be to your advantage to find yourself a good art house, gain its trust and confidence, and stick with it. In many cities, these art studios are the major source of advertising design and layout. Smaller agencies often cannot afford to retain a full-time art director and rely on the studios to do their layouts for them.

Artists and Illustrators

The time will inevitably come when you and your department will be asked to come up with a piece of fine art—say, an anniversary portrait of the chairman of the board, or an impressionistic painting for the cover of your annual report. It is often surprising, even in smaller communities, how many fine artists are available. The first place to go is your art studio. The proprietor probably knows everyone in town who paints. If you have a shop that sells art materials, the proprietor will doubtlessly know who paints, their styles, and how much they are likely to charge.

Another excellent source, if there is a nearby college or university, is its department of fine arts. There will be excellent people on the faculty, and it is quite likely that some of their students would love the chance to do a job for you, at a modest price.

TV and Radio Production

A radio announcement or commercial is relatively easy to produce. What is difficult is a *good* radio commercial. That takes talent. Most local radio stations are good at putting together commercials. They have all the equipment in their studios, plus people who are experienced writers and producers. Many radio station reps sell prospects by doing a commercial and then letting the prospect hear it when they call. Unlike local TV, local radio tends to be pretty good. If your firm has an advertising agency, it too is prepared to write and oversee the production of a commercial for you.

Today almost all TV footage is produced by film houses or studios. These range from the big West Coast studios to smaller local ones. Check the ones in your community. You will find them listed in the Yellow Pages under "Motion Picture Producers and Studios." It is important for you to learn their capabilities. What kind of equipment and technicians do they have? Are they prepared to do location as well as studio shots? And, of course, what are their prices?

If you were responsible for producing a 15-minute film to be used in a fund-raising drive, you would go to one of these studios. But for shorter, simpler subjects, your local TV station can be helpful—and inexpensive. You may have to arrange studio time to suit the station's convenience, but a simple "stand-up" message can often be taped for as little as $100.

Sound Studios

You'll find these in the Yellow Pages under "Recording Service—Sound and Video." You ordinarily associate these with recording artists making a "side." They have sophisticated audio equipment and can blend as many as sixteen bands of sound. Sound studios can also locate singers and musicians for you and set up the whole recording date. They know every songwriter in town, too. The "jingle" or theme song is just as effective for getting across a public service idea as it is for plugging a soft drink or a pizza parlor.

Outdoor Advertising Companies

The 24-sheet people have a greater capability than providing space for signs. They have their own studios and artists and can create the sign itself. Your art studio can also do this, but you might get a better price with the outdoor company's studio, since it is their space you are renting. Outdoor is a very special medium. The message has but a few seconds to get across. Creating the illustration and copy requires the services of people who are familiar with the medium and its limitations.

Photograph Houses and Photographers

You will find a variety of photographers in your community. Like printers, their capabilities and prices cover a wide range. Your choice will depend on what kind of picture you need and how much you are willing to pay for it.

An excellent source of competent and fairly priced photography is the photographic department of your local newspaper. Many staff photographers will welcome the chance to do some freelance work. They have the equipment and know what they are doing.

Your community also has photographic studios. These people are prepared to do outdoor location shots, or shots on sets prepared in their own studios. For a picture that must be specially posed in a certain situation, it is necessary to call upon their skills. Many of them have "set dressers," people who prepare the interior location at which the picture is made. They are particularly important when special or dated settings are required. They know what should be on the set, what the people in the picture should be wearing, and where the proper clothes and furnishings can be obtained.

A great deal of danger lurks in special and period pieces. Get one thing wrong, and the result can appear ridiculous. If your picture should be shot in the interior of a sailing yacht or an early railroad parlor car, beware. You can be sure someone will be going over the scene with a magnifying glass, searching for errors. When they find one, they often address the letters to the president of your company.

Stock photo houses produce and catalog photographs for almost every conceivable situation. They have quality photos of people in all kinds of real-life situations. At $15 to $25 apiece, these photos are a handy source of "instant illustration" for a great variety of pieces you might be called on to prepare.

Your town may be fortunate enough to possess a photographer who carries the initials "ASMP" on his or her business card. The letters stand for the old name of the organization—American Society of Magazine Photographers. Today it is called the Society of Photographers in Communication, and its members include the top people in the field. If you cannot locate one in your neighborhood, write to ASMP at 10 East 42 Street, New York, N.Y. 10017, and ASMP will help you find someone near you.

ASMP photographers do not come cheap—$1500 or $2000 is not unusual for a single picture. But if the job you are doing should reflect quality, these are the people you will want to work for you. Annual reports, of course, always demand quality work. A brochure for a condominium development, books and brochures for localities and countries, and literature for an elegant resort all justify the expense of retaining outstanding photographic artists. Often the cost of the illustrations can be justified by the length of time the piece will be in use.

Direct Mail Houses

These organizations can be very helpful to the public relations person. Look in your Yellow Pages under "Letter Shop Service." When you have to do a large-scale mailing of any kind, they can help. Large organizations, such as labor unions, political organizations, and industry associations, as well as many businesses, have their own built-in letter shop service.

What the letter shop does is take over the entire mechanical part of the mailing process. It will put your addresses on tape, place them on the envelope, "stuff," close, and seal the envelope, postage meter the letters, and deliver them to the proper post office. It will obtain mailing lists for you and can zero in on any particular zip code area or set of streets you might desire. With the experience they have, direct mail houses can give you lots of advice about the tricky field of mail order and direct mail.

Research

As we have emphasized, a proper research capability is absolutely essential to the public relations function. You *must* have the facts in hand before you launch any public relations project. Much of this research you can organize and carry out by yourself. When you cannot, there are organizations that will do the work for you. Like everything else, they will vary in cost and capability. In your Yellow Pages you will usually find them listed under "Market Research and Analysis."

The number and quality of researchers will depend on the size of your community. In smaller cities, particularly popular test market areas, you will find that many of the research services are correspondents for larger organizations. That is, when a wide sampling must be done on a particular research project, the company carrying out the project will enlist the aid of its correspondent researchers in various parts of the country. Other firms are purely local and have the advantage of knowing their home market intimately.

Another source, if you have a nearby college or university, is the marketing department faculty. Most of these people have a good knowlege of research and can carry out a project for you. In addition, most universities have research directors of their own. One of them might be induced to do a freelance job for you. Do not lose sight of the fact that most marketing students and teachers will welcome the opportunity to perform a "real" job, often for the benefit of the experience. If you want to use one of the really big companies in the field, look in the *Journal of Marketing Research.* There you will find advertised the services of a number of first-rate research firms capable of performing a job anywhere in the world.

Exhibit Builders

Listed under "Display Designers and Producers" in the Yellow Pages, these companies will design and construct a custom-built display for use at conventions, exhibits, or fairs. The importance of a well-built and designed exhibition booth cannot be overstated. If you have ever walked through the exhibition hall at a trade show of any kind, you will understand the problem. Your booth is competing for attention with a hundred or more booths. It takes an outstanding exhibit to get people to stop, inspect, and chat—which is what you are there for. Moreover, you want something that reflects the character, or image, of your organization. Display builders can give you valuable ideas. They are intimately acquainted with their trade and what goes on in it.

You may also be responsible for the literature available at your booth. Remember, the less expensive pieces are for the "collectors," often kids. The more elaborate brochures are kept under the counter and are brought out for the more serious customer.

Hotel Managers, Maitre d's, and Bartenders

Hotel and restaurant people can be helpful in a variety of ways. Reservations for banquet rooms, meeting rooms, and private suites are sometimes hard to come by. Public relations people are often expected to perform miracles. In larger communities, the banquet manager or sales manager is the one you will want to know particularly well. Resort operators may also be important. Many companies hold their annual sales meetings at exotic resorts, and the task of making all the arrangements may fall to the public relations department. The logistics problems involved can be sobering.

In public relations, much of our work goes on over luncheon or dinner. When dining with important clients, you will want to be able to command a good table (at certain restaurants, some table locations are more prestigious than others) at a good restaurant. Careful cultivation of the maitre d' will assure you of both excellent service and seating. As a business expense, you can justify generous tipping to the staff. Many maitre d's prefer to get theirs as a "Christmas present"—once a year and, of course, in cash.

Do not forget the bartender. Many public relations people who dine with clients regularly have worked out certain arrangements with bartenders. The three-martini lunch can take years off your life, as most people in the business recognize. If you think it advisable, make sure your bartender understands that your before-lunch cocktail should be nonalcoholic.

Freelance Writers

You will probably have little trouble locating good artists and illustrators in your community, but not writers. For some reason, good writers are hard to come by, particularly good *specialized writers*. It is assumed that you yourself are perfectly capable of producing a clearly written and well-constructed news release. But the time may come when you need something out of the ordinary: a special speech, a poem, or a humorous essay. Not everyone can write these. Not everyone can write even one or two of them. The best speech writer is often stumped when called upon to produce humorous verse for greeting cards.

Try your advertising agencies first. Advertising writers often develop a command of a number of writing styles—the nature of their work on varied products demands it. Your college or university English department may be able to send you someone. But there is no simple solution to freelance writer problems. Perhaps an ad in one of the writer's magazines such as *Writer's Digest* will produce results.

Actors and Models

If your town has a model agency, you are off and running. Unfortunately, only the larger creative centers such as New York, Chicago, and Los Angeles have agencies that truly represent and arrange work for all kinds of professional models. What other cities have is modeling schools which will, of course, book their students into jobs. But there is a world of difference—and cost—between the agency-represented photographer's model and the person who yearns for a modeling career. However, you may seldom need the high-priced fashion model. What you are much more likely to need are attractive youngsters who can staff an exhibit booth, distribute samples, convey cards at sales meetings, or act as hosts at company functions. For these jobs, your local modeling school should be able to fill the bill. If you have no modeling school, temporary-help agencies might be able to help you.

Actors and actresses present much less of a problem. In New York, where there are lots of theaters—and lots of temporarily unemployed theater people—you will find them performing a variety of tasks while waiting for the next curtain to go up. Many of these temporary jobs are public-relations-related. Since these people are personable, articulate, and "quick studies," they can be depended on to do a good job.

But even in smaller communities, there are more stage-talented people than you may suspect. If your city has an amateur theatrical group, a "little theatre," go see the director and ask for help. She or he probably will have a card file containing all the acting talent in town. Often these people will work for very little, since they are not union members. And you may be surprised at how much talent they display.

City Hall

There are a number of officials in city government whose friendship can help you avoid some headaches. You just cannot go out and hold a parade, for example. It has to be licensed. This is true for the use of all community facilities—parks, playgrounds, streets, stadiums, auditoriums. There are times when you will want to make arrangements with the police, too: an escort for a VIP, or getting a street closed to traffic when you are taking a special shot.

If you are planning something that will reflect honor or credit on the community, you will have little trouble getting cooperation. In fact, on many of these projects you ought to be able to work with your counterpart at city hall or the chamber of commerce.

Ticket Brokers, Box Office People, and Guardians of the Press Box

The ability to come up with two-on-the-aisle for a hit show or a box on the fifty-yard line at a big game is a skill to be learned by public relations people. Your company, like most, may do a great deal of entertaining. Getting someone into a show that is "sold-out-for-weeks" can impress even the most blasé person.

Other public relations people can often help you, particularly when you can return the favor in some way. Public relations people for shows, circuses, fairs, and other events usually carry around a pocketful of passes to be distributed where they will do the most good. Some larger communities have ticket brokers who usually hold a few seats for special situations. The people who staff the box offices at your local auditorium or theater can be very helpful, particularly when it comes to locations.

A seat in the press box is always impressive and sometimes can be arranged by friends in the sports department or by the broadcast crew. The booth will usually have a major domo who looks after the reporters' needs, sees that the free lunch doesn't run out, and admits only those with the proper credentials. It is good practice to do this person a favor from time to time, too.

Typographers

When you want a piece of copy set in type, you send it to a typographer, together with the specification of the size and character of type you desire (Cheltenham Bold, 14 point). Many typographers will also prepare "camera ready" art for you. This means they will paste illustration and typeset copy in place, ready for the photograph from which the engravings will be made.

You should familiarize yourself with some of the common typefaces. Old English, for example, is what you often see on invitations and diplomas; while Barnum, as you might expect, is that typeface you associate with circus posters.

Silk Screen Houses

These companies make signs and posters in limited numbers by a method known as silk screening. The colors are extruded through a fine screen onto the cardboard or poster paper. Colors are usually primary and designs simple. This is the place to go when you need a few dozen announcement posters.

Advertising Specialty Vendors

Advertising specialties are all those little reminder items that convey the company's name—calendars, pens, pencils, key chains. Get one of the vendor's catalogs, and you will be astonished at the number of these items they can provide. In addition, you ought to know the store in the community that supplies cups, awards, medals, and plaques. There will be many occasions when you will want to come up with a special award to an honored guest or an employee who has done an outstanding job.

SUMMARY

There are a number of people around town upon whom the public relations person must rely. Most of them can be found in the Yellow Pages. Here is a partial list of the most important ones:

Printers
Art services
Artists and illustrators
Broadcasting production studios
Outdoor advertising companies
Photographers
Direct mail houses
Research
Hotel personnel
Ticket brokers

KEY TERMS

Printers   Market research and analysis
Art services   *Journal of Marketing Research*
Film house   Exhibit and display builder
Sound studios   Banquet manager
24-sheet poster   Freelance writer
Photographic studio   *Writer's Digest*
Set dresser   Model agency
Location shot   Modeling school
Stock photo   Ticket broker
ASMP   Press box attendant
Direct mail house   Silk screen house
Typographer

THE WAY IT HAPPENED

Our medium-sized city has at least four excellent art services. We have more art studios, but these are the outstanding ones. This seems to happen where there are a number of small advertising agencies who cannot afford to keep a regular art director on staff. As a result, they turn their graphic art work over to the studios, who develop in a very healthy way.

I found this out when I went into business for myself and needed letterheads, business cards, invoice forms, and so on. I thought it was something the printer did for you.

But a friend pointed out to me, "Your letterhead *is* your calling card, and you want to have it reflect as much class as possible." So I went to a design studio he recommended. I could see a lot of the stuff they were working on for their clients: posters, advertising layouts, even a menu for a top-notch restaurant.

They did a great job of design for me and I never regretted going to them. After all, the design of your company name on the card or letterhead is something you live with for a long time.

A PERSONAL PROJECT

Unless you live in a particularly large city where everything is available, it would be well to check the services you have on hand in your own community.

Review all the services mentioned in this chapter and then make a list of those that are immediately available. You may find that some of them are not available—a little theater, a letter house, or a market research firm, for example. In this case, list the *nearest* one available.

READING TO BROADEN UNDERSTANDING

Almost every field mentioned in this chapter has its "index," "yearbook," or "list." These tell, in exhaustive fashion, who does what and where they are located. See, for example, the *Standard Rate and Data*, for a number of mediums, or *Broadcasting/Cable Yearbook*. Usually, the Yellow Pages will show you what services are available locally.

10

HOW PEOPLE SEE THINGS, THINK ABOUT THEM, AND ACT ON THEM

OVERVIEW AND GOALS

In this chapter we look at the problem of "moving people's minds." You will see why changing people is so difficult—and why we are so firmly "set" in our ways. We will examine perceptions and attitudes, images and beliefs, and behavior, all of which are related. Finally, we will look at some popular theories about attitudes and behavior. When you have finished this chapter, you should be able to

> *Define* and *differentiate* perception, attitude, image, belief.
>
> *Appreciate* why your own perceptions and beliefs are so difficult to alter.
>
> *Understand* the three theoretical approaches that attempt to explain perceptions and attitudes.

In public relations we often apply learning principles in the messages we create in order to reach a particular public. We want them to "learn" that our candidate deserves their vote. We try to "educate them" to the idea that our cause is worth contributing to or that our company deserves their trust and confidence. But once we have succeeded in "teaching" someone something, we cannot sit back with a self-satisfied sigh. Because in "educating" people we have opened up a floodgate—the floodgate of *thought*. It is a factor no public relations person can afford to forget.

When we ask people for their vote, or their money, or their confidence, we invite them to *consider* what we are offering. Is the candidate worthy of a vote? What do I think about him or her and the rival candidates? Is this a worthy cause? Does it appeal to me, and would I be willing to put my money into it? Do I want to believe you and give you my trust? What have you done in the past to gain my confidence? What are you likely to do in the future? These are the kinds of issues you are up against as a public relations person. Your message is not going to be received by open, uncluttered minds. It is going to be received by people who have biases, preconceptions, misinformation, prejudices, uncertainties, resolute convictions, and unshakable beliefs.

I do not know whether or not there is a cult that believes the moon is made of green cheese, but I know there is a cult of true believers for everything else, from shaving your head and collecting money in airports, to eating nothing but "natural" plants and grains. You may have a little trouble getting across your tale of a new Messiah or the joys of eating charcoal-broiled steaks from corn-fed Nebraska cattle. And you might have a little trouble convincing someone from Michigan that the best football in the country isn't played in the Big Ten.

In some cases, there is not much we can do with these people. Their biases and beliefs are just too strong and deeply entrenched for us to make a dent. Fortunately for public relations people, there are many more individuals whose mind sets *can* be changed, whose ideas and preconceptions are *not* unalterable. These are the people whose minds are not really cast in concrete and who are surprisingly amenable to logical argument.

If we are to change the way people think of things, despite their beliefs and prejudices, we are going to have to understand them and what seems to be going on in their minds. This is not a particularly easy job. No one has ever really *seen* a prejudice; we only see the evidence of it. Although it is possible to discover why a person clings so tightly to a teddy bear, in public relations we do not enjoy the advantages of having one person at a time to analyze. We must deal with thousands at once. What we are going to try to do now is to understand the ways in which people see things and feel about them—their perceptions and their attitudes—and how they act as a result.

Perception—The Particular Way We See Things

We become aware of things around us usually through our eyes and ears. Of course, we can also become aware that the person sitting next to us has had a garlic sandwich for lunch. In any case, our senses have brought to our minds an awareness of something around us—a person, a football game, or an ambulance siren warning us to get out of the way. Having *sensed* these things, our minds give them meaning. The person is nice-looking, the football game will be an enjoyable couple of hours, the siren reminds us that accidents happen.

But for another person, the meanings may be quite different. The "nice-looking" person may seem threatening. The prospect of a football game may be boring. Sirens mean fire engines, not ambulances. Each of us has our own *particular* way of perceiving things based on past experience and knowledge. Though our own perceptions may differ quite radically from our neighbor's, there is nothing unusual about them as far as we are concerned; they make a great deal of sense to us.

They not only make sense, they are a necessity, for they represent the world around us—*our* world—and our particular relation to it. We are very comfortable with our perceptions. Changing them not only becomes an un-comfortable process, it can also be seen as a threatening one. I have seen people get up and walk out of a room rather than endure a threat to a perception. When challenged to distinguish their favorite drink from among four or five popular brands, people find it unbelievable that they cannot recognize the one they perceive to be the best. They actually become quite disturbed when told they cannot. A beer company took advantage of this phenomenon in some recent advertising. It ran a taste test among those who perceived a rival brand to be the best and drank it regularly. In the test beer drinkers of the rival brand were asked to try, blindfolded, their favorite and the advertiser's brand. Of course, each time about 50 percent of those who perceived theirs to be best chose the other brand. This enabled the brewer to point out that even many of the dedicated drinkers of brand X preferred the other.

Sometimes things are just too painful for us to recognize. We refuse to see them, or we see them in a way that is comforting to us. We may not see someone as physically unattractive, but as someone with an interesting per-sonality. We find it difficult to accept the news that a deacon has embezzled the church funds. The people who exploded the latest bomb in Beirut are thought by some as terrorists—and by others as freedom fighters. Note that all this perceiving takes place in our minds. It's all in the way you look at it.

Our perceptions screen things out. You could drive for miles and never "see" a classic sports car like the MG-TC. Then one day a friend of yours gets you interested in old sports cars. You begin reading *Road and Track* and *Car and Driver.* Before long, there is not an MG, Jag, Porsche, Lambroghine, or Morgan that you miss as you drive along. Just as you bar certain undesired things from perception, you admit certain others selectively. This is important for people in public relations. It is very close to the principle of market segmentation or target markets in marketing. We are not anxious to waste time and effort on those who will never conceivably buy a product. Nor are public relations people wise to devote effort to reaching those who will screen the message out. Like the marketer, we cannot always get our message before the public whose attention and interest we will be sure of. But we can be discriminating. Wealthy people whose children have gone to private schools and are now graduated from college are unlikely to have much interest in promoting a new bond issue for public schools. But you will have little trouble getting the attention of a young couple of modest income with 4- and 5-year-olds.

If our perceptions did not filter and screen the mass of information from outside, we would probably go out of our heads. So our perceptual apparatus works for us. It not only keeps certain perceptions out and lets others in, but it also arranges and categorizes things for us. We have one perceptual categorization for "oil companies" and quite another for "service stations." We also have perceptions regarding individual service stations—convenience, service, personality of the proprietor. The United Fund was very wise in doing this categorization for us, in reverse. We no longer have to distinguish among our perceptions of dozens of different charities appealing to us for support. We give once and contribute to an acceptable perception—charity. Of course, a lot of other worthy causes, now somewhat beyond our perception, may be left out in the cold.

Sometimes it is difficult for people to grasp something as large and complicated as a department store, a corporation, or a cause. It is here that the public relations person can go to work. For he or she can supply cues that will help the perception along. Stores have been known to scent themselves with a gentle perfume that immediately generates the perception of "class" and "style." It may be very difficult to have a perception of a corporation that builds electric motors for a variety of uses. But the corporation that stepped in and bailed out the local ball club when it was about to go under is something everyone can understand. The statistics of population growth and food supply may be emotionally flat. But the picture of one weeping child and an empty bowl opens pocketbooks.

Six blind men, as the fable said, touched an elephant, and each "saw" the animal differently. So it is with us. We live in the world of our particular perceptions. Fortunately for public relations people, middle-class Americans possess many of the same perceptions. But you do not have to move far from this group before the perceptions begin to differ markedly. The way the black teenager in a ghetto sees the world is certainly far different from the way a white teenager in suburbia sees it. We are not only a "melting pot" of peoples, we are a melting pot of perceptions too.

Attitudes—And What They Do

If each of us has his or her own set of perceptions (or hangups, or predispositions, or prejudices), then we also have the attitudes that give them expression. In fact, *attitudes* have been defined as "mental readiness or implicit predispositions that exert some ... influence on a fairly large class of evaluation responses."[1] We express these attitudes by doing something or saying something. If my attitude toward you is favorable (because my perception is a positive one), I will vote for you and stand up and argue for you. And when someone mentions your name, I will feel good about you and be proud that you are my candidate. I *believe* in you. I am emotionally wrapped up in you and your cause. Any challenge to you is a challenge to me, personally. If the challenge persists, I feel threatened and I may lose my temper.

But suppose something should happen—you are caught accepting a bribe—and I should lose my belief in you. I will feel sad and disappointed. I no longer can speak up in your behalf. You will not get my vote in the next election.

Psychologists have said that it is important for us to understand that our thinking, our feeling, and our behavior are closely tied together. As you can see in the case of the dishonest politician, when the "stimulus" (bribe-taking) occurred, our attitude shifted—and so did our feelings, our thoughts, and our actions. But the results of our attitudes do not always come in such a neat, predictable manner. Let us take our dishonest politician again. My belief in him has been badly shattered and I feel terrible about it. But I still vote for him. Why? As we said, things are not always neat and simple. In the politician's case, many other stimuli affect my attitude toward him, and thus my behavior. I may be convinced that his opponent is a bum. I may know I can count on him to look after the interests of my business. He may even have promised me a political plum of some kind once he has been elected. This happens in real life all the time. Politicians are indicted and convicted of all sorts of misbehavior. In the next election, to everyone's consternation, their constituents cheerfully send them back to their job. It is as though they were saying, "He may be a bum, but he's *our* bum!"

Other investigators[2] point out that attitudes often govern our *intentions.* But our actions do not always follow our intentions. Intentions must be taken into consideration before we jump to a conclusion as to what a person's behavior might be, based on his or her known attitudes. The reason for this, it is said, is that we usually pause to consider the *consequences* of behavior. So behavior can be blocked by any number of outside factors, including the consideration of what the consequences might be. In the case of the politician, we might find the snow 12 inches deep on election day. Though we had every intention of going to the polls and voting, the prospect of shoveling out the driveway negates that intention. However, consequences must also be taken into consideration. What will be the consequences if you do not stir yourself and vote? This politician is in a position to help you if he is elected. Suppose he is defeated by one vote? Suppose it becomes known that you did not

[1]Philip G. Zimbardo, et al, *Influencing Attitudes and Changing Behavior* (Reading, Mass: Addison-Wesley, 1977), p. 20.

[2]Martin Fishbein and Icek Ajzen, *Beliefs, Attitudes, and Attention.* (Reading, Mass.: Addison-Wesley, 1977) p. 291.

bother to show up at the polls? What is going to happen the next time you appear at his office, hat in hand, to ask a favor?

Now, to make the public relations person's job just a little tougher, it is possible for people to hold opposing attitudes about the same subject. In fact, it is quite possible for us to have a whole complex of attitudes battling for first place in our behavior-making process. What, for example, is your attitude toward intercollegiate football?

1. *It is fun to watch, but I wouldn't want to devote all the time and energy it takes to play on the team.*

2. *It raises a great deal of money and supports the rest of the athletic program. But $8 a ticket is too much for me.*

3. *Football is great for the alumni—keeps their enthusiasm and interest up.*

4. *It is too professional—all those jocks on scholarships. I prefer rugby, a real amateur sport.*

5. *It is our college team and we should support it, even though we get the worst seats in the stadium.*

6. *With midterms coming up, I would probably be better off spending that three hours sitting in the library.*

But are you going to the game? (the ultimate behavior). Your attitudes sway you one way and another. And then a *new* factor is introduced. Your best friend from home and her father are coming up for the game. They have an extra ticket. Would you like to go to the game? Of course you would— *and you do.* Your attitude toward your friend overcame all the negative attitudes about professionalism and rotten seats and costs and time.

What this adds up to for the public relations person is this: You may think you have won a convert because you have changed an attitude. But you can never be sure. You can only be fairly certain of the results when you have changed the *strongest* attitudes and the *majority* of attitudes. If as a public relations person you work on a fund-raising drive, you will discover what a vast difference there is between pledges (attitudes and intentions) and donations (behavior). Often it will be necessary for you to give the pledgee several nudges before he or she makes good. Professional fund-raisers, or experienced amateurs, know all about this. Human frailty is often involved. Carried away by the music, the wine, and the speeches, Mr. Jones comes marching down the aisle waving a pledge of $10,000. The room is wild with cheering. Mr. Jones is walking on air. But next day, he has second thoughts. That is why, when he arrives at his office, he finds a smiling representative from the fund drive waiting for him.

The Theories behind Changing Attitudes

As I am sure you can see, perceptions and attitudes, feelings and beliefs and behaviors, are the very life blood of public relations. Unfortunately, we cannot take a belief apart to see what makes it tick. Nor can we label all the moving parts of an attitude. The best we can do (and it is a pretty good best) is to theorize about what is happening on the basis of what we can see.

As we noted, the perceptions and attitudes that lead to behavior take place in the mind. And there is a great deal we still do not know about the human brain and how it works. Come back in 50 years, the neurologists tell us, and we can give you a pretty good blueprint of what goes on. Until then, we will have to be satisfied with theories. Ignore the fact that theories differ. That is what they are for—to speculate about and choose the one that makes the best sense. Fifty years from now, we might find that they *all* make sense, and that each made an important contribution to our understanding.

We will examine several of these theories. Is this impractical scientific "junk"? It sure isn't. It is what lies at the very heart and soul of our profession, and we had better understand it. There are a great many public relations practitioners (and marketing, sales, and advertising people) who have a pretty good grasp of what things work. But often they do not know *why* they work. They are thankful when they win, and puzzled when they lose. The true professional knows the *why* as well as the *how.* Therefore it is in our interest to try to understand that most essential element of public relations—attitude change.

The Yale Approach

Carl Hovland, a psychology professor at Yale University, headed the team that put together this theory. If you are a student of advertising, you will find much in it that is familiar. It analyzes the components of persuasion, which changes our beliefs. Presenting arguments, whether they be for a product or a cause, is *persuasion.*

The Yale approach distinguishes four kinds of processes that determine how well a person will be persuaded to a particular point of view:

1. Attention. *Obviously I must get you to listen to me if I am going to persuade you.*
2. Comprehension. *I must present my argument in terms you will understand.*
3. Acceptance. *You are more willing to accept my persuasion if what I have to offer will answer your needs in some way.*
4. Retention. *I must present my arguments so effectively that you will remember them.*

This, as you can see, is a mixed bag. Almost *all* processes—learning, adoption, problem-solving—start with some form of attention. Comprehension comes straight from the communication process, as you have already seen. I must encode my persuasive message in such a way that you will be able to decode it properly. Acceptance is a combination of those elements sales and advertising people recognize as *desire* and *conviction.* If I am to persuade you to buy something from me, I must arouse your desire to have it by making you see the benefits you will derive from it. (This skin cream will make you more beautiful. A vote for candidate X will keep you from being unemployed.) But I must also provide you with reasons why you can believe before you will accept. (The most beautiful women in Hollywood use it. Economists tell us deficits and interest rates must be brought down for us to have economic recovery.)

Retention is part of learning theory and is something all sales and advertising people are concerned about. Do you learn a fact for just long enough to get it down on the exam paper? Or will it stay with you for the rest of your life? Television commercials are repeated night after night in an effort to strengthen retention. Remember the public relations person who said, "I tell them what I'm going to tell them, then I tell them, then I tell them what I told them."

The Yale approach also points out four variables that will have an effect on the impact of a persuasive effort. You will recognize these too from your study of communication.

1. *The* source and its authoritativeness. *This is why we offer testimonials in advertising. This is why the character and reputation of your spokesperson is so important in public relations.*

2. Communication. *Communication involves more than simply "encoding" and "decoding." It involves the* impact *of the message—how strongly it falls on the ears of those who are listening. This is the creativity in selling and persuading. There are many ways to say things; there is one memorable way, as Abraham Lincoln demonstrated at Gettysburg.*

3. Audience. *People vary as we have noted. There are those who cannot be budged, and there are those who are open-minded and amenable to persuasive argument. You may find yourself up against a hostile audience some day, people deeply committed to a cause. You will have as rough a time as Secretary Watts has had before the members of the Sierra Club.*

The Group Dynamics Approach

Those of you who have studied marketing will immediately recognize this approach as the same as the influence of peer groups—or family or neighbors—on buying behavior. Just as our group plays a part in influencing our buying decisions, so it plays a part in altering our perceptions, attitudes, and beliefs about many things. Sociologists recognize that *conformity* is a very powerful influence in our lives. The pressure to be "one of the gang" is hard to resist. The nonconformist runs the risk of punishment and rejection. As you will recall from Chapter 3, liking and respect and acceptance are things we all very much need. This mind set of perception, attitudes, and behavior, when governed by the crowd, can be extremely difficult for the public relations person to overcome. You are faced not only with an attitude that may be inflexible, but often with the threat of being ostracized.

Other people than those in our immediate crowd can affect our attitudes and beliefs. People we look up to and admire can be very influential. We tend to try to think the way the "best people" think. You can see why thought leaders are so important in public relations. The *New York Review of Books* is a publication devoted to book reviews and activities in the literary world. It is read by intellectuals—writers, critics, and serious readers. Its advertising content, as you might expect, is almost exclusively publishers and books. Yet recently a small foreign country took a full-page ad to explain its political position. Why the *New York Review of Books?* Obviously because the country wanted to reach and change the minds of intellectuals who can influence others. Public relations people for clubs and restaurants understand this herd instinct, too. They know that if they can induce the right people (society figures, sports stars, writers) to patronize an establishment, they will draw those who want to be identified with writers, or athletes, or beautiful people.

Cognitive Dissonance Theory

Cognitive dissonance is well known to students of marketing. It is what happens when we are "torn" between two choices. It also occurs after a purchase when we begin to have doubts. A *cognition* is the way we think about or regard things. When two cognitions come in conflict, we hit a *dissonance,* or a sour note. From a psychological point of view, we feel a discomfort we wish to relieve.

The discomfort of our dissonance will vary with the importance of the cognitive elements. To relieve our tension, we often explain to ourselves that "it's no big deal"—and maybe it really isn't—and we refuse to get upset. But when we are going out on a limb—making a decision about job, or marriage, or school—then the dissonance becomes strong and we suffer. We are truly torn by indecision. We can also become worried and distracted when we have "a lot on our minds." That is, we are affected by several dissonances going on at once. It is well not to let these dissonances pile up, for we all have a limit to our tolerance. When they become too loud, we may try to crawl into a bottle, or impale ourselves on the end of a needle. Every instinct tells us to run away from dissonance.

Because those whose attitudes and beliefs we are trying to change are subject to dissonance, and therefore may actually "run away" and be lost to any chance of conversion, we must make every effort to reduce the dissonance and the discomfort. Believe me, the one who *feels* the dissonance is going to want all the help he or she can get, so it is up to us to supply it. Retail salespeople become very adept at this. When you are hesitating between two items, the salesperson may suggest, "Why not take both?" Your pocketbook is lighter, but your cognitive dissonance has disappeared too. Of course you could eliminate the dissonance by not taking either, and this is something the salesperson would like to avoid at all costs.

The salesperson may help you rid yourself of your tensions by helping you to *rationalize* your decision. "The items may be expensive, but think what they are going to do for your appearance." And, as we have seen, he or she may convince you that buying two is no big deal. The salesperson may also realize that it is easier at this point to sell you something to go with the item. This is called *cognitive overlap.* It simply means that there is more relationship (and thus less dissonance) between the "buy this to go with that" decision than the "buy this and that" decision.

All these marketing and sales situations have counterparts in public relations. We know it is much easier for people to walk away from a decision than make it. So we must prevent them from leaving. ("If you really believe in the preservation of our lakes, now is the time for you to stand up and say so!") We know they will rationalize their way out, if possible. ("It sounds like a socialistic idea to me.") So we must present the idea in acceptable terms. We know that the mere mention of some ideas can frighten people ("I'm not going down to the blood bank and let them stick needles in me. Besides, I *need* my blood.") Then we point out to the person that the members of his church are marching on the blood bank tomorrow to save a kid's life and that they assume he is going to be with them.

Other theories also help to explain behavior based on attitudes and perceptions. In all of them, as in the ones noted here, we all would recognize elements from our own experience. Perhaps "50 years from now" it will turn out that all our theories are part of the explanation.

SUMMARY

In public relations, the people we appeal to do not have uncluttered minds. They have a full set of biases, preconceptions, prejudices, convictions, and unshakable beliefs.

Frequently we must overcome this mind set. To change the way people think, we must understand how their minds work—how they are brought to their beliefs and prejudices.

Perceptions are the particular way people see things. We need perceptions: They represent our world. We do not like to have them disturbed. We screen other perceptions out; we see things our way.

We express our perceptions in attitudes. And we reveal our attitudes in words and actions. But, perversely, we do not always follow our attitudes.

Other forces may overcome them. So ultimate behavior is not always predictable.

There are several theories behind attitude change. The Yale approach analyzes the components of persuasion. The group dynamic approach stresses the role played by groups in altering or determining perceptions. Cognitive dissonance theory shows how the discomfort of conflict (dissonance) in our minds can be relieved by changing perceptions and attitudes.

KEY TERMS

Perception	Yale approach
Attitude	Attention
Behavior	Comprehension
Feeling	Acceptance
Intention	Retention
Belief	Group dynamics approach
Cognitive dissonance	Mind set

THE WAY IT HAPPENED

One of the better-known examples of image-perception-attitude changing involves Marlboro cigarettes. In fact, it was literally a sex change.

Cork-tipped Marlboros used to be regarded as strictly a woman's cigarette. A dedicated Lucky Strike or Camel smoker wouldn't be caught dead with a pack of these "effeminate" cigarettes in his pocket.

Marlboro rattled along with its small, specialized share of the market for some time. Then new marketing management came in and decided it was time to challenge the "big four" who controlled most of the market—as a he-man's cigarette!

Marlboro's advertising was given the task of transforming the cigarette's image from female to male. In place of languid beauties dangling Marlboros from their fingertips, there appeared the "Marlboro Man." Most memorable was the hard-bitten, wind-burned cowboy, squatting on his heels before the fire, clutching a Marlboro in his work-gnarled hand. The tattoo between thumb and forefinger on that hand became the very symbol of Marlboro's masculinity.

A PERSONAL PROJECT

One of the public relations person's greatest problems is that his or her publics' perceptions vary so much. We cannot assume that just because we and all our friends regard something in a particular way that the rest of the world regards it that way. Very often this is not so.

For example, there is a very popular Italian dish called calamari. It is made of squid. Would you eat a squid? What is your perception of squid as a food? Or for that matter snails?

See if you can prepare a list of 10 objects which, like squid, have the widest swing in attitudes as a result of their different public perceptions.

READING TO BROADEN UNDERSTANDING

Current issues of the *Journal of Applied Psychology* and *Psychology Today* are likely to have articles on attitudes, perceptions, and beliefs.

RUSS, FREDERICK A., and CHARLES A. KIRKPATRICK. *Marketing* (Boston: Little, Brown, 1982). Chapter 5, "The Psychology of Consumer Behavior," contains some good material on attitudes and perceptions in relation to buyers.

See also texts in use in your college on selling, advertising, marketing, and consumer behavior. All of them will have material on attitudes and perceptions, images and beliefs.

11

SPORTS

OVERVIEW AND GOALS

We begin now to look at public relations in action—what happens in a single field, in this case college and professional athletics. Now that we are moving from the theoretical to the practical, you will see how the theory plays a role. When you have completed this chapter, you should be able to

> *Appreciate how a knowledge of one's publics and how to communicate with them is of real practical importance to the public relations person.*
>
> *Recognize many of the standard techniques used today in both college and professional sports publicity.*
>
> *Apply these techniques if and when you are in a position to do so.*

Up to this point you have been learning about the mechanics of public relations: the tools the public relations person must have to carry out the job, the people and things he or she must know to make public relations work. Now we examine public relations at work. You are going to see how all the facts you have learned thus far are utilized to achieve results in a number of different fields.

This is not an encyclopedia of all the possible public relations techniques one might use. Rather, it is a sampling of real-life examples from various fields so that you can see how the pros do it. As in sales promotion, there are a great many standard publicity techniques. You will see some appearing time after time in such fields as sports, food, and finance. But remember: As in sales promotion, a special premium is attached to the new, fresh, exciting idea.

The Sporting Life

Sports is big business. In the case of professional football and baseball, it is *very* big business. TV's insatiable appetite for weekend sports shows has pulled many a "minor" sport into the big time: bowling, gymnastics, skiing. Moreover, business has discovered that the sponsorship of sports is an excellent public relations vehicle. We have a two-way street. We create publicity to publicize an event, and the event helps to publicize us. College and professional bowl games are heavily promoted and publicized. For days before the event, the papers are filled with press release stories on the players, the coaches, and the game.

But the game is also a great publicity event for the city in which it is being played. In fact, most college bowl games are backed by local business interests, and may have been originated by them. "New money" is brought into town. The charms of the city are exploited by the cameras. The colleges themselves are being publicized. During the half-time break, there will be segments (prepared by the public information office of the college) showing the activities and accomplishments of the college in classroom and laboratory.

College athletic teams must have publicity, as we will see. But these teams also generate tremendous publicity for their colleges. Over the years, Notre Dame has built a great reputation as a football power. But the publicity generated by football has also given the university a chance to stress to the public its tremendous intellectual accomplishments as an important seat of learning.

Every now and then, a small school from nowhere will organize a booster club, raise some money, and get itself some tall guys who can shoot baskets. Wonder of wonders, there they are a couple of years later at the Garden, fighting it out with the Marylands, the NCLAs, the Indianas, and the Brigham Youngs, for a place in the finals. All of a sudden "Old Toogaloo" is on *everybody's* lips.

FIGURE 11-1   Football programs are an important part of the university's public relations effort. The programs do far more than give the "name and number of each and every player," as the vendor says. They contain pictures of university officials, reviews of its activities, and usually a message from the president. They are also an important source of income: $1.50 × a stadium full of Iowa rooters six or more times a season ain't hay.

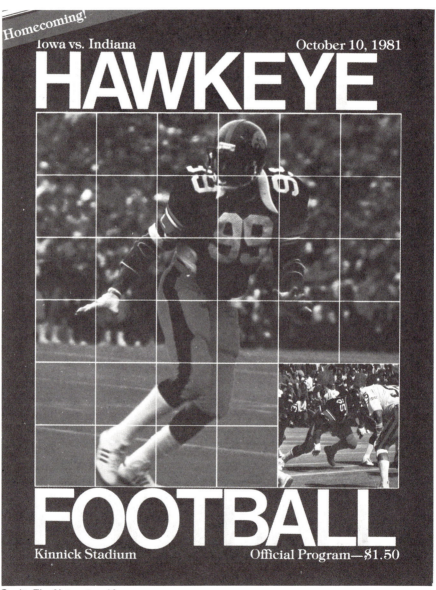

Credit: The University of Iowa.

FIGURE 11-2   Intensive lobbying for All-American honors is not unusual. Colleges and university public relations people want to make sure sports editors do not overlook the qualities of their particular star. "The Record Breaker," produced by Kim Kelly, the assistant sports information director of Clemson University, in behalf of Perry Tuttle is an outstandingly original approach. Designed in the manner of record jackets, it has a trick photo of Tuttle on the front and a list of his accomplishments on the back. Note the final "sell" to the editor in the lower right-hand corner: "Perry Tuttle the Record Breaker—An All-American Candidate. Cast Your Vote Now!" The design, paper, color photography, printing, and engraving for a job like this does not come cheap. Also note the sports writer's column in Figure 11-4.

FIGURE 11-2   *continued*

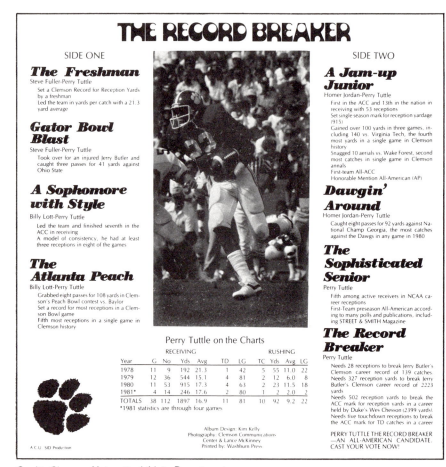

THE RECORD BREAKER

SIDE ONE

The Freshman
Steve Fuller-Perry Tuttle
Set a Clemson Record for Reception Yards by a freshman
Led the team in yards per catch with a 21.3 yard average

Gator Bowl Blast
Steve Fuller-Perry Tuttle
Took over for an injured Jerry Butler and caught three passes for 41 yards against Ohio State

A Sophomore with Style
Billy Lott-Perry Tuttle
Led the team and finished seventh in the ACC in receiving
A model of consistency, he had at least three receptions in eight of the games

The Atlanta Peach
Billy Lott-Perry Tuttle
Grabbed eight passes for 108 yards in Clemson's Peach Bowl contest vs. Baylor
Set a record for most receptions in a Clemson Bowl game
Fifth most receptions in a single game in Clemson history

SIDE TWO

A Jam-up Junior
Homer Jordan-Perry Tuttle
First in the ACC and 13th in the nation in receiving with 53 receptions
Set single season mark for reception yardage (915)
Gained over 100 yards in three games, including 140 vs. Virginia Tech, the fourth most yards in a single game in Clemson history
Snagged 10 aerials vs. Wake Forest, second most catches in single game in Clemson annals
First-team All-ACC
Honorable Mention All-American (AP)

Dawgin' Around
Homer Jordan-Perry Tuttle
Caught eight passes for 92 yards against National Champ Georgia, the most catches against the Dawgs in any game in 1980

The Sophisticated Senior
Perry Tuttle
Fifth among active receivers in NCAA career receptions
First-Team preseason All-American according to many polls and publications, including STREET & SMITH Magazine

The Record Breaker
Perry Tuttle
Needs 28 receptions to break Jerry Butler's Clemson career record of 139 catches
Needs 327 reception yards to break Jerry Butler's Clemson career record of 2223 yards
Needs 502 reception yards to break the ACC mark for reception yards in a career held by Duke's Wes Chesson (2399 yards)
Needs five touchdown receptions to break the ACC mark for TD catches in a career

PERRY TUTTLE THE RECORD BREAKER —AN ALL-AMERICAN CANDIDATE. CAST YOUR VOTE NOW!

Perry Tuttle on the Charts

Year		RECEIVING					RUSHING			
Year	G	No	Yds	Avg	TD	LG	TC	Yds	Avg	LG
1978	11	9	192	21.3	1	42	5	55	11.0	22
1979	12	36	544	15.1	4	81	2	12	6.0	8
1980	11	53	915	17.3	4	63	2	23	11.5	18
1981*	4	14	246	17.6	2	80	1	2	2.0	2
TOTALS	38	112	1897	16.9	11	81	10	92	9.2	22

*1981 statistics are through four games

Album Design: Kim Kelly
Photography: Clemson Communications
Center & Lance McKinney
Printed by: Washburn Press

A.C.U. SID Production

Credit: *Clemson University Athletic Department.*

The College Sports Information Director

Let us begin close to home and examine some of the kinds of public relations carried out by a college sports information office.

Who are the "publics" involved? The alumni, of course, thousands and thousands of them of all ages—from the "oldest living" to the latest graduates. Students and their parents, who certainly have a vital interest in the college. The faculty, and quite possibly faculty of other schools. Townspeople, particularly if the school is located in a smaller community. High school students and, as far as the coaches are concerned, high school athletes. People of money and influence throughout your area who might "adopt" the college as their own (the subway alumni).

When a member of the team is declared an All-American, when the team wins a conference championship or gets invited to a bowl game, it makes a tremendous splash. The waves extend for miles. The loyal alumni swell with pride, and their contributions to the alumni fund increase in size. The morale of the student body is enhanced. Graduating high school seniors (many of whom like to be associated with "winners," even though they do not participate themselves) think more seriously about attending the school. As for recruiting high school athletes, the assistant coaches find the doors open much more easily when they represent a champion.

The trouble is, All-Americans and conference championships and bowl games and all their wonderful publicity effects do not come along every day. Sometimes it is necessary to do some hard and persistent public relations work. Let us say you are the athletic department information officer for a medium-size Midwestern college. You've never had an All-American or received a bowl bid. You are usually one of the respectable runners-up in your conference. What are some of the things you might be doing to keep the money, the interest, and the adrenalin flowing?

Spreading the Good Word

One of the first things you would do is to set up and put into action a *speaker's bureau.* Enlisted in your speaker's bureau will be officials from the athletic department, coaches, and players. You will, of course, have filmed highlights of past games that they can take along with them.

Booking your speakers will be done in conjunction with your alumni clubs, who will want speakers and movies themselves, as well as the Quarterback Clubs and other organizations in your area they can spot for you. You will find that your head coach is an old hand at the game and has a complete repertoire of jokes and comments. Of course, if you have someone as fast on his feet as Lou Holtz (Arkansas), you are twice blessed. The assistant coaches learn fast—after-dinner speaking comes with the profession—but some of the players may need a lot of help. Classroom and playing field obligations make if difficult to send players on speaking engagements. If possible, parade the players before the hometown folks and relatives—they'll appreciate it.

You also hold special background meetings for the press. These meetings are very much like the background meetings held for members of the press corps in Washington in which they are "filled in" on the background of certain events. You will have selected the key sports editors and writers in your area and invited them for a luncheon or dinner. Your invitation will make it clear that this is a special event for special people and an RSVP (acknowledgement)

FIGURE 11-3 **Here is the table of contents of a regular season press guide. This 156-page book is an elaborate and complete guide, as you can see from the items covered. These books are prepared in the spring and by midsummer are arriving on sports writers desks all over the country. They are also offered to alumni for a modest charge.**

Table of Contents

1

Awards and honors

Beaver Stadium

Bowls

Coaches

Opponents

Penn State

Results and records

Season preview (1981)

Season review

Credit: The Pennsylvania State University.

FIGURE 11-4 This column, by Mike Szostak of the *Providence Evening Bulletin*, is remarkable. It gives us not only an insight into the preparation of a sports promotion piece, but some thoughtful comments by others on the whole business of the pushing of All-American candidates by the sports information office. Truly, this has become a "whole marketing strategy." Note in the fourth column the mention of other gimmicks. Of course, one of the best "gimmicks" is four quarterback sacks in one game by a defensive tackle.

Sports

Providence, RI

B Section

The Evening Bulletin
Wednesday, Nov. 4, 1981

Mike Szostak

Often gimmicks, publicity behind the making of an All-American

Behind many an All-America football player stands a good publicist.

Ask Perry Tuttle.

Clemson's terrific wide receiver and All-America candidate has found his way into the files of hundreds of sports writers and broadcasters not because of his pass-catching exploits but because of Kim Kelly's ingenuity.

Miss Kelly, Clemson's assistant sports information director, is a young woman with a Madison Avenue flair for the imaginative. She has packaged Tuttle as a recording studio might package Chuck Mangione or George Benson and promoted him to writers from Boston to Los Angeles.

As the nation's sporting press prepares to play its version of The Name Game, her gimmick stands helmet and shoulder pads above the colorless flyers and pamphlets now clogging newsroom mailboxes. If Perry Tuttle makes All-America, he owes Kim Kelly a dinner.

"We like to develop a whole marketing strategy," Miss Kelly explained yesterday from her office at Clemson.

"If you get something real different, you're going to get their attention. You might not get their vote, but at least they will recognize and remember the player," she said.

'Hits' on the flip side

Miss Kelly's attention-getter is "The Record Breaker," a 12 x 12 album "cover" she designed. On the full-color front sits Tuttle, broken records strewn at his feet. He letters "PT" printed boldly in football. Were a horn instead of a football resting between his legs, Tuttle could pass as a contemporary of Mangione or Benson.

On the flip side, framing a full color-action photograph, are Tuttle's hit recordings. Side One: The Freshman. Gator Bowl Blast. A Sophomore with Style. The Atlanta Peach. Side Two: A Jam-up Junior. Dawgin' Around. The Sophisticated Senior. Beneath each title is a brief description. "Set Clemson record . . . Led the team . . . First in ACC . . . Set single season mark . . . First-team preseason All-America STREET & SMITH."

And beneath the picture are statistics, "Perry Tuttle on the Charts."

Started project in June

The project is a perfect example of the marketing of an All-America candidate.

"It's not something we take too lightly here," Miss Kelly said.

She spent $4,000 producing the album, a black and white pamphlet hyping linebacker Jeff "The Judge" Davis and offensive lineman Lee "ACC's Strongest Athlete Ever" Nanney, an 11 x 14 poster of The Judge in a jurist's robes and a flyer on Nanney.

"We started in June targeting which Clemson athletes might make All-America," Miss Kelly explained. "They gave me a budget and told me to promote them any way I wanted to."

She was listening to a Teddy Pendergrass album one summer day when lightning struck.

"I got to wondering if it would work out," she said. "Perry is a flashy, flamboyant guy. We took some pictures and I thought, 'Why just make it a poster?' So I fiddled around with the idea of the songs and the stats."

Big hypes cost big money

Miss Kelly and her staff took two days to stuff, seal, stamp and address 1,000 envelopes. They went to those on the Clemson mailing list, to many members of the football writers' association and to newspapers with a minimum circulation of 55,000.

The gimmick worked. Writers from foreign turf ("You're calling from Providence?" she said with a laugh) are asking about Perry Tuttle.

"Perry loved it. He's very personable and outgoing, and you can do a lot with that kind of athlete," Miss Kelly said.

You can do a lot with that kind of money, too.

"What we spend is a drop in the bucket for other schools," exclaimed Phil Langan, Brown's sports information director, alluding to the fact that major

colleges often spend big bucks promoting their athletes.

Langan produced a flyer on Steve Jordan, Brown's All-Ivy tight end and an AP All-America honorable mention last year. Five hundred copies cost him $40. His first mailing went to about 100 media representatives. If Jordan plays well in Brown's last three games, Langan plans two more mailings. Total cost of the project: $150, "probably what they spend on a typist for a week," Langan said wryly.

"But I think it's an honest approach," he added.

Gimmicks don't always work

Langan hyped four third-team AP All-Americas in his stops at Ithaca, Princeton and Cornell, proving the old flyer routine can help. Other SIDs have resorted to match books, cigars, film clips, slides and repeated telephone calls to push their players.

But gimmicks are not always necessary.

"We try to make people aware in our weekly release," said Reid Oslin, SID at Boston College, which has yet to produce a football player with a gimmick.

"By producing information, we get our share of the accolades," Oslin said.

And a gimmick, however ingenious, does not guarantee an All-America.

Langan told of an SID who spent about $15,000 a decade or so ago hyping two players, both of whom eventually played professional football but did not receive the honors the school had anticipated.

Langan paused, respectfully.

"The guy got canned."

Credit: Copyright 1981, The Providence Evening Bulletin.

159

is requested. You will inform them what members of the coaching staff and athletic department will participate. Your guests will understand that much of what they are about to learn is "inside information" and possibly not attributable for direct quotes.

With very few exceptions, the members of the press will honor your request for confidentiality. If your people have a star running back whose knee is not expected to last the season, you would not want the news trumpeted far and wide. But the coaches *can* say, "As you know, Jones's knee was operated on this spring. We'll probably be using him sparingly the first part of the season." The press will get the idea. You will win a lot of them to your side when you tell them: "It's a little early for this, and we'd appreciate it if you keep it under your hat for awhile, but we have a freshman on the squad who is the greatest thing since 'Crazy Legs Hirsh.' You won't see him till midseason, but when No. 28 appears, have your binoculars in focus!" Sports columnists, who get a tremendous amount of readership in most communities, love this kind of "inside dope." After all, it helps them write with that air of infallibility most sports writers cherish.

Band Days, Alumni Clubs, Game Tours

For state-oriented universities, the institution of *Band Day* was made to order. Dozens of outstanding high school bands are given the chance to demonstrate their talent, strutting and tooting before as many as 80,000 people. It is a great thing for the kids, their parents, and the schools. Many of these youngsters have never been on a college campus before. The excitement is tremendous. Of course the ultimate thrill comes when the whistle blows, the drums begin to thump, and the Blue and White of Logansport High comes swinging down the field to the cheers of thousands.

Never underestimate the power of a high school band. After all, there are more of them—majorettes, flag bearers, baton twirlers, to say nothing of musicians—than there are football players. Band is a big and important activity in most high schools. With all the parents, teachers, and students involved, it reaches to the heart of every community. You will enlist *all* the facilities of the college to see that these kids and their teachers have the best time possible.

Almost all colleges and universities have alumni offices whose job is to keep track of the thousands of alumni, keep them up to date on the activities of the college, and solicit their financial support. As public relations director of the athletic department you can be a big help, especially when speakers visit the various clubs around the country. The alumni strongly identify with stars of the past, and if you can supply one, together with some old game films, you will help fill the hall. Many of the "greats" stay in college administration, so you should not have any trouble reaching them. The importance

FIGURE 11-5   An information sheet for the press is prepared and distributed for each game. In this one, pertinent information on all aspects of the game and the individual teams that might be of help to reporters in doing the story is supplied.

Penn State

Sports Information
234 Recreation Building
University Park, PA 16802

David L. Baker
Sports Information Director

Mary Jo Haverbeck
Assistant Sports Information Director

Richard E. Sapara
Assistant Sports Information Director

PENN STATE - WEST VIRGINIA   October 18, 1981

Sixth game: Penn State (5-0) faces West Virginia (5-1) at Beaver Stadium, University Park, Pa., Saturday, October 24, 1981. Kickoff is 1:30 p.m. EDT.

Estimated attendance: A capacity crowd of 84,000 is expected for the 48th meeting of the two Eastern independents. The Beaver Stadium record is 84,585 against Nebraska Sept. 27, 1980.

ESPN coverage: ESPN will distribute the Penn State-West Virginia game throughout the country to 12.2 million homes. John Sanders, play-by-play, and Fred Miller, color, are the ESPN announcers. This will be Penn State's fourth ESPN appearance this season. The Lions are 5-0 in ESPN games the last two years. The game will be televised Sunday, Oct. 25 at 1:30 a.m. and 1:30 p.m.; Monday, Oct. 26 at 9 p.m.; and Tuesday, Oct. 27 at 11 a.m.

Additional radio-TV coverage: The Penn State Football Television Network (Ray Scott, play-by-play, and George Paterno, color) will distribute the game to 14 stations in the Northeast and the USA Network and Modern Satellite cable systems, which reach more than 12 million homes. The Penn State Football Radio Network (Fran Fisher, play-by-play, and John Grant, color) will broadcast the game to 79 stations in a four-state area.

Penn State last game: Penn State boosted its record to 5-0 with a 41-16 victory over Syracuse in the Carrier Dome last Saturday. Junior tailback Curt Warner set a single-game Penn State rushing record, carrying for 256 yards in 26 carries. Sophomore quarterback Todd Blackledge completed 10 of 11 passes for 121 yards as the Lions rolled up a season-high 513 yards total offense. The Penn State defenders sacked Syracuse quarterbacks eight times.

West Virginia last game: Senior quarterback Oliver Luck threw three touchdown passes to lead West Virginia to a 27-6 win over Virginia Tech in Morgantown last Saturday. Passing accounted for all WVU scores as tailback Mickey Walczak also threw for a touchdown. Luck finished with a 17-for-26 performance for 265 yards. The Mountaineer defense limited the visitors to seven first downs and 131 yards total offense.

Penn State results and schedule: Defeated Cincinnati, 52-0; defeated Nebraska, 30-24; defeated Temple, 30-0; defeated Boston College, 38-7; defeated Syracuse, 41-16; Oct. 24, West Virginia, Oct. 31, at Miami, Fla.; Nov. 7, at North Carolina State; Nov. 14, Alabama; Nov. 21, Notre Dame; Nov. 28, at Pittsburgh.

West Virginia results and schedule: Defeated Virginia, 32-18; defeated Maryland, 17-13; defeated Colorado State, 49-3; defeated Boston College, 38-10; lost to Pittsburgh, 17-0; defeated Virginia Tech, 27-6; Oct. 24, at Penn State; Oct. 31, East Carolina; Nov. 7, Temple; Nov. 14, Rutgers; Nov. 21, at Syracuse.

Coaches: Penn State's Joe Paterno has compiled a 16-year record of 146-31-1 for an 82.2 winning percentage. He is the nation's winningest active coach (based on percentage) for coaches with a minimum of 10 years experience at a major college and fourth among active coaches in career victories. He ranks eighth on the all-time chart in percentage (10 years as a head coach). Paterno has taken 10 consecutive Penn State teams to bowl games and 13 of his 15 Lion squads have played in post-season contests. Don Nehlen is in his second season at West Virginia; he has a record of 11 wins and seven losses. Nehlen previously served as head coach at Bowling Green for nine seasons, compiling a 53-35-4 record at the Mid-American Conference school His 11-year collegiate record is 64-42-4.

(continued on reverse side)

FIGURE 11-5   continued

The series: Penn State has won 22 consecutive games against West Virginia to take
a 38-7-2 lead in the series that started in 1905. West Virginia's last victory was a 21-7
decision at Morgantown in 1955. Penn State owns an 11-4-1 record in Morgantown and a 27-3
record at Penn State. The Lions have won all 13 games in the series that have been played
in Beaver Stadium and have won 15 straight home games against the Mountaineers.

Last meeting: Penn State held off a furious fourth-quarter rally to edge West
Virginia, 20-15, at Morgantown Oct. 25, 1980. The Mountaineers' kicking game kept them
in the game and Walter Easley's run closed the gap to five points in the final minutes of
the game. WVU recovered an onside kick, but Giuseppe Harris intercepted a pass to end
the losers' final threat. Fullback Booker Moore highlighted the Lion offense, rushing
for 112 yards in the rainy weather.

Penn State offense: Penn State is averaging 302 yards rushing, 135 yards passing,
437 yards total offense and 38.2 points per game. Tailback Curt Warner is averaging
167.6 yards rushing per game with 115 carries for 838 yards (7.3 average) and eight
touchdowns. Tailback Jon Williams (227 yards) and fullback Mike Meade (220) provide
running balance. Quarterback Todd Blackledge has completed 35 of 68 passes (51.5 per
cent) for 607 yards, six touchdowns and four interceptions. Split end Gregg Garrity
(9-171), tight end Mike McCloskey (8-134-2) and flanker Kenny Jackson (6-178-3) are the
leading receivers.

Penn State defense: Penn State's defenders are permitting 137.6 yards rushing, 127
yards passing, 264.6 yards total offense and 9.4 points per game. The Lions have allowed
only one rushing touchdown in five games. Linebacker Chet Parlavecchio (22 solos, 11
assists) and safety Mark Robinson (15 solos, 11 assists) are the leading tacklers.
Defensive end Walker Lee Ashley leads the team with five sacks. Eleven different players
have interceptions in the first five games.

Penn State kicking: Punter Ralph Giacomarro and placekicker Brian Franco provide
the Lions with two outstanding weapons. Giacomarro has averaged 44.2 yards per kick,
while Franco has kicked 10-of-11 field goals and 21-of-22 extra points.

West Virginia offense: The Mountaineers are averaging 149.7 yards rushing, 209.7
yards passing, 359.4 yards total offense and 27.2 points per game. Tailbacks Curlin Beck
(262 yards) and King Harvey (176) lead the West Virginia running game. Quarterback Oliver
Luck has completed 51.3 per cent of his passes (96 of 187) for 1,163 yards; he has thrown
nine touchdowns and has been intercepted six times. Wide receiver Rich Hollins (24-491-5)
and tight end Mark Raugh (24-245-1) are the top receivers.

West Virginia defense: West Virginia is surrendering 110.3 yards rushing, 106.7
yards passing, 217 yards total offense and 11.2 points per game in the first six contests.
Linebackers Darryl Talley and Dennis Fowlkes are the top defenders. The Mountaineers
have intercepted 14 passes and have allowed only one rushing touchdown in the first six
games.

West Virginia kicking: Punter Jody McKnown has averaged 37.8 yards on 36 kicks this
year. Placekicker Murcat Tercan has hit on five-of-12 field goal attempts and has been
successful on all 20 extra point tries.

West Virginia travel plans: The Mountaineers will bus to State College Friday, Oct.
23, for an afternoon workout. The team headquarters is the State College Holiday Inn
(814 238-3001). The team will return to West Virginia immediately after the game.

Penn State Sportsline: Recorded comments from Penn State football coach Joe Paterno,
members of the Nittany Lions' staff and team are featured daily on the Penn State Sportsline. A different message is available on the telephone by 2 p.m., Monday through Friday.
During the football season, a Saturday morning update and a Saturday evening post-game
message will be available. This is a service to the media and the telephone number
should not be released to the public. The Penn State Sportsline telephone number is
814 238-0281.

* * * * *

Credit: The Pennsylvania State University.

FIGURE 11-6   When a college is selected for a bowl game, the wheels in the sports information office really begin to spin. A press book must be prepared for the event. Here is the contents page from Penn State's press guide for the 1982 Fiesta Bowl game. Note the detail that must be covered in this brochure, and the press conferences that have been arranged with coaches and players. Says Dave Baker, Penn State's sports information director: "As the season progressed, it was obvious that Penn State was going to be selected for a bowl game. With time restrictions an important consideration, much of the material had to be prepared during the season. All of the material had to be at the printer one week before the final game to insure a delivery date of December 18, so we could mail 1,000 copies nationwide. More than anything else, the job is planning. I needed to have all the background material ready to go to produce all the player sketches, season wrapup, and outlook on the Fiesta Bowl in the three days, following the Pittsburgh game."

1982 Fiesta Bowl Guide

1

Editors: Dave Baker and Dick Sapara

Press Conferences

December 26 — Penn State football coach Joe Paterno will hold a press conference on Penn State's arrival day at Mountain Shadows, the Nittany Lions' team headquarters during the week of Fiesta Bowl XI. The press conference will be held approximately one hour after the team arrives at the hotel. Contact Fiesta Bowl publicity director John Junker for more information. Players will not be available at this time.

December 27 — Penn State will hold a press conference the first hour of the team's first practice in Arizona. Team members and coaches will be available for interviews, photographs and filming at Scottsdale Community College that day. Starting time for practice will be announced by Penn State sports information director Dave Baker at the December 26 press conference at Mountain Shadows. Penn State practices will be closed the remainder of the week.

December 29 — Penn State football coach Joe Paterno will be available for interviews prior to the Tempe Chamber of Commerce-Temple Diablos Press Brunch at the Fiesta Inn in Tempe. Paterno and USC coach John Robinson will begin the press conference at 9:30 a.m. with the brunch scheduled to start at 10 a.m. Players will not be available at this time.

December 31 — Three Penn State players will be available at 11 a.m. in the press room of the Phoenix Civic Plaza, prior to the Fiesta Bowl Kickoff Luncheon at noon that day. The Penn State sports information staff will assist reporters who wish to interview other players, prior to the start of the luncheon.

Special requests for interviews — Special requests will be handled as time permits. Requests should be made through sports information director Dave Baker and assistant sports information director Dick Sapara.

Credit: The Pennsylvania State University.

FIGURE 11-7   The coach's comments on the football team are always of interest to alumni. Note, in this letter, the emphasis on the much-appreciated participation and behavior of the Clemson fans.

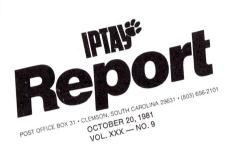

FIRST-CLASS MAIL
U. S. POSTAGE
PAID
CLEMSON, S. C. 29631
PERMIT NO. 5

FIRST CLASS MAIL

IPTAY Report

POST OFFICE BOX 31 · CLEMSON, SOUTH CAROLINA 29631 · (803) 656-2101
OCTOBER 20, 1981
VOL. XXX — NO. 9

TEXTILE BOWL

The annual football game between N. C. State and Clemson is being designated as the Textile Bowl as part of the observance of Textile Week.

A large commemorative trophy will be presented annually to the winning team and will remain in that team's possession for a year. The trophy is a gift of the Textile Hall Corporation.

The Textile Manufacturers Association in North Carolina and South Carolina will also present a $500 scholarship to each school in the name of each team's most outstanding player in the game.

Additional presentation will be made during halftime ceremonies.

The special designation of this game as the Textile Bowl is made in recognition of the unique contribution the two universities have made to America's textile industry.

FIELD HOCKEY CONTINUES TO WIN

Clemson's field hockey team continued its winning ways this week as they took third in the Virginia Tech Invitational and defeated William and Mary. The Tigers' loss column came at the hands of thirteenth-ranked Virginia in a tiebreaker, 0-1. In the Virginia Tech tournament, Clemson defeated Pfeiffer 1-0, lost to the eventual champs Trenton State, 1-2, and shutout Longwood 3-0. On Tuesday, they faced the toughest team they have played all season, Virginia. After two seven-minute overtimes and two-penalty stroke tiebreakers, Virginia finally beat the Tigers 1-0. The next day, Clemson defeated another ranked team, William and Mary 3-1. The Lady Tigers' record now stands at 10-3-0 and they travel to Charlotte where they face Duke on Wednesday.

NEW STATION IN MEBANE, N. C.

Tiger fans in the Mebane, N. C. area will be happy to learn that radio station WHNI is now carrying Clemson football. We appreciate the cooperation of the people at WHNI and the advertisers in the area who have made this broadcast possible.

Published weekly after each football game and monthly during January, February, March, April, May and August

Sent to all IPTAY members in the interest of education thru athletics.

Clemson Athletic Department
P. O. Box 31 / Clemson, SC 29631

BILL McLELLAN
Athletic Director

JOE TURNER
Executive Secretary of IPTAY

ALLISON DALTON
IPTAY Report Editor

Team Statistics

	CU	DU	CU	Opp
First downs rushing	14	5	70	37
First downs passing	11	13	40	56
First downs penalty	0	5	3	9
Total first downs	25	23	113	102
Rushing attempts	59	36	349	242
Net yards rushing	323	82	1358	568
Passes attempted	20	28	98	161
Passes completed	14	17	53	80
Passes had intercepted				18
Net yards passing	240	243	891	936
Total number of plays	79	64	447	403
Total Net yards	563	325	2249	1504
Number times punted				40
Average punt	31.5	40.5	43.7	40.5
No. of punt returns	5	5	18	10
Average Punt return		2	61	8.0
No. of kickoffs returned	3	10	10	15
Average kickoff return	16.7	45	20.4	15.9
Yards lost by penalty	83	16	383	132
Fumbles		3	13	22
Fumbles lost	4	2	7	12
Touchdowns passing		1	4	2
Touchdowns rushing	4	0	15	0
TD's interception return	0	1	0	2
Total touchdowns	5	1	19	1
Safety	0	1	0	5
Field goals	1	1	8	2
Extra points, kick	5	0	19	0
Extra pts. run or pass	0	0	0	0
Total points	38	10	157	31

Individual Statistics

	Plays Rush	Yds. Rush	Tot.	Att. Pass	Com. Pass	Yds. Pass	Tot. Plays	Tot. Yds.	TD
Austin	87	466	24	94	51	840	181	1094	3
Jordan	87	254	30	0	0	0	66	303	1
McSwain	66	303	27	0	0	0	53	202	0
McCall	33	116	18	0	0	51	33	116	0
Mack			16				7	58	0
Gasque			7	0	0	0	2	43	0
Tuttle	0	0	24	0	0	0	0	0	0
Gaillard	0	0	0	0	0	0	0	0	0
Magwood	12	32	6	0	0	0	12	32	0
Crite			6						

RECEIVING

	No.	Yds.	TD
Tuttle	22	391	1
Magwood	11	214	0
Gaillard	7	97	0
Diggs	6	59	0
Stockstill	5	75	0
Alley	3	43	0
Austin	1	8	0
McSwain	1	4	0

SCORING

	TD	PAT	FG	Tot.
Jordan	4	0	0	24
Austin	5	0	0	30
Paulling	0	18	3	27
Tuttle	3	0	0	18
Igwebuike	0	1	5	16
McSwain	2	0	0	12
McCall	2	0	0	12
Mack	1	0	0	6
Magwood	1	0	0	6
Crite	1	0	0	6

FIGURE 11-7   continued

IPTAY Report

Vol. XXX   October 20, 1981   No. 9

The Coach Says...

Dear IPTAY

We were very excited about the opportunity to play Duke at Wallace Wade Stadium this year. Last year we felt we played a good first half and then totally lost our concentration in the second half. We had been waiting a year to improve on our showing against Duke. We were pleased that we played with great intensity this year. We feel our offensive team showed great improvement and our defensive team improved also. Our kicking game, with the exception of punting, also showed improvement. We feel that we can work out our punting situation in the future, however. Since we didn't punt until late in the game that might have affected our timing.

We were really proud of the great crowd Clemson had in Durham. It actually looked like there were nearly as many Tiger fans in Wallace Wade Stadium as there were Duke fans. We continue to appreciate your loyal support and it is truly outstanding. I know you all appreciated, as I did, the fine comments Coach Bestwick of Virginia made about you Clemson fans. When you go away and see fan conduct that is not equal to yours it really makes us proud of Clemson and the way you conduct yourselves and the way you treat our visitors.

We had a lot of respect for Duke going into Saturday's game. They had been playing well and we knew they had a lot of good players returning. Duke's young quarterback, Bennett, did an excellent job for them. We tried several ways to rush him and confuse him and I think our coaches had done an excellent job preparing for Duke.

I am really proud of our defensive coaches and the defensive team for all they have accomplished this year. I feel Joe Glenn and Bill Smith are both doing a good job for us at defensive end. Edgar Pickett is also doing

(Continued on page 2)

CLEMSON DEFEATS DUKE 38-10

More than a third of the 26,000 fans in Wallace Wade Stadium in Durham Saturday for Duke's homecoming appeared to be attired in Orange. The number of fans following the Tigers on the road becomes more impressive each week. The "Two Plus Orange" is an impressive show.

The Clemson offense lost little time Saturday proving to everyone that the defense is not all that got the Tigers ranked 6th in the nation.

Clemson marched 64 yards in seven plays the first time it got the ball to take an early 7-0 lead when Paulling kicked the PAT. That first touchdown came on a four yard run by Crite.

Duke controlled the ball six minutes before the Tigers got it back except for one play when the Tigers gave it up on a fumble.

The next time Clemson got possession on their own 20 they moved the ball 77 yards in 15 plays using about seven minutes but had to settle for a 20 yard field goal by Paulling to make the score 10-0 Clemson.

Duke took the ball on their own 20 and controlled it four plays before they fumbled and Davis recovered on the Duke 49. Clemson scored eight plays later when Austin carried in from 15 yards out and Paulling made the PAT to give the Tigers a 17-0 lead with 9:05 remaining in the half.

Clemson gave the ball up on an interception the next time they had possession but Bennett threw a long pass on first down and Kinard intercepted at the Clemson two yard line. On second and three at the Clemson 19 Austin went up the middle and broke loose for a 77 yard run before being tripped up from behind at the Duke four. Three plays later Jordan sneaked over from one yard out to make the score Clemson 24 and Duke 0 after Paulling added the PAT.

Duke took the kickoff and moved to the Clemson two yard line in seven plays where Headen threw Bennett for a 10 yard loss and Duke was forced to go for a 29 yard field goal which was good to make the score 24-3 in favor of Clemson at the half.

Clemson took the second half kick and engineered a 59 yard drive in 13 plays with Austin scoring from two yards out. Paulling added his fourth PAT of the day to give Clemson a 31-3 lead.

Duke was able to move the ball on their next possession 79 yards in seven plays and scored on a 21 yard pass. The PAT was good to make the score Clemson 31 and Duke 10.

(Continued on page 2)

Cliff Austin

Jeff Davis

Homer Jordan

Terry Kinard

FIGURE 11-7 *continued*

THE COACH SAYS . . .
(Continued from page 1)
a good job. Andy Headen continues to play well and we are real pleased that he continues to stay healthy. Mark Richardson is doing a good job backing Headen.

Our defensive line has improved as much as any area on our team. Dan Benish is a much improved player and Ray Brown is a good player backing him up. Jeff Bryant and Jim Scott are doing a good job on the other side at tackle. Our nose guards, Devane and Perry continue to do an outstanding job. Devane has been a very pleasant surprise. Triplett and Rembert are both playing well at linebacker and it looks like Rembert comes up with an interception every time he gets in the game. Davis and Cheek are also doing a good job on the other side at linebacker. Jeff Davis continues to be our leader on defense and we feel like his play has a lot to do with how well our defensive team plays.

Our secondary is still playing well and they kept everything in front of them at Duke except on the one play when Duke scored. That was simply a perfectly executed play. Hollis Hall, Ken Brown, Anthony Rose, Rod McSwain, Jeff Suttle, Billy Davis, and Terry Kinard are all doing an excellent job for Coach Holloman's group. We missed Tim Childers because he had some bruised ribs this past week. We look forward to having him back for the N. C. State game.

Our defensive team has played absolutely great this year and they have shown consistent improvement since the second half against Wofford. They go into every game with a lot of confidence and that makes a lot of difference in comparing to what we did a year ago.

Our offensive team played very well against Duke. In our team meeting Sunday afternoon our coaches all agreed that we had never had better effort from our wide receivers: Stockstill, Magwood, Alley, Tuttle, and Gaillard. Gaillard came back after being out two weeks with a turned ankle and twisted knee and played great. They were going out knocking people down as well as catching the ball.

Our tailbacks had a good game. Cliff Austin had 178 yards and looked like the Cliff Austin we saw as a freshman before his knee surgery. Chuck McSwain came back to do another job and we are fortunate to have backs like Austin, McSwain, McCall, and Mack. It was also good to get Crite into action at the wingback spot on our goal line attack. He can also help us at fullback and tailback if the need arises. He made a nice run Saturday on the reverse play and got a touchdown for us.

Jordan continues to play well and we

think he is as good a quarterback as we have had at Clemson in a good while. We think he will continue to improve and he is showing good leadership for our offensive team. We are very fortunate that he has played well in every game this year.

Our offensive line is continuing to improve and probably showed the most improvement this past week that they have shown all year. Fisher, Gary Brown, Farr, Butcher, Berryhill, Mayberry, Clark, Nanney, Ellis, and Massaro are all coming off the ball well and giving second and third effort which is enabling us to get the yardage we have been getting in the last two games. This past week our total offensive yardage was 563 which is the third best in Clemson's history and it came against a pretty good defensive team. Duke had just come off two good defensive games.

There are lots of things we still want to accomplish. Our team does have increased confidence, but we know we have a big challenge coming up with N. C. State this week. We can't brag on our young players enough. They are attempting to do everything we ask of them. They are showing steady progress and are developing into a total team and we hope to reach our potential before the season is over. It will probably take our best game of the year to do well against State this week.

Our kicking game this past week was especially good for Paulling who had one field goal and was good on all five extra points. Igwebuike continued to give us good kickoffs.

Our entire staff is grateful for the fine effort our young athletes are giving. We feel like their performance should make our entire university proud as well and the families and friends of our athletes. I feel like our entire staff is to be commended for an outstanding job in preparing our team each week. Our staff accepts their responsibilities so well and each one carries out his duties in a way that has enabled us to be well prepared for every one of our opponents each week in the season. I am proud of the job each of them is doing and I hope you are.

We are all proud to be ranked sixth in the nation and we hope we can continue to improve.

We all look forward to seeing you in Clemson Saturday. We are truly proud to be able to represent such a fine institution and such a fine group of fans. It really makes us feel good to be coming back to Death Valley where you all can see what we believe will be another great game.

Thank you for your continued support.

Danny Ford

TIGERS DEFEAT DUKE . . .
(Continued from page 1)
Clemson's next possession resulted in a touchdown on a five play 65 yard drive. The final 29 yards were covered with a pass from Jordan to Tuttle in the end zone. Paulling added the PAT to make the final score 38-10.

Austin rushed for 178 yards on 19 carries in the game. Jordan had 47 yards rushing and passed for 198 yards to give him 245 yards total offense. Jordan was good on 13 of 19 attempts passing. The Tigers had a total of 563 yards in the game.

Kinard had six solo tackles for the Tigers and two pass interceptions. Jeff Davis was credited with three solo hits and 10 assists to lead the defense.

CROSS COUNTRY WINS

The third-ranked Clemson men's cross country defeated 13th-ranked Tennessee and in-state rival Furman in a match held on the Clemson course behind the Jervey Athletic Center Sunday afternoon.

The final scores were: Clemson 23, Tennessee 32, and Furman 82.

The win puts the Tigers' dual meet record at 2-0.

LADY NETTERS SWEEP LEAGUE OVER THE WEEKEND IN N. C.

Clemson's Womens' Tennis team cleaned house in the ACC this past weekend defeating North Carolina-Chapel Hill 5-4 on Friday, Duke 7-2 on Saturday and finishing up on N. C. State 9-0 on Sunday. Clemson's top three netters suffered losses at North Carolina, but King's trio of Melissa Seigler, Lori Miller and Jane Neville all took their matches.

The Lady Tigers, now 6-1, stand undefeated in league play 3-0. They play at the ACC tournament next weekend in Duke.

PT THE RECORD BREAKER

The Clemson SID's office has its newest release, "PT The Record Breaker", ready for national distribution. Hopes are high that it will make the top 10. "PT The Record Breaker" is a unique piece prepared to tout Perry Tuttle for All America honors. The piece looks like a long-play record album and is really professional looking. 1500 extra copies were prepared for sale and you may purchase one this Saturday prior to the N. C. State game at the program booths inside the stadium. Cost of the unusual poster is $3.00 each or two for $5.00.

This will be a collectors item. No additional copies will be printed.

FIGURE 11-7 continued

SOCCER CONTINUES TO WIN

For the first time since 1978, Clemson's Tigers won their own tournament with a 2-1 victory over Cleveland State to capture the eighth Clemson Invitational.

The Tigers were aided by two Mo Tinsley goals which earned him Most Valuable Player honors.

In the second half, both teams were stymied in the midfield as both defenses played a fine game during the first half of the final period.

The win ups the Tiger record to 9-1 on the season. The next game for fourth-ranked Clemson will be on Friday night, October 23 as they take on Davis & Elkins at 7:30 p.m. here on the Clemson field.

In the Consolation game, South Florida handed the Mountaineers of Appalachian State their second loss by a 2-1 score.

MEN'S TENNIS TEAM FINISHED THIRD IN SAN ANTONIO

Clemson's men's tennis team finished third in an eigth-team tournament in San Antonio Texas over the weekend. Chuck Kriese's team defeated SMU in the first round of the Miller High Life Collegiate Team Championships by a 6-3 count. In the second round Southern Cal, the team that eliminated Clemson from the NCAA tournament last May, topped the Tigers by the same score, 6-3. Clemson then defeated Trinity of Texas in the third-place match, 8-1. Clemson will be at the SIU-Edwardsville Fall Tennis Classic this weekend.

WOMEN'S CROSS COUNTRY WINS

The Clemson women's cross country team took three of the top 10 places to win the Indiana Invitational. This was the biggest invitational win ever for the Lady Tigers as both sixth-ranked Tennessee and ninth-ranked Purdue were in the field.

The scores in order of finish were: Clemson 41, Tennessee 67, Purdue 75, Kentucky 114, Alabama 151, Ohio Track Club 170, host Indiana 194, and Ohio State 244. There were also nine other schools competing.

The Tigers were led by All-American Cindy Duarte, who finished the five kilometer course in a time of 17:03. Duarte finished third overall. Other Tigers finishing high include: Judith Shepard (5th) 17:12; Kerry Robinson (6th) 17:18; Stephanie Weikert (13th) 17:40; Jennifer Briscoe (14th) 17:41; and Laurie Montgomery (15th) 17:44.

CLEMSON LINEUP vs. DUKE

Offense:

SE—Perry Tuttle, 15 Jeff Stockstill
LT—61 Brad Fisher, 68 Gary Brown
LG—60 James Farr, 62 Brian Butcher
C—63 Tony Berryhill, 52 Massaro
RG—74 Bob Mayberry, 70 Brian Clark
RT—77 Lee Nanney, 64 Ellis
QB—3 Homer Jordan, 11 Gasque
FB—32 McCall, 27 Kevin Mack, 38 Crite
TB—7 Austin, 35 McSwain
WR—2 Frank Magwood, 89 Kendall Alley
WR-TE—41 Gaillard, 85 Diggs,
    80 Wurst, 81 K. D. Dunn
PK—18 Igwebuike, 6 Paulling

Defense

LE—84 Bill Smith, 53 Joe Glenn
LT—71 Dan Benish, 72 Ray Brown
MG—94 William Devane, 66 Perry
RT—99 Jeff Bryant, 67 Jim Scott
RE—12 Andy Headen, 92 Richardson
SLB—82 Triplett, 90 Rembert
WLB—45 J. Davis, 55 Cheek
LE—29 Hollis Hall
RC—21 Anthony Rose, 28 R. McSwain
SS—23 Jeff Suttle, 9 Ken Brown
FS—43 Terry Kinard
P—5 Hatcher

DEFENSIVE STATISTICS

Player	GP-GS	Tot	Hits	Ast	TL-Yds	Sacks
J. Davis, LB	6-6	86	56	30	4-13	2-11
Kinard, FS	6-6	55	46	9		
Triplett, LB	6-6	53	31	22	4-7	1-2
Bryant, DT	6-6	45	35	10	10-38	4-31
Hall, DB	6-6	34	26	8	2-3	
Benish, DT	6-6	33	24	9	6-21	1-8
Childers, SS	5-5	28	17	11	2-14	1-10
Headen, DE	6-6	28	18	10	3-19	3-19
Perry, MG	6-0	23	16	7	5-22	1-17
Suttle, SS	6-1	22	20	2	2-14	1-11
Devane, MG	6-6	21	16	5	2-12	2-12
Smith, B., DE	4-2	16	6	10	2-19	2-19
McSwain, R., DB	6-0	15	10	5	1-1	
Glenn, DE	6-4	10	5	5	3-20	2-20
Pickett, DE	6-0	9	5	4	2-20	2-20
Rembert, LB	6-0	9	8	1	1-5	
Rose, CB	6-6	9	7	2		
Richardson, DE	6-0	9	3	6		
Scott, DT	5-0	6	5	1	1-8	1-8
Brown, Ray, DE	5-0	5	2	3	1-1	
Lindsay, LB	5-0	5	2	3		
Cheek, LB	6-0	5	4	1	1-3	
Martin, DB	6-0	4	2	2		
Brown, Roy, DE	5-0	3	3	0		
Davis, B., FS	6-0	3	2	1		
Milton, DE	1-0	1	1	0		
Meeks, LB	1-0	1	1	0		
Arrington, CB	6-0	1	1	0		

PBU's (25) Hall 6, J. Davis 4, Headen 3, Kinard 2, Rose 1, Suttle 1, Rembert 1, Triplett 1, Childers 1, Bryant 1.
RECOVERED FUMBLES (12) Perry 2, J. Davis 2, Suttle 1, Glenn 1, Pickett 1, Ray Brown 1, B. Smith 1, Bryant 1, Headen 1, Hall 1.
CAUSED FUMBLES (12) J. Davis 4, Bryant 2, Triplett 2, Ray Brown, Smith 1, Kinard 1, J. Scott 1.

CLEMSON-USC CLOSED CIRCUIT

Ticket manager, Van Hilderbrand, reports brisk sales of tickets for the closed circuit showing of the Clemson-USC game since tickets went on sale last week.

The game will be shown in Littlejohn Coliseum and only 7000 tickets will be sold. The tickets are $7.00 each and are general admission. The tickets may be purchased at Jervey Athletic Center ticket office between the hours of 8:30 a.m. and 4:30 p.m. Monday through Friday.

BASKETBALL SCRIMMAGE

Bill Foster's Tiger basketball team will hold an Orange & White scrimmage next Saturday prior to the Wake Forest football game, so it will be beneficial for all Tiger fans to get to Clemson early. Foster's club will begin the scrimmage at 10:30 A.M. in Littlejohn Coliseum. The Tigers also will have a game on November 14, following the Maryland football game. Foster's club will meet Marathon Oil in an exhibition game starting at 4:30 P.M. in Littlejohn Coliseum. There will be no admission charge for the Orange & White scrimmage next Saturday.

Credit: Clemson University Athletic Department and IPTAY.

of alumni support grows as the financial squeeze tightens. And the importance of athletics to that support should not be underestimated.

Travel people discovered a long time ago that college groups—students, faculty, alumni—are great prospects for packaged tours. There are all kinds of reasons for tours—to examine the flora and fauna of the Galapagos Islands, to visit European art museums, or to attend an important out-of-town football game. As sports public relations, you will work with the tour people and make every effort to promote the package to alumni. Both you and the travel agency profit. You are particularly anxious that alumni support at the game be as strong as possible. You want them to have a wonderful time, too, even if your side loses. If you are playing on a "foreign field," be sure the ticket manager does not "pepper" your ticket allotment, thereby diluting the effect of your team's followers. It has been known to happen. Insist on a block. Then when your team scores, the TV cameras will pick up *all* the pompoms.

Making News

Your college "market area" probably contains dozens of small-town weekly newspapers. Often these papers are desperately shorthanded. They rely on and are grateful for what is known as *boilerplate.* This is preset copy in mat or type form which the editor can simply drop into a spot in the paper. You will find that a column or sports letter in this form from the athletic office of the college will usually be published, especially if it is offered on a regular basis. Stress the local angles, especially the progress and performance of the players on your squad from the smaller towns. The pride of the townspeople in their boy or girl who made good is an important public relations force for you.

There are among the students certain influential people—class officers, members of honor societies, and outstanding people in the classroom and on the playing field. An occasional letter to these opinion leaders, taking them into your confidence, can often be important. A few years ago, one of the East's great football powers was struck by a series of scandals. The school had always taken great pride in the unsullied record of its program and in the integrity of the scholar-athletes who represented them. Now the situation was like a bad joke. Sports writers didn't miss the irony of the situation. With shouts of glee, they jumped on the "nice nellies" and their "holier-than-thou" attitude. It was a very bad time for the athletic department information office people. They needed every tool they could find to rally press and public, students and alumni behind them. The coach, one of the most admired men in his profession, called the press in and took the blame on his own shoulders. He admitted that, in the eagerness to recruit superior players, the element of character had sometimes been overlooked—and it was he who had been careless. Most of the sports writers rallied to his side, because they knew he spoke from the heart and had not tried to "stonewall" or cover up anything.

Your university, which has been playing games since the days of Walter Erkersal and the Flying Wedge, undoubtedly has a college Hall of Fame. You will play up the induction of a new member for all it's worth—right out there in the middle of the field at half-time. There is a lot of nostalgia and sentiment involved in these presentations, and the people in the press box will not overlook any of it. Some of the best sports columns are woven from memories.

Picture day is another "institution." On one of the first days of fall practice, everyone suits up in the new uniforms and lets the press photographers go at it as long as they want. There is a variation on the "presidential handshake picture" that can be used here. When the president goes visiting, all the local celebrities who voted for the right party are lined up—literally. Each one steps forward and shakes the president's hand; click goes the camera shutter, and the next person moves up. A couple of weeks later, each receives an autographed photo of himself or herself shaking hands with the president of the United States. Something to frame, hang on the office wall, or show your grandchildren. On picture day, alert your favorite boosters to be present so that young Johnny (who will be a booster himself in a couple of years) can have his picture taken with a tackle draped over his shoulder. This picture is going to take you a long, long way. Every kid in Johnny's school will see it. Maybe the local press will publish it, and it will hang on the wall in Johnny's house for many years. A lot of people are going to have a very warm feeling.

The annual *press book* is a preseason information guide sent to sports writers all over the country. It contains a review of the team and the season schedule. There are pictures, statistics, and personal profiles of the players, and in some cases much more. The preseason press books for the bigger football and basketball teams tend to be quite elaborate slick-paper, four-color productions. Many colleges get further mileage out of them (and help reduce costs) by making them available to alumni.

Gathering Support

Booster clubs are organizations of local businesspeople (who may or may not be alumni) who have a vested interest in seeing to it that your college has a good athletic program. Your relationship with the members of the booster club may be ambiguous—you want to be close to them, but not *too* close. In some cases, the coach's job—and *your* job—may hang on the relationship with the boosters. Their demands are usually not great—good seat locations, sideline or press box passes, and small privileges. But never forget that these people often have a lot of political clout. They tend not to be philosophical about losing. You must keep an eye on them. Theoretically they are "independent," but if they commit some awful blunder, you and the people in your department are the ones who suffer. If you follow sports closely, you know that there have been cases in which booster clubs inflicted wounds the public relations department had trouble closing.

FIGURE 11-8   The bowl game press book often has to be gotten together in a hurry, though much of the statistical information is already set in type. The University of Miami displayed originality in die-cutting this book in the shape of a peach—a gesture that no doubt delighted the Peach Bowl management.

FIGURE 11-8   *continued*

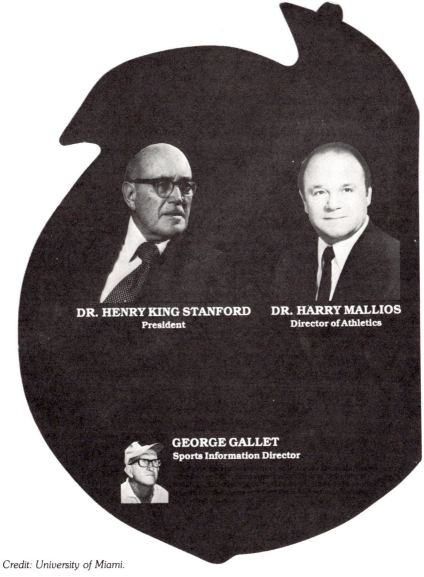

DR. HENRY KING STANFORD
President

DR. HARRY MALLIOS
Director of Athletics

GEORGE GALLET
Sports Information Director

Credit: University of Miami.

You can do yourself a lot of good around the state by letting important business interests know that you are setting aside blocks of tickets for them. Preseason group reservations of this kind can be important. Business firms put these to good use with employees, executives, and customers.

It will probably fall to the lot of your office to set up pregame festivities. The on-campus bonfire and rally is tradition, primarily for the students. The pregame luncheons and dinners, however, are attended by guests and alumni. The coaches and players will be there, as well as the band and the cheerleaders. Make sure the leaders have a place at the head table. The price of admission should cover the costs of pompoms, banners, and souvenirs.

Your college bookstore carries a wide variety of merchandise bearing the college name and seal: glasses, ash trays, running shorts, caps. You should encourage the sale of these items, and make use of them yourself whenever possible. The alumni of your college are dispersed to the four corners of the earth. They can, literally, carry your name far and wide. (Remember the prisoner in the American embassy in Teheran with the "Ohio State" sweatshirt?)

Homecoming Day is one of the oldest traditions we have, and it usually falls on an autumn weekend with a football game as one of the main attractions. This is one of the few times when you will have this many alumni together in one place in a happy checkbook-opening mood. You and your staff should make every effort to coordinate with all those who are trying to provide the alumni with a good time. Set up tours of the athletic facilities. Provide special tables at the college dining facilities for ex-players on your teams—a separate one for each sport, if possible. Have players on hand at key spots—gym, A.D.'s office—to chat with visitors. Try to have a sports-related souvenir on hand for every child—this weekend is often a family affair.

Tailgating began years ago with pregame drinks and sandwiches spread out on a station wagon tailgate. Today, outside many stadiums, the parking lots often look like trailer parks. You should see to it that these supporters of your team are kept as comfortable and happy as possible. What you have on your hands is a house party. All the normal facilities must be in place: police security, fire protection, first-aid and emergency ambulance service. Set up a "city hall" nearby where people can bring their problems and get them solved quickly. Get members of the band and college chorus to act as minstrels, serenading the people with college songs. You can impress a lot of people and send them home happier—even when your side loses by 20 points. Most important, they will look forward to the next home game.

Dress Code

This may sound silly, but it's not. When your teams are on the road, they are the representatives of your institution. The impression they make *off* the field may be more lasting than the one they make on. Stress to your

FIGURE 11-9 **A typical announcement from a professional football club. The sports desk will be literally showered with these from March 1 until the Super Bowl game is played the following January—one reason for making *your* release as interesting and newsworthy as possible.**

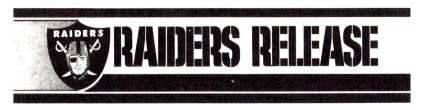

FOR IMMEDIATE RELEASE
(Mailed Monday, March 1, 1982)

RAIDERS ANNOUNCE 1982 PRESEASON SCHEDULE

OAKLAND, CALIF. - Home games against the Green Bay Packers and Cleveland Browns are featured on the Raiders 1982 preseason schedule which also includes the annual summer battle against the 49ers - this year in San Francisco - and a road game against the Detroit Lions.

The Raiders open the 1982 preseason schedule on the road against the NFC Western Division San Francisco 49ers, winners of Superbowl XVI, in Candlestick Park on Saturday night, August 14th. The following weekend the Raiders travel into the midwest to take on the Detroit Lions of the NFC Central Division on Saturday night, August 21st, in the mammoth 80,000 seat Pontiac Silverdome, site of Superbowl XVI. The Lions only missed the 1981 playoffs on a three-point loss in the season's final game.

The preseason home opener for the Raiders will be on Saturday night, August 28th when Bart Starr brings out his 1982 edition of the Green Bay Packers. The NFC Central Division Packers, off to a shaky start in 1981, came on strong to win six of their last eight games last season, finishing 8-8 and just missing a playoff berth.

The exciting Cleveland Browns will provide the opposition for the preseason home finale for the Raiders on Saturday night, September 4th. The last time these two American Conference rivals met was in the dramatic AFC Playoff game in Cleveland's frozen Municipal Stadium on January 4, 1981 when the Raiders triumphed 14-12 to earn a berth in the AFC Championship game enroute to an eventual World Championship of Professional Football.

1982 PRESEASON SCHEDULE

Saturday	August 14	at San Francisco 49ers	6 p.m. (PDT)
Saturday	August 21	at Detroit Lions	5 p.m. (PDT)
Saturday	August 28	GREEN BAY PACKERS	6 p.m. (PDT)
Saturday	September 4	CLEVELAND BROWNS	6 p.m. (PDT)

(all kickoff times are listed in Pacific Coast Time)

The NFL 1982 league season is scheduled to get underway on Sunday, September 12th. Dates and times for the games will be released by the NFL office when the official schedule is announced in April. The 1982 opponents for each team have already been determined based on the final standings from the 1981 season:

1982 RAIDERS OPPONENTS

HOME GAMES	Away Games
CLEVELAND BROWNS	at Atlanta Falcons
DENVER BRONCOS	at Baltimore Colts
KANSAS CITY CHIEFS	at Cincinnati Bengals
LOS ANGELES RAMS	at Denver Broncos
MIAMI DOLPHINS	at Kanaas City Chiefs
NEW ORLEANS SAINTS	at San Diego Chargers
SAN DIEGO CHARGERS	at San Francisco 49ers
SEATTLE SEAHAWKS	at Seattle Seahawks

Credit: Oakland Raiders Football Club.

coaching staff, if necessary, the importance of having every player well-shaved, well-combed, and well-polished. Many schools provide the traveling squad with blazers carrying the college crest. When your team gets off the plane and comes through the airport, you do not want them to look as though they had just been released from a work gang. They are not tramp athletes, they are students—and they should look like gentlemen and ladies. They are, after all, your ambassadors-at-large. One of your greatest nightmares as a sports information officer can take place on the road—and there is not much you can do about it. Just let one student get involved in a traffic accident or a barroom fight, and it will be on the front page in the morning. It will be up to you to pick up the pieces, and you hope you have some past favors that can be called in.

The Professional Sports Information Director

There is much in this job that resembles the work of the person in the amateur ranks. In fact, many professional, network, and wire service people get their early training in college public relations offices. There are some differences, however. The "bottom line" in professional sports is a lot more immediate than it is at the college level. In college, you are striving to present your institution and its people in the best possible light. As you have seen, there are many ways you can do this, not all of them directly related to the box office. Sure, if you do your job right, eventually it will show in bigger donations and better attendance, and better alumni support and better enrollment, too.

In pro sports, the immediate preoccupation is *always* the box office. "Counting the house" is something the front office does automatically. Let attendance begin to slide, and people lose their jobs. As you may have noticed, the average big league manager has the life expectancy of a lion trainer. Fortunately, they keep getting rehired as coaches, scouts, and managers for rival teams.

As a professional team's information officer, neither you nor management expects the gentler treatment reserved for the college teams. The very volume of ink devoted to your team, particularly during the season, far outweighs anything the colleges get. Much of what you are going to get can be pretty horrifying. Never mind, it goes with the franchise. There are a lot of sports writers, broadcasters, and sports columnists who will take fiendish glee in holding your team up to ridicule. After all, controversy sells papers

---

FIGURE 11-10   As anyone who has ever watched a car race knows, corporate sponsorship is highly visible. Here is a press release from the Coca-Cola 12 Hours of Sebring. Although the race may belong to Coca-Cola, you can see at the bottom of the release form that others are along for the ride, too.

NEWS FROM THE:

Coca-Cola

12 HOURS
OF SEBRING

For Further Information:
PRESS CONTACT: Bruce A. Czaja
P. O. Box 2044, Sebring, Fl. 33870
Telephone (813) 655-2525

FOR IMMEDIATE RELEASE:
March 2, 1982

EARLY 12 HOUR TEST DAY SET FOR SUNDAY MARCH 7

Sebring, FL--A special early test session has been scheduled for competitors in the Coca-Cola 12 Hours of Sebring on Sunday March 7. The test session, utilizing the 1.4-mile Sebring "short course" will be held in conjuction with the Skip Barber Racing School Race Series.

The test sessions will be open to the public beginning at 1:00 in the afternoon. Spectators will be able to see cars test for the 12 Hours, which is being run for the Camel GT Endurance Championship, and for the Champion Spark Plug Challenge sedan race. In addition, two 30 minute Formula Ford races will be held in the Barber Racing Series.

Admission to the test day and races is $2.00, with all of the proceeds going to the 30th Anniversary Race Committee which is working on various activities connected with race week in the Sebring area.

The scheduled practice and qualifying for the 12 Hours weekend begins on Thursday March 18. Qualifying for the top 40 starting positions in the 12 Hours will be held that afternoon. A qualifying race for the remaining starting positions in the race will be held on Friday afternoon.

The 30th running of the Coca-Cola 12 Hours of Sebring International Grand Prix of Endurance is scheduled to begin at 11:00 AM on Saturday March 20. The race will attract the top sports car teams and drivers from the world over, searching for Camel GT points and an expected $100,000 in prize money and contingency awards.

Tickets for the 12 Hours are now on sale at all Sears stores in Florida with race information available at Datsun dealers or where Coca-Cola products are sold.

---30---

Credit: The 12 Hours of Sebring, Sebring Motorsports International, Inc.

and gets readership. There are people out there at typewriters who cannot lift a bat, let alone swing one. Yet they will not hesitate for a moment to second-guess your manager on a decision in last night's game. There is not much you can do about them except kid them along and praise their rhetoric.

You will not be donning the pinstripes of Madison Avenue or the New York Yankees right away. But there are a whole lot of minor league and smaller city franchises in a variety of sports that can use all the help they can get. For some of them, it is a daily fight just to stay alive. Farm clubs can often depend on the parent organizations to pick up their losses. But most are expected to pay their own way—or at least demonstrate promise—or perish.

The competition for the fan's dollar is rugged. Even with readjusted schedules, such as football in the spring or summer, there is often another game in town looking for the same customers you are. Free and paid TV are very hard to compete with. But don't blame the broadcasters. They have killed some audiences, but they have created many others, with big box offices and salaries to match. You may find yourself working for an ice show or gymnastics tour that exists only because of the TV contract.

Let's say you are getting your start in a smaller city with a new sports franchise. What are some of the things you would do?

Community Involvement

The name of the game for the local sports franchise is community involvement. The more people—the more families—have a rooting, or following, interest in your team, the better off you are. The community takes pride in its professional sports franchise. The presence of the team enhances the image of the city. Just as the team has a stake in them, so they have a stake in its success. The chamber of commerce, as well as the city council, are going to do anything reasonable to help you. Keep in mind that the failure of a sports franchise hurts everyone.

1. *Personal appearances.* Look at the "Events Today" column in the local newspaper, and you will see the extraordinary number of luncheons and meetings that go on every day in your community. A great many of them are service clubs, such as Kiwanis or Redmen. Their entertainment chairperson is often hard-pressed to find good speakers. If he or she does not find one, club attendance falls off. So they will probably welcome you with open arms—particularly if you can supply an informed and interesting speaker. Try to keep members of the coaching staff and team at the speaker's table as much as possible. Do not send them out cold and unrehearsed. If they have no laugh-provoking sports anecdotes, it is up to you to supply some. Make sure the ultimate sell is always in there: "This is an exciting game in clean surroundings suitable for the whole family. Come out and support us. You'll have a wonderful time!"

2. *Clinics.* Getting your players into a teaching situation is a great goodwill builder. It is also a good way to win the youth of the community, who are

FIGURE 11-11   The front and back covers of the media guide for the Vancouver **Whitecaps**. Labatt is a Canadian brewer. Companies find sponsoring an entire team a good public relations device. This does not occur in major league baseball and football, of course, but it is not unknown in soccer. The Boston Teamen, before the franchise was moved, were backed by the Lipton Tea Company.

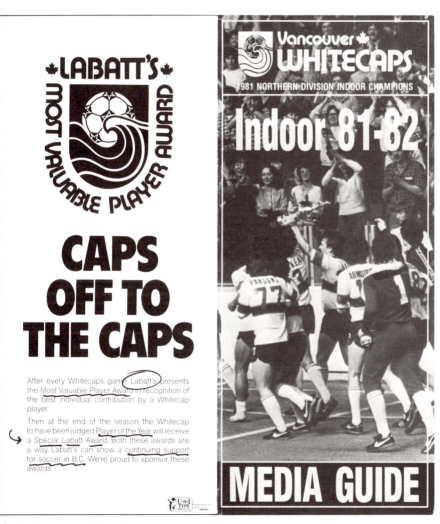

Credit: Vancouver Whitecaps.

essential to your success. It also means you are going to be manufacturing *knowledgeable* fans—the very best kind. Visit schools, youth organizations, and teams with players teaching the basics of the game: how to field a bunt, how to head a soccer ball.

3. *Youth leagues.* In baseball, you will find teams already made to order for you—Little League and Babe Ruth League. But in such sports as soccer, you may find yourself starting from scratch. Here is where you have a great chance to build a following. Kids who have been coached by your players are going to insist that Dad take them to the home games. Try to have games scheduled early enough so that youngsters will not be kept up on a school night.

4. *Off-season coaching.* You may be able to get closer involvement with the community through off-season coaching assignments at local schools. Gym classes often provide high school coaches with the opportunity to develop skills during the off-season. The player-coach becomes an established part of the community.

5. *Special nights.* On Family Nite, every adult accompanied by a child gets in for half-price. You can also have *giveaway nites.* The "free beer" nights set up by some clubs are not recommended because they can get out of hand. Keep the freebies kid-oriented, if possible. Have enough so that no one goes home emptyhanded. Here is a clever switch on the comeback premium (one steak knife with every refill). Some clubs give away parts of uniforms—caps one week, shirts the next. These are relatively inexpensive kid-size uniforms.

6. *Caps and Shirts.* The use of the old-fashioned round-crowned baseball cap, apparently started by the Pittsburgh Pirates "family," has spread. Today it is possible to buy one of these caps with the name and colors of hundreds of teams. The same is true for jerseys. You can buy all professional football team jerseys *with* the name of your favorite player. Make sure the concessionaires and sports shops in your community have a plentiful supply, along with bumper stickers, buttons, pennants, and so on, for your team.

7. *Openings.* You are going to want to stage opening day or night with all the hoopla possible. Public officials, business leaders, and other influential people will be in the bunting-draped box seats. A high school band or two should be on hand, and a local singer to sing the anthem. A local pastor will give the invocation. Perhaps you can give a VIP party beforehand with a top league official saying a few words.

8. *Reservations.* Preferential treatment should be given to business block-seat holders and established regulars. A letter telling them you are setting aside seats for them for a particularly important game will be appreciated.

Figure 11-12   **Here is an unusual press release about a man who has issued a thousand press releases himself. The story of the retirement party and the warmhearted regard of the football club must have touched every Dolphin fan. Note how his importance to the club is stressed, how he was one of the first key persons hired by Robbie, the owner, and how they are leaving the door open for him to serve with them in the future. Also note their generous accolade: ". . . a legend in the world of sports publicity."**

PRESS INFORMATION
MIAMI
DOLPHINS

For Immediate Use, January 18, 1982

CALLAHAN RETIRES AFTER 16 SEASONS WITH DOLPHINS

Charles M. Callahan, who has publicized the Miami Dolphins since their inception as an American Football League expansion team in 1966, will be honored February 8 at a retirement party, Dolphins owner Joseph Robbie announced today.

Callahan was the second key person hired by Robbie in the fall of 1965 as the club was organized. That season, Callahan concluded 20 years as the sports publicity director at the University of Notre Dame.

Callahan, 66, will be designated the Dolphins' Publicity Director Emeritus, Robbie said, and he will handle special assignments. He may assist at training camp when he is available.

Robbie gave this evaluation of Callahan's service to the Dolphins:

"Charlie Callahan is an important part of the Notre Dame and Miami Dolphins tradition. He has been attached to champions in the field of college and professional football during the 36 years he has beat the drums for the Fighting Irish and the Dolphins as perennial contenders in the merged National Football League.

"Joe Thomas and Charlie Callahan were the first two key employees of the Miami Dolphins when the franchise was formed. They gave instant credibility to the franchise which has been as successful as any in the NFL since the merger occurred in 1970.

"When Charlie informed me of his retirement last August, we asked him to remain with us through the 1981 season. We have also suggested to Charlie that he return to training camp whenever he can and handle the special assignments which he does best.

"Charlie Callahan is a legend in the world of sports publicity. We are pleased that he will still be with us. His relationship with top sports writers around the country is a warm, human and sentimental attachment in which we all like to share."

Callahan, a 1938 journalism graduate of Notre Dame, served four years in the Army Air Corps, mainly in sports promotion, before accepting the Notre Dame post in 1946. In the succeeding 20 years, he promoted the Fighting Irish sports program under football coaches Frank Leahy, Terry Brennan, Joe Kuharich, Hugh Devore and Ara Parseghian. He promoted five Heisman Trophy winners in Johnny Lujack (1947), Leon Hart (1949), John Lattner (1953), Paul Hornung (1956) and John Huarte (1964).

With the Dolphins, Callahan witnessed the formative years (1966-69) under George Wilson and the remarkable success (1970-81) under Don Shula when the Dolphins won consecutive Super Bowls in 1972 and 1973.

Charlie and his wife Betty will celebrate their 36th wedding anniversary in June.

Credit: Bob Kearney, Miami Dolphins, Ltd.

FIGURE 11-13 Page from a preseason football press brochure from the University of Nevada, Reno. Here they take the opportunity to introduce their athletic administration to sports writers. This is a nice touch, since *assistants* to the AD are often little-known people.

Athletic Administration

DICK TRACHOK
Athletic Director

University of Nevada athletics and the name Dick Trachok are synonymous. For five decades, as a star halfback in the 1940's, the university's head football coach in the 1950's and 60's, and as the UNR athletic director in the 70's and 80's, Trachok has been both the driving force and the guiding hand of the Wolf Pack athletic program.

The quality of the UNR program — from its emerging national prominence to the caliber of its coaching staff — is traceable directly to Trachok. His latest achievements are the Nevada State Legislature's approval of the proposed 12,500 seat, on-campus basketball and special events center and UNR

capturing the Big Sky Conference's All-Sports trophy in 1980-81 after just two years in the conference.

Among his other accomplishments during his 12-year tenure as athletic director is the development of the highly successful Wolf Club booster organization, which is among the leaders nationwide in annual donations to a university athletic department.

Trachok was inducted to the University of Nevada Athletic Hall of Fame in 1975 in recognition of his achievements as a player, coach, and administrator. Originally from Pennsylvania, Dick and his wife Fran have three children — Rick, Margo and Cathy.

CLAYT RABEDEAUX
**Assistant Director of Athletics
Promotions/Fund Raising**

Rabedeaux joined the UNR athletic department in 1975 as director of the Wolf Club with a perfect background for the promotion and fund-raising position: coaching and sales. A graduate of the University of Iowa in 1959, he was a high school coach for nine years. Before coming to UNR, he was national sales manager for SRA Educational Publishing Co.

In 1978, Rabedeaux was named an assistant athletic director, his duties now encompassing the Wolf Club, athletic promotions, and sports publicity. The club is now considered among the largest university athletics fund raising organizations in the West, last year raising approximately $650,000.

Rabedeaux has three sons — Jeff, Jack, and Jason.

TOM REED
**Assistant Athletic Director
Business**

Tom Reed was named UNR athletic business manager in 1977 after coaching the secondary for the school's football team for five years. His status was elevated to assistant athletic director one year later.

An All-Far Western Conference defensive back for the Wolf Pack in the late 1960's, Reed was a graduate assistant coach for two

years before taking the full-time coaching position in 1972. That same year he completed his MA degree in school administration/physical education.

Reed is an avid marathon runner who recently qualified for the 1982 Boston Marathon. He has one daughter, Ayme, age 5.

JOHN LEGARZA
Coordinator of Women's Athletics

Appointed to the position in 1977, Legarza has an impressive background in coaching at both the high school and college levels. He has been the UNR golf coach for eight years, his teams claiming several conference championships, and was an assistant basketball

coach at UNR in 1974 and '75.

Legarza graduated from UNR in 1958 and received his MA here in 1960. He and his wife Nadine have four children — Kim, Mike, Sherry, and Matthew. Mike is a member of the Wolf Pack basketball team.

6

Credit: University of Nevada-Reno.

9. *Films.* Make sure official press photographers get sideline passes and make it just as easy as possible for your local TV camera crews to operate so that highlights of the game get on the news shows. You should also have made short films of various lengths suitable for cable, community TV, or instructional use.

SUMMARY

Sports, whether professional or amateur, is a highly competitive big business. Every college of any size has a sports information director who is responsible for sports publicity. This person deals with a particular set of publics: alumni, students, parents, faculty, townspeople, high school students, and "subway" alumni.

The sports information director has a number of ways of communicating: speaker's bureaus, press meetings, band days, appearances at alumni clubs, game tours, boilerplate columns and stories, and many others, including elaborate press books.

The duties of the professional team's sports information director are similar, though the public is more general—often the whole community. Here the target is community involvement. Families are important, especially youngsters. The information director uses such devices as personal appearances by players and coaches, clinics, youth league and school coaching, family nights, and caps and jerseys for the kids, among others.

KEY TERMS

College sports information director
Speaker's bureau
Background meeting
Band day
Alumni clubs
Game tours
Boilerplate columns
Awards, picture day, press day
Booster clubs

Press books
Brunches, rallies
Homecoming day
Tailgating
Personal appearances
Clinics
Off-season coaching
Special nights

THE WAY IT HAPPENED

I drove by the ball park of our local double-A baseball team the other night and was astonished to see that the place was jammed. Even though the team is a contender this year, they are usually lucky to draw 1500 fans. Tonight, from grandstand to bleachers, there wasn't an empty seat!

Then, as my car climbed the ramp to the freeway, I looked back and saw a strange sight. I saw, in the middle of the infield, what seemed to be a big chicken cavorting about!

The symbolic animal, a costumed student, has been part of the college football scene for years. Everything from mountain lions to 'gators help lead the cheers.

But it fell to a genius to combine the costume of an animal with the talents of a highly professional clown. The San Diego Chicken's act brings the house down—and *fills* it.

For the local ball club, it provides a wonderful shot in the arm and attendance reflects it. The publicity fallout is remarkable too. The Chicken is a nationally known figure, and many fans have seen him on TV. When he comes to town, it is a newsworthy event.

Like all good actors, the Chicken charges well for his performance—but to the club, he's worth every cent they pay him.

A PERSONAL PROJECT

Often a small college or a community college will have trouble getting "ink" in the local press for the feats of its sports teams. This is often particularly true of so-called minor sports, such as cross-country or women's volleyball. Sometimes they are lucky even to get mentioned in the scores column.

Pick out one of your college's sports teams now in action—one of the more obscure ones, if possible. Dig up an angle and write a press release that will put your team on the front page of the sports section.

Suggestion: Suppose it turned out that one of the center forwards is an exiled Iranian princess who was taught soccer by her brother while in hiding in Greece. Her American college debut marks the first time she has ever played without wearing the traditional veil.

Just an idea.

READING TO BROADEN UNDERSTANDING

BRONZAU, ROBERT T. *Public Relations, Promotions, and Fund Raising for Athletic and Physical Education Programs* (New York: Wiley, 1977). An excellent, carefully researched job that ought to be on every sports information director's desk, and probably is. If you are interested in going into the field of sports publicity, this is a must.

HOLTZMAN, JEROME (ED.). *No Cheering in the Press Box* (New York: Holt, Rinehart and Winston, 1974). What 18 of our leading sports writers have to say about their profession.

PESTOLESI, ROBERT A., AND WILLIAM ANDREW SINCLAIR. *Creative Administration in Physical Education and Athletics* (Englewood Cliffs, N.J.: Prentice-Hall, 1978). See Chapter 9, "Politics and Public Relations."

WOY, BUCKY, WITH JACK PATTERSON. *Sign 'em Up Bucky* (New York: Hawthorne Books, 1975). Adventures of a sports agent, with lots about sports publicity woven into the stories.

12

CORPORATE PUBLIC RELATIONS

OVERVIEW AND GOALS

We turn now to what is probably the most pervasive of all public relations activities—that within the corporation. The chances are that if you go to work in this field, you will be working for a corporate body. This is where modern public relations started, with giving "relations with the public" advice to the great corporate leaders of the day. When you have completed this chapter, you should be able to

> **Understand** some of the ways public relations functions within the corporation.
>
> **Appreciate** how public relations plays an important role in the communications process within a business organization.
>
> **See** how corporate public relations is directed outside the organization.
>
> **Distinguish** between corporate advertising and advocacy advertising.

You might point out that the baseball club, of which we have been speaking, *is* a corporation, and you would be quite right. But now we are going to discuss corporate bodies—businesses that have a somewhat different set of publics than sports enterprises: employees, customers, stockholders, politicians, neighbors, and the general public.

Of course, these businesses, like the sports teams, are vitally interested in "selling seats." But they are also very much interested in such things as perceptions, attitudes, images, and their positioning in the world they live in. The means they use to affect our perceptions and attitudes may not be quite as flamboyant as those used by the sports teams. In sports, the line between promotion and publicity is often a fine one. When we give out caps and shirts to kids on a special night, that is a promotion to get people into the ball park. But when the kids wear the caps and shirts around town with the team name emblazoned on them, that is publicity.

Public relations does play a big part in the promotion of products, too. In the next chapter, we will see how the combination of publicity and promotions works in selling products. First, however, we will examine public relations from the corporate point of view. We will imagine that you have just gone to work in the public relations department of General Mills in their corporate headquarters in Minneapolis. What would you find?

Corporate Subjects

There are a number of constant, recurring situations in the daily life of the corporation that you will be expected to handle. These are the daily "bread-and-butter" affairs that will be ground into image-building publicity for your company. Let's examine some of them:

1. *New personnel, promotions.* When a new and important person joins your company, or when there are executive promotions, this is often a newsworthy item. Just *how* newsworthy may be up to you. You may be able to get six lines on the business page, or you may generate a front-page story with photographs. Your executive picture file should be up-to-date and of good quality. Try to avoid the wooden poses and retouched photos that make the person look frightened and much younger. The fact that the company has a new president may not be exactly world-shaking, except in the trade press. But the fact that he won a battlefield promotion for bravery in Vietnam may catch the editor's eye. A probing interview (not a review of his official biography) will often turn up interesting and newsworthy facts.

2. *Significant statements.* Most organizations, including some very small ones, have some knowledgeable specialists on staff. These include engineers, scientists, sociologists, economists, chemists, and business historians. Often what these people have to say is not only authoritative, but extremely interesting to the public—particularly in terms of current events. For example, an economist with your firm may have something to say on a subject

FIGURE 12-1 Financial statements by corporations are important to business editors. In addition to the financial facts, they offer an opportunity for corporate officers to make significant and newsworthy statements. Gordon C. Hamilton, manager, public relations at Texaco, was good enough to point out, "The basic information for these releases is assembled by the comptroller's department, and the final versions are subject to extensive review by public relations, by the legal department, and by executive management."

Public Relations
2000 Westchester Ave
White Plains, N.Y. 10650
(914) 253-4177

NEWS FROM
TEXACO INC.

TEXACO REPORTS RESULTS

FOR FOURTH QUARTER AND YEAR 1981

FOR IMMEDIATE RELEASE: THURSDAY, JANUARY 28, 1982.

WHITE PLAINS, N.Y., Jan. 28. - Texaco Inc. announced today that consolidated worldwide net income for the fourth quarter of 1981 was $507 million, or $1.96 per share, compared with $500 million, or $1.86 per share, for the fourth quarter of 1980.

Net income for the year 1981 totaled $2,310 million, or $8.75 per share, compared with $2,240 million, or $8.31 per share, for the year 1980.

Revenues for the fourth quarter of 1981 amounted to $14.7 billion, compared with $14.1 billion for the same quarter of 1980. For the year 1981, revenues were $59.4 billion, compared with $52.5 billion in 1980.

The above 1980 results exclude the extraordinary credit from the sale of the Company's interest in Belridge Oil Company.

Commenting on these results, John K. McKinley, Chairman and Chief Executive Officer, stated: "The fourth quarter saw a deepening of the worldwide economic recession. A substantial reduction in petroleum demand was caused by these sluggish business conditions and by reduced consumption. These factors exerted downward pressures on petroleum prices. Operating in this business environment, the Company could not fully recover in the competitive marketplace the increases in crude oil prices which were announced by Saudi Arabia at the end of October, retroactive to October 1, 1981."

Commenting further on the economic picture, Mr. McKinley observed: "The present business outlook for 1982 in the United States, Canada, and Western Europe is not very encouraging. During the first half of this year, it appears that petroleum operating margins will continue under pressure. An upturn in overall business activity is not generally expected until later in the year."

FIGURE 12-1   *continued*

-2-

A significant factor in the 1981 fourth-quarter results was a Last-in, First-out (LIFO) inventory drawdown earnings benefit of $113 million, after related income tax effects. The Company's program, begun early in the year, to reduce its inventories to more efficient levels achieved a reduction of 16 percent during 1981 to a year-end total of about 200 million barrels. A LIFO inventory drawdown benefit of $454 million, after related income taxes, was realized during 1981. For the year 1980, net income included a LIFO drawdown benefit of $99 million.

Fourth-quarter 1981 results include a $43 million charge, after applicable income taxes, in connection with the shutdown of the Lockport, Illinois refinery. This high-cost facility was surplus to the Company's needs and not economical in the face of declining petroleum demand.

Net income for the fourth quarter of 1981 included losses in foreign currency translations of $21 million, compared with losses of $26 million in the same quarter of 1980. For the year 1981, foreign currency translations resulted in gains of $57 million, compared with losses of $69 million for the year 1980.

The Texaco Chairman made the following observations on the Company's earnings performance for the year 1981:

-   Net income represented an 8.4 percent return on average total assets of approximately $27.5 billion and a 17.6 percent return on average stockholders' equity of approximately $13.1 billion.

-   The Company's earnings per gallon on all petroleum and products sold worldwide averaged 3.5 cents.

-   Worldwide capital and exploratory expenditures, including the Company's equity in expenditures of nonsubsidiary companies, were $3,691 million in 1981, an increase of $616 million, or 20 percent over such expenditures of $3,075 million in 1980.

FIGURE 12-1   continued

-3-

- The U.S. "windfall profit" tax amounted to $1.1 billion in 1981, compared with $305 million in the year 1980. This tax became effective March 1, 1980.

Functional Breakdown

The worldwide net income of $2,310 million for 1981 consisted of $2,308 million in operating earnings and $2 million in nonoperating items (including general corporate items as well as interest income and expense).

These operating earnings consisted of $2,199 million from petroleum and natural gas operations, $81 million from petrochemical operations, and $28 million from non-petroleum activities. Of the operating earnings for petroleum and natural gas, $2,059 million was generated by exploration and producing operations, and $140 million by manufacturing, marketing, and supply activities.

Geographical Segregation

On a geographical basis, net income attributable to operations in the United States for the fourth quarter of 1981 was approximately $190 million, or 37 percent of worldwide net income. Net income attributable to operations outside the United States for the 1981 quarter was approximately $317 million, or 63 percent of worldwide net income.

For the year 1981, net income attributable to U.S. operations was approximately $931 million, or 40 percent of worldwide net income, while net income outside the United States amounted to approximately $1,379 million, or 60 percent of worldwide net income.

Comments on U.S. Results

Earnings from operations in the U.S. for both the fourth quarter and the year 1981 improved over earnings in the same periods of 1980. The improvements were realized from producing activities primarily resulting from increased crude oil prices due to decontrol and higher prices for natural gas. The benefit from

FIGURE 12-1   *continued*

-4-

higher prices of crude oil and natural gas was offset somewhat by an 8 percent
decline for the year in gross liquid production and a 7.5 percent decline in
natural gas sales volumes.   There also were increased production costs due
primarily to the "windfall profit" tax and increased exploratory expenses,
including dry hole costs, associated with an expanded exploration program.

Manufacturing and marketing results in the United States during 1981 were
less favorable than they were during the comparative fourth quarter and full
year of 1980.   Lower petroleum demand and depressed product prices reduced the
Company's operating margins.   The price increases on petroleum products that
were attained early in the year were substantially eroded as the year
progressed.   Prices were especially soft in the fourth quarter, particularly for
gasoline and residual fuel oil.

Comments on Results Outside U.S.

Producing operations outside the United States were improved for the year
1981 compared with 1980, while down somewhat for the comparative fourth-quarter
periods.   There were revisions in the estimated effects of arrangements with
certain producing countries in both 1981 and 1980.   The comparative year and
fourth-quarter results were improved due to higher crude oil production in the
United Kingdom and Angola, while adversely impacted by increased dry hole
expenses.

Manufacturing and marketing operations outside the United States reflected
the adverse effect of reduced petroleum demand and soft product prices.   Overall
earnings for these operations in 1981, both for the full year and in the fourth
quarter, were lower than they were during the same periods of 1980.   The overall
strengthening of the U.S. dollar against major currencies during 1981 and Saudi
Arabia's crude oil price increases in the fourth quarter further eroded the
dollar operating margins.

FIGURE 12-1 *continued*

-5-

<u>Petrochemicals</u>

Worldwide petrochemical earnings for 1981 were $75 million, compared with $77 million for 1980. The comparative earnings improvement that had been achieved during the early half of the year eroded during the latter half of the year. In particular, the poor performance by the United States automobile and housing industries adversely impacted the petrochemical business. For the fourth quarter of 1981, petrochemical earnings worldwide were $13 million, representing a substantial decline from fourth-quarter 1980 earnings of $29 million.

-xxx-

Note: Tables for the fourth quarter and year are attached.

Net income ($000,000)	Fourth quarter			Year		
	1981	1980	Increase (decrease)	1981	1980	Increase (decrease)
United States:						
Petroleum, natural gas, and other	$184	$109	68.2 %	$ 881	$ 793	11.1 %
Petrochemical	6	20	(70.3)%	50	41	23.0 %
Net income, United States	190	129	46.8 %	931	834	11.7 %
Per cent of total net income	37%	26%		40%	37%	
Outside United States:						
Petroleum, natural gas, and other	310	362	(14.5)%	1,354	1,370	(1.2)%
Petrochemical	7	9	(16.1)%	25	36	(30.2)%
Net income, Outside United States	317	371	(14.6)%	1,379	1,406	(2.0)%
Per cent of total net income	63%	74%		60%	63%	
Total net income:						
Petroleum, natural gas, and other	494	471	4.6 %	2,235	2,163	3.3 %
Petrochemical	13	29	(52.9)%	75	77	(2.0)%
Total net income, excluding extraordinary credit	$507	$500	1.2 %	$2,310	$2,240	3.1 %
Extraordinary credit:						
Gain on sale of interest in Belridge Oil Co.					402	
Total net income, including extraordinary credit				$2,310	$2,642	
Net income per share						
Total net income, excluding extraordinary credit	$1.96	$1.86	5.4 %	$8.75	$8.31	5.3 %
Total net income, including extraordinary credit					$9.79	
Average number of shares outstanding (000,000)				264	270	
Number of shares outstanding at end of period (000,000)				259	269	

TEXACO

FIGURE 12-1   continued

	Fourth quarter			Year		
	1981	1980	Increase (decrease)	1981	1980*	Increase (decrease)
Other Financial Data						
Revenues ($000,000)	$14,700	$14,100	4.1 %	$59,400	$52,500	13.1 %
Net income per dollar of revenue	3.5¢	3.6¢		3.9¢	4.3¢	
Net income per gallon on all petroleum and products sold worldwide	3.2¢	3.0¢		3.5¢	3.4¢	
Average total assets ($000,000)				$27,514	$25,212	
Net income as % of average total assets				8.4%	8.9%	
Average stockholders' equity ($000,000)				$13,126	$11,374	
Net income as % of average stockholders' equity				17.6%	19.7%	
Capital and exploratory expenditures ($000,000) Texaco Inc. and Subsidiary Companies						
United States	$ 730	$ 669	9.2 %	$ 2,196	$ 1,655	32.7 %
Outside United States	333	437	(23.8)%	951	1,036	(8.2)%
Total	1,063	1,106	(3.9)%	3,147	2,691	16.9 %
Equity in nonsubsidiary companies Total, including equity in nonsubsidiary companies	192	123	56.3 %	544	384	41.6 %
	$ 1,255	$ 1,229	2.2 %	$ 3,691	$ 3,075	20.0 %
Cash dividends paid ($000,000)	$ 194	$ 174		$ 740	$ 661	
Dividends per share	75¢	65¢	15.4 %	2.80	2.45	14.3 %
Taxes ($000,000)						
Income taxes	$ 239	$ 195	22.5 %	$ 1,892	$ 1,878	.7 %
Windfall profit tax	208	102	101.5 %	1,120	305	266.5 %
Other taxes	1,615	1,604	.8 %	6,366	5,895	8.0 %
Total taxes	$ 2,062	$ 1,901	8.5 %	$ 9,378	$ 8,078	16.1 %
Currency translation gains (losses) included in net income ($000,000)	$ (21)	$ (26)		$ 57	$ (69)	

*Excludes the effect of the sale of the Company's interest in Belridge Oil Company in the first quarter of 1980.

TEXACO

	Fourth quarter		Year	
	1981	1980	1981	1980
Operating data – including interests in nonsubsidiary companies				
Gross production of crude oil and natural gas liquids – (000 BPD)				
United States	409	448	432	468
Other Western Hemisphere	247	267	268	270
Eastern Hemisphere*	2,328	2,534	2,488	2,578
Total	2,984	3,249	3,188	3,316
Refinery runs – (000 BPD)				
United States	832	908	836	902
Other Western Hemisphere	328	398	363	426
Eastern Hemisphere	943	1,159	1,012	1,205
Total	2,103	2,465	2,211	2,533
Petroleum product sales – (000 BPD)				
United States	906	1,022	901	980
Other Western Hemisphere	437	490	449	483
Eastern Hemisphere	1,281	1,376	1,306	1,361
Total	2,624	2,888	2,656	2,824
Natural gas sales – (000 MCFPD)				
United States	2,495	2,556	2,672	2,881
Outside United States	280	231	259	222
Total	2,775	2,787	2,931	3,103

*Includes crude oil purchases provided for under special arrangements with certain producing countries

TEXACO

FIGURE 12-1   continued

193

FIGURE 12-1   continued

Public Relations
2000 Westchester Ave
White Plains, N.Y. 10650
(914) 253-4177

NEWS FROM
TEXACO INC.

TEXACO DECLARES DIVIDEND

FOR IMMEDIATE RELEASE: THURSDAY, JANUARY 28, 1982.

WHITE PLAINS, N.Y., Jan. 28. – Directors of **Texaco Inc.** today declared
a quarterly dividend of 75 cents a share, payable March 10 to shareholders of
record as of February 8.

-xxx-

N/11182

Credit: Reprinted by permission from Texaco, Inc.

that interests us all these days. Business editors are always interested in this sort of thing, and the more controversial and offbeat the better. Sometimes it may fall your lot to create, or at least encourage, the significant statement. Often scientists are reticent. What may be wondrous to the ordinary person is quite commonplace to them. They are surprised that anyone is interested.

3. *Methods, procedures.* The trade press, particularly, will be interested in any new processes or procedures your company has. Not all of these can be publicized, of course. On the other hand, you may be doing the entire industry a favor in publicizing a new trend or a new method.

4. *New plant openings, groundbreakings.* You may have your hands full with these events. A number of important people will be involved and all must be looked after. VIP's, speakers, microphones, refreshments, press, all have to be moved around with precision. Sometimes it is advisable to appoint "guides" who make sure everyone does the right things and does not get lost in the process.

5. *Gifts, charities, solicitations.* Most of these will be routed through your office, and some can be a nuisance. If you are fortunate, your organization will have definite guidelines in the form of a policy statement regarding contributions. Otherwise, you are on your own and in a vulnerable position. Which do you give to, and which do you refuse? What is likely to be the outcome of your action? United Fund has solved part of the problem, but not all of it. There may be local causes that deserve all the help you can give them. There are others that are nothing less than rackets, with some promotor lining his or her pockets. Beware of "complimentary ads" in publications that never seem to appear.

Decisions on political contributions are usually left to top brass. If your company has a political action committee (PAC), so much the better.

6. *New product developments.* You may have a chance to be a real hero here. It does not happen very often, but each year someone comes up with a self-developing camera, a toothpaste loaded with fluorides, or a pocket calculator that does everything up to square roots. When this happens, you may have to fight off the people who want to do stories on your new baby. If it is a new way of cleaning ovens, baking bread at home, or making old brass glitter, you will have no trouble getting space in a wide variety of women's interest and "shelter" magazines.

More often you are likely to have a new feature that you will wish to translate as a new consumer benefit. Your R&D people (research and development) are constantly seeking ways in which your company's products can be made more attractive to the consumer—and thus more competitive. New improvements and features are added each year to prolong the life span of products. Look at the progress of the can opener from thumb-jabber to attractive, electrically operated instrument that does everything but whistle "Dixie."

7. *Civic activities.* If your company is in a city like Minneapolis, or even a much smaller community, you can bet they have their thumb in the civic pie. Your job is to make everyone just as aware of this as possible. You may support a men's or women's softball team with the name of your company emblazoned on their jackets. There may be an intercompany bowling league in town. For years, Phillips Petroleum Company of Bartlesville, Oklahoma, supported an AAU basketball team.

FIGURE 12-2   Finding new uses for a product is a well-known marketing technique for increasing sales. Here is the same idea in a news release from an industry association. They are selling the soup that *uses* meat as an ingredient.

Exclusive to You in Your City

Winning Ways with Meat
Release No. 2 Pix. No. 4060-6
March, 1982

                Satisfy Appetites with Easy Old-Fashioned Beef Soup

    The "good old days" in grandma's kitchen are usually remembered in one of

two ways. Those with an eye for the practical question if the results really

merited the long hours of hard work under difficult conditions. But the roman-

tics remember only the marvelous aromas, delicious flavors and the loving care

that went into the preparation.

    Probably the one dish that best captures these nostalgic memories is home-

made soup. Just the mention of it brings visions of grandma fussing over a

huge kettle of soup that had been simmering lazily for hours on the back of the

range.

    Fortunately for today's homemaker, it is still possible to create a soup

with all the goodness of grandma's but without all the work. Pot o' Flavor is

hearty beef, barley and vegetable fare that blends the quality of the past with

the convenience of the present.

    Preparation starts simply as beef shank cross cuts simmer in water without

preliminary browning. Then the soup begins to take shape quickly with the help

of easy-to-use onion soup mix. The mix, supplemented with sage and peppercorns,

gives the soup a quick flavor boost. Barley and vegetables--carrots, celery and

cabbage--are added during the gentle cooking and the flavors merge and develop.

                                (more)

Consumer Services Department, Gay Starrak, Director
NATIONAL LIVE STOCK AND MEAT BOARD • 444 N. MICHIGAN AVE. • CHICAGO, ILLINOIS 60611 (312) 467-5520

Credit: National Live Stock and Meat Board.

Other enterprises may attract your company. Downtown development, public housing, pollution control, auto safety, drug and alcohol abuse, safety on the streets, and voter participation are just a few of the civic projects to which your company might wish to lend its support.

8. *Subjects of trade interest.* In addition to the publicity designed to position you in the public's eye, there will be many occurrences of interest to the professionals in your business. A new design for store layout would be of considerable interest to *Progressive Grocer.* Your new advertising agency and its plans might find a place in the pages of *Advertising Age.* Almost anything innovative you do in the various departments will be of intense interest to someone.

Communication within the Company

One of your most important publics is other employees. Modern management recognizes the vital role played by two-way communication within the corporate organization. It is much more than simply communication for communication's sake; what we are talking about is the essence of modern management philosophy and its goal of productivity.

Today, most companies encourage a far greater level of participation in organization matters than has been the case in the past. Indeed, experience in Scandinavia, West Germany, and Japan has shown that the lessons of the Mayes, Fayols, and other students of management have been learned: With greater involvement and participation comes higher productivity. Involvement and participation cannot exist without communication. Let us look at some of the ways you will help this happen.

1. *The traditional suggestion box.* Suggestion boxes have been in existence for years. At first, they were literally boxes with slots into which workers dropped their suggestions. Today's suggestion box is a far more sophisticated matter. In industry, it will often involve meetings, on a regular basis, between floor workers, supervisory management, and middle management people. Management literature contains many case histories of the happy results that can accrue from this procedure. Often it will fall upon you to make the arrangements for such a meeting, or to suggest to management the desirability of doing so.

   Suggestion meetings pay off handsomely if properly handled. Employee dignity and self-image are improved. A greater sense of loyalty and participation is evident. A better working rapport is developed between managers and workers. A clear channel of upward communication is established. Problems are indicated and can be dealt with before they become too hot to handle. All this, of course, tends to develop better employee public relations, in addition to the time and money-saving suggestions that are produced.

2. *The grapevine.* One of the most pervasive—and dangerous—kinds of communication within an organization is the *grapevine rumor.* Tall tales get started and spread with incredible speed. One way to handle these is to keep *your* ear to the ground to catch the first tremors. Often you can anticipate such stories and counter them with the truth.

Rumors are often the result of fear or hysteria. A simple fact, such as the retirement of a company officer, will get blown up into a rumor that the company is about to be sold. Rumors ought to be squelched as quickly as possible. A source of established credibility (often you) is one way. The truth, served up immediately, is another.

Sometimes rumors are of the "poison-pen" type. Recently, one of America's leading food distributors was the victim of a mail campaign accusing it of indulging in witchcraft. The company's recourse in such a case is to attempt to apprehend the writers and to bring them to court. Rumors, unfortunately, are often a source of excitement—"Hey, have you heard the latest?" And rumormongers often provide themselves with a much-needed sense of importance. The person who always claims to be "in the know" is a familiar figure in many organizations.

3. *Employee publications.* A sure way of reaching your company public is through the employee magazine or newspaper. This may be edited by your office, but there should be as much employee participation as possible.

These media are great for accomplishing several important goals in employee relations: maintaining morale and company pride, keeping informed on company changes and accomplishments, and creating a better rapport between worker and management. In addition, this is the vehicle of choice when a rumor is to be scotched and the facts set forth.

4. *Pictures.* Photography will play an important role in your company publication, of course. But pictures anyplace—on a bulletin board, for example—can play an important role. Pictures of groundbreakings, celebrations, and other events are good subject matter. Candid, unposed shots of people simply doing their jobs are popular and get a lot of attention.

5. *Welcome handbooks.* Orientation brochures prepared for new employees will usually be done by your office, and they help set the tone for the entire organization. The "welcome brochure" is usually done in a light, amusing manner, often with cartoons. It should be clearly and simply written at about a tenth-grade reading level.

These handbooks can do a great deal of good. For one thing, they allow management to state company policy in clear, unequivocal language. This includes policy regarding employees as well as policy regarding customers. It is a great morale-booster, too, for people who are apprehensive and a little confused, perhaps on their first job. They will find out about vacation and sick leave, payday and benefits, work hours, and even where the rest rooms are.

6. *Friends and relatives.* Never forget the power of the people behind the people behind the machines. The employee's wife, children, friends, and neighbors are of utmost importance to you. Their opinions and attitudes can reflect the attitudes and opinions of your employee throughout the entire neighborhood. They are much closer to you than you may think. Though your employee is but one person in a family, several others depend on that paycheck. In some instances, the whole community may depend on your payroll. Your company, if it is wise, recognizes that it has a certain degree of social responsibility.

In any case, your department can do your organization a lot of good by recognizing that employees do have people who are close to them, and who therefore can influence them. Company bowling leagues or softball leagues serve to bring employees' families together. Many companies have

FIGURE 12-3   This is an excellent example of how a corporation can build good public relations through a message to the public on a subject of interest to all drivers. Note that this message is presented as "Customer Information." It does something else, too. It helps to spike the idea that car manufacturers are against installing seat belts because of the added cost. Shell Oil does this kind of message on TV with its driver education campaign.

CUSTOMER INFORMATION FROM GENERAL MOTORS

HOW TO SAVE YOUR LIFE
AND THE ONE NEXT TO YOU

OVERCOMING YOUR PSYCHOLOGICAL RESISTANCE TO SEAT BELTS MAY BE THE KEY.

The facts are startling. Experts estimate that almost half of all automobile occupant fatalities and many serious injuries might have been avoided if the people had been wearing seat belts. That's because most injuries occur when the car stops abruptly and the occupants are thrown against the car's interior or out of the car. Belts reduce this risk.

Many people say they know the facts, but they still don't wear belts. Their reasons range all over the lot: seat belts are troublesome to put on, they are uncomfortable, or they wrinkle your clothes. Some people even think getting hurt or killed in a car accident is a question of fate; and, therefore, seat belts don't matter.

If you're one of those people who don't use belts for one reason or another, please think carefully about your motivations. Are your objections to seat belts based on the facts or on rationalizations? **Here are a few of the common rationalizations.** Many people say they are afraid of being trapped in a car by a seat belt. In fact, in the vast majority of cases, seat belts protect passengers from severe injuries, allowing them to escape more quickly. Another popular rationalization: you'll be saved by being thrown clear of the car. Here again, accident data have proved that to be untrue—you are almost always safer inside the car.

Some people use seat belts for highway driving, but rationalize it's not worth the trouble to buckle up for short trips. The numbers tell a different story: 80% of all automobile accidents causing serious injury or death involve cars traveling under 40 miles per hour. And three quarters of all collisions happen less than 25 miles from the driver's home. **When you're the driver, you have the psychological authority to convince all of the passengers that they should wear seat belts.** It has been shown that in a car, the driver is considered to be an authority figure. A simple reminder from you may help save someone's life.

Another common myth: holding a small child in your arms will provide the child with sufficient protection during a crash. The safety experts disagree. They point out that even during a 30 mph collision, a 10-pound child can exert a 300-pound force against the parent's grip. So please make sure Child Restraint Systems are used for children who aren't old enough to use regular seat belts.

If you're an employer, encourage your employees to wear seat belts. At GM, we've made it a matter of policy that everyone riding in company-owned vehicles is expected to wear lap and shoulder belts. We heartily support the program initiated by the National Highway Traffic Safety Administration to encourage the use of seat belts. So please fasten your own belt, and urge your family and friends to follow your example. Even the best driver in the world can't predict what another driver will do.

This advertisement is part of our continuing effort to give customers useful information about their cars and trucks and the company that builds them.

General Motors

Chevrolet • Pontiac
Oldsmobile • Buick
Cadillac • GMC Truck

GM PAP P20105
7" x 10"   b/w
Magazines

N W Ayer Incorporated

Credit: Reprinted with the permission of General Motors Corporation.

annual outings and picnics at which everyone, including the chairman of the board, participates.

A personal letter home to spouse or parent on the occasion of some special event regarding the employee is more appreciated, sometimes, than you might think. All of us want our loved ones to be proud of us. Open house for families is another good morale builder. This is not practical in every business, but where it is, a tour that gives families an idea of just what the breadwinner does—and the importance of and skills required on the job—brings everyone a lot closer.

7. *Displays.* Many employees never see the end results of their labors. It is often difficult for them to envisage the contribution they may have to an overall effort.

Posted pictures, or an automatic slide film projector can often be used to show company products in action. You can build a slide film presentation from company photographs, write the narration and place it in cafeterias and employee locker rooms.

8. *Special situations.* You and your department should be prepared with contingency plans to help handle unexpected situations. Note that these situations are *unexpected,* not *unknown.* Fires, floods, plant closings, strikes, and accidents occur with some regularity in business and industry. You should have a standing plan ready when trouble strikes.

When any unusual situation occurs, media people will want their questions answered in a hurry. In most cases, it is you who will have to supply the answers. As we noted earlier, a straightforward, honest approach, within the bounds of company policy, is usually best. Let us look at some examples. A few years ago at a college, a professor was assaulted and robbed on campus. The college's public relations department indulged itself in an orgy of mishandling. Though this was not the first assault to occur in the campus's high-crime area, the public relations people attempted to play the incident down. When the victim's spouse was approached, his reaction was highly critical of the college and its security force. But when the next edition of the paper appeared, it was quite apparent that the spouse had been "gotten to" by someone. The victim's partner no longer remembered making the critical statements and had little or nothing to say to the press. The reporter sensed what was going on and took pains to see that readers were aware of it. The incident did the college's public image little good.

The public relations department of a large corporation, being more professional, handled one of these situations in a far better manner. It had a contingency plan ready, and put it into action. It was well it did, because the "situation" was to become the subject of a nationwide television broadcast, witnessed by millions. This big manufacturer had decided to move one of its operations to a foreign country, where labor costs would be much lower. The move would throw about 250 American operators out of work and have a devastating effect on the economy of the small town in which the factory was located.

The broadcast did little to arouse sympathy for the company, particularly since so many old and loyal (and efficient) employees were faced with such a bleak future. It helped little when an officer of the company pointed out that the company had an obligation to shareholders, too. But what did help to alleviate a very negative situation was the contingency plan the company was able to put into operation. It had a program for relocation, reemployment, and retraining. It would not keep all the employees off the unemployment rolls, nor assure that their income would be the same as previously. But the plan was given good coverage at the end of the program and helped take some of the sting out of what could only be regarded as an "unfortunate" situation.

9. *Labor relations.* Labor relations is so special that your company may retain an inside specialist or an outside consulting firm to handle problems. Sometimes the inside specialist in labor may be in your department, often with a title having little to do with labor relations. This is usually true if your company has been carrying on unrelenting warfare with labor unions for a period of years. In most industrial companies, however, the crunch only comes each year or time when both parties sit down at the bargaining table. Your job here is likely to be a delicate one. The company is going to want to make its position clear. This is usually done through paid advertising space, letters to the editor, or statements to the press in press conferences or interviews. Remember that you are in the position of a lawyer stating a case to the public while the trial is still going on. Certainly you do not want to say anything that will enrage or insult the opposition. What you say should be in the *public's* interest; you should state, clearly and calmly, just what the issues are, and the importance of a quick and reasonable solution. Do not hold anyone up to ridicule, or imply that anyone who does not agree with your point of view is not only an idiot, but un-American.

Community Relations

Your company has a special and intimate relationship with the people in the community—that of good neighbor. So the relationship is certainly going to be one of your immediate concerns. Most companies want to maintain good community relations because it makes life easier for everyone. In a large community, you may not be so noticeable. But in smaller communities, you are likely to have more impact. What you do and say is important to everyone. This is particularly true in the so-called company towns—communities dependent on the payroll of a single company. There are a great many more of these towns than you might imagine in the South, in the Midwest, and in the Far West. In these places your visibility is *very* high.

What can you do to demonstrate your responsibility as a member of the community? After all, you cannot hold everyone's hand and contribute to every cause. Let us look at some of the things you can do.

1. *Pollution and ecology.* These are some of the hottest questions you may be called upon to handle. The cleanliness of our air, land, and water and the preservation of our natural resources are matters of impassioned debate and political maneuvering. Your company already is operating within the strictures of state and federal regulations. The point is that when there is an oil slick on the water, a smell in the air, or a beer can on the lawn, everyone notices it and starts pointing fingers.

Often spills and smells are accidental. There is little you can do but tell the public, with all speed possible, of the efforts your company is making to clean up the situation. Often companies publicize their policies. Millions of dollars are sometimes spent in these efforts. Lumber companies tell of

FIGURE 12-4   Recruitment of new, promising people is one of the functions of the personnel department. The very future of the organization depends on it. Just how "aggressive, self-starting young men and women like yourself" regard the Kinney Shoe Corporation and its products is going to have a great bearing on the success of the company's recruiting efforts. Note that Kinney is offering young people an opportunity with "six of the most dynamic names in footwear and apparel retailing. Names that America looks to for quality, value, and service."

Kinney's specialized retail shops are and can be an exciting career for the person who has the desire and ambition to be successful.

Expand your own horizons . . . Kinney may just be the career you're looking for. Maybe you've overlooked Retailing in the past because you have the wrong notion of what Retail is all about. Kinney retailing is an extremely fast-pace career, demanding only those individuals who can handle responsibility as soon as they enter the field.

We provide an opportunity not only for fast promotion, but the challenge of running your own business.

Credit: Kinney Shoe Corporation.

their tree farms, steel companies of smoke-control equipment, container people push the return and recyclable idea.

2. *Civic and political matters.* As has already been mentioned, your company will be expected to participate in local civic and political matters. As members of the chamber of commerce and other civic bodies, executives from the company will play an important role in such things as games, conventions, and city improvement and rehabilitation. It is your job to see that credit is received where credit is due.

3. *Education.* There is much you can do in cooperation with the educational institutions, public and private, in your community. *Scholarships* should be made available, especially for the sons and daughters of employees. *Grants and awards* can be given for special projects, particularly in fields of special interest to the company. It is quite possible that a company executive will be asked to serve on a school board or board of trustees. *Photographic exhibits* of the activities of the company will probably be welcomed in classes in engineering, chemistry, data processing, or management. *Career literature* concerning the company or industry is always welcome in schools. People in career planning will give such brochures lots of display and will put them to good use.

   You will want to cooperate with local schools regarding learning opportunities for employees. The schools will usually be more than happy to work with you. In turn, employees will greatly appreciate the opportunity to continue their education on a part-time basis. Many companies are taking advantage of community college day and night classes, with resulting goodwill from both schools and employees. Many companies also encourage their employees to participate in school organizations.

4. *Summer employment and internships.* A program that brings students into the organization on a part-time basis cannot help but do you a lot of good. A small paycheck can bring a lot of goodwill from student and parents. It is also an excellent way to help the personnel department develop prospective full-time employees who can make a real contribution to the company. If there is a Junior Achievement or a similar organization in the community, this program would be a good tie-in.

Corporate Advertising

Advertising by the corporation can be placed in two categories: *institutional* advertising, and what has become known as *advocacy* advertising. There are several differences between the two.

Institutional advertising is like standard advertising. It is attractive in artwork and layout and contains a message over the corporate name and trademark. It appears, usually in large space, in magazines and newspapers. Institutional ads are also used on commercial time on TV and radio. The point for you to remember about institutional advertising is that it advertises the company—the institution—and not its products. The subject matter of these institutional ads is, therefore, pure public relations: "We want you to think better of us because. . . ." Your department will probably have little to

FIGURE 12-5 It is to the interest of every industry to bring the "brightest and the best" into its field. Promoting interest in its field also makes for excellent image building with customers and clients. In most colleges, you can find brochures such as this one from The Upjohn Company in the career opportunity section of Student Services. Shown is a sample page from the brochure.

What is a Pharmacist?

You hear the word "pharmacist" and immediately picture the white-jacketed man or woman who is always available to dispense health-giving prescriptions. Certainly he or she is a well-known member of the health team and a leader in the community. However, opportunities are so varied that a pharmacist may make his career in several areas other than retail pharmacy.

This science called pharmacy is an applied physical science. The pharmacist knows medicines and the art of compounding and dispensing them. He also has learned to identify, select, analyze, preserve, combine, and standardize these same medicines. Doctors and the lives of their patients depend on his integrity and scientific knowledge.

These professional abilities, plus a knack for business, make up the retail pharmacist as we know him. From 80 to 90% of the 110,000 pharmacists in the United States either own or work in retail pharmacies throughout the country.

Opportunities on the increase

Another and much smaller group of pharmacists is employed in hospital pharmacy work. Because of specialized features in this field, post-graduate courses in hospital pharmacy are being offered in increasing numbers of colleges.

The government also employs pharmacists in the Public Health Service and the Armed Forces.

Other men with pharmacy degrees are found teaching in the more than 75 accredited colleges of pharmacy in the United States. This is another field where advanced degrees are helpful.

An area which has a growing need for pharmacists is industry. This includes pharmaceutical manufacturing, which has in recent years relieved the busy retail pharmacist of many manufacturing duties.

In this category is The Upjohn Company, where pharmacists are found in various areas of research, development, manufacturing, control, and marketing. The work of the pharmacist is essential to our business. To the pharmacist, the work is challenging, worthwhile, and satisfying.

Varied challenges in research

Like the retail pharmacist, the industrial pharmacist is concerned with compounding drugs. In industry though, the pharmacist frequently works on problems of developing formulas and processes for compounding new products and dosage forms.

New drugs must be available in the most practical form for use by patients and physicians. A drug may be formulated in any

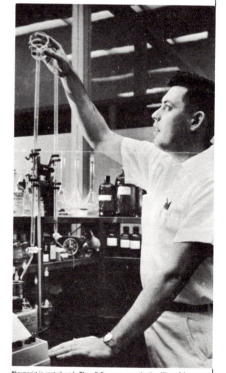

Pharmacist in control work. Glenn Kelley prepares a titration. His work involves analytical research to develop control methods for new products.

Credit: Courtesy of The Upjohn Company.

FIGURE 12-6   Study this ad carefully as a classic example of corporate institutional advertising. Note that it is "Tenth in a Series"—a good indication of Motorola's belief in consistency in building a favorable public perception for itself. But this institutional ad is interesting for another reason. Considering the state of the economy and of American industrial productivity, the headline is a real shocker: ". . . outperform anybody in the world." In publicly embracing the concept of participative management, Motorola has staked out a powerful public relations stance for itself. Not every company is enthusiastic about PMP. But Motorola is laying it right on the line. It's getting way out front compared to much of American management. If Motorola is right, and can continue to make it work, it will be in a wonderful public relations position.

FIGURE 12-6   continued

At Motorola, that's a long-held belief. More than that, it's a long-term business principle. We've been operating on this principle for at least fifteen years. And we've coined a name for it. We call it Tool Management Culture (TMC).

TMC means supplying every employee with the best equipment to do the job. From pencils to computers. TMC also means investing the resources to make it work. And invest we do. Of 1981's capital expenditures of $317 million, nearly 70% was put behind TMC.

But it also takes employee understanding and motivation to make TMC work. Because employees are the prime movers in recommending new tools, methods and techniques.

That's where our Participative Management Program has been a tremendous help. Because this program not only makes every employee a member of the management team, it allows them to make recommendations to improve their own productivity.

As participants in management, Motorola people know that better tools produce better quality, higher productivity, increased demand in the marketplace. And that helps reduce costs, preserve jobs, and make the company's products more competitive.

Take our Communications Sector for example. With thousands of people in the field servicing land mobile communications products with dozens of separate pieces of test equipment, our people saw a need for something

Motorola's R2001. In one "in-the-field" test unit: a signal generator; a frequency modulation, and RF power meter; a spectrum analyzer; a duplex generator; RF memory tables; a code synthesizer; an audio frequency counter; a digital voltmeter; an oscilloscope; and a sweep generator.

better. So they invented the R2001, a single in-the-field test unit that could handle 12 functions in one test unit.

There isn't another piece of service equipment like it. Amazingly, it not only services all Motorola's land mobile communications products, it can service anyone else's. As a result, the R2001 has expanded the test equipment market for us, in addition to providing a better tool for our own people.

Clearly, it's for reasons like this we're a world leader in land mobile communications. And it's also an example that proves our point.

Giving people the right tools can help a company work a lot smarter. But to give them the right tools, you've also got to give them their heads. And once you do that, they'll help you compete with anybody at home or abroad.

(M) **MOTOROLA** A World Leader in Electronics.

Quality and productivity through employee participation in management.

© 1982 Motorola Inc. Motorola and (M) are registered trademarks of Motorola, Inc.

Credit: Motorola, Inc.

do with the creation of these ads. They are generally produced by the advertising agency. Their subject matter is always chosen to enhance the reputation of the company.

Advocacy advertising is a different matter, and your department is quite likely to be involved in it. Advocacy ads are gaining in use and popularity. Though they occupy advertising space and time, they much more closely resemble editorials and, in fact, will most likely appear on the editorial page. When the company, or one of its executives, decides to take a stand on a political or social issue, more impact than a letter to the editor may be required. Therefore, larger display space is taken for what is, in effect, an editorial. On radio or TV, it may be an "answer" to an editorial position taken by the station.

Advocacy ads can be dangerous stuff. You may please a lot of people with your stand, but you may also rub a lot of others the wrong way. Basically, what you have to say will be in your own self-interest. But if you can demonstrate in your argument that your self-interest and the public self-interest coincide, you are on pretty firm ground. There is nothing wrong in an insurance company defending the 55 mph speed limit or a shipping company advocating channel dredging—*if* the public can be made to see the benefit.

SUMMARY

Corporate public relations includes a number of "bread and butter" subjects that must be handled each day. These include promotions and new executive arrivals, special statements by the company, new industrial processes or procedures, plant openings and groundbreakings, charitable support, and civic activities.

There is also a job to be done in communications within the company. These activities may take the form of handling suggestions and rumors, editing employee publications and placing displays, and being prepared to handle special situations that may occur within the organization. Many companies have special labor relations departments, though public relations inevitably gets involved.

On special occasions, companies will take a story to the public by means of paid time or space in broadcast or print media. This may take the form of institutional advertising, nonproduct advertising that seeks to enhance the company's image and reputation. Advocacy advertising, on the other hand, seeks to put forward a particular point of view held by the corporation.

FIGURE 12-7   This ad, from Mobil Oil, is representative of what is probably the best-known and most widely read advocacy campaign in the country. One of its distinctions is the regularity with which the ads in this campaign appear—usually one or two a week, in the same position adjacent to the editorial pages. These Mobil Oil "advocacy" ads treat a variety of subjects—social, economic, and political. Often they are controversial, but the writer leaves no doubt as to where the company stands.

Black tie and   blue jeans...

...Brahms and ballet... musicals and Molière...cool jazz and sizzling drama. It's as international as grand opera, and as "down home" as the Cotton Club.

We're talking about the John F. Kennedy Center for the Performing Arts, the nation's first and only national cultural center, a showcase for performances from America, and from cultures far beyond our shores.

Join the millions of visitors who pass through this artistic melting pot on the Potomac, the theater for all Americans. It's an invitation to excellence.

And ponder an invitation of another kind: to business concerns, perhaps one you're associated with, to help support the continuance of this unique Center. Why unique? Well, consider other well-known temples of culture like the Royal Shakespeare Company, La Scala, the Bolshoi Ballet, and the Paris Opera. All are government-subsidized. The Kennedy Center receives virtually no government funding for its wide-ranging programs.

By contrast, the Center provides education and public service programs, which touch the lives of millions of Americans, and thousands of free and half-price tickets each year to students, the elderly, the handicapped, the military and citizens with low fixed incomes—all in order to insure that the performing arts are not limited to an affluent minority. Funding for such varied programming cannot be met through ticket sales

alone. That's why The Corporate Fund for the Performing Arts at Kennedy Center was established in 1977. It's a voluntary association whose Board of Governors, composed of principal officers from 24 major U.S. corporations (including Mobil), works to keep the curtain up at America's premier showcase.

Corporate contributions mean that the Center can mount new American dance, theatrical and musical productions, while bringing to this country—often for the very first time—the best the rest of the world has to offer. The gift your company makes will also enable the Center to reach out to people in communities around the country. It helps develop new talent, new works and new audiences; sponsors touring programs for children and youth in various cities; aids dance companies and theater groups; and helps fund the American College Theatre Festival, which involves some 450 colleges and universities. Corporate gifts also sponsor many other grass-roots programs, including one that seeks to expand black and other minority participation in the performing arts.

To find out how your company can help, please write to Mr. Charles L. Brown, Chairman, Board of Governors, The Corporate Fund for the Performing Arts, The Kennedy Center, Washington, D.C. 20566. Make show business your business, too.

Mobil

This ad appeared in The New York Times of June 3, 1982.

© 1982 Mobil Corporation

Credit: Mobil Oil Corporation.

FIGURE 12-8   This is the cover of a recruitment brochure—a fairly elaborate one—used by the Army Air Force Exchange Service. Look in your college employment office book rack for more of these.

Credit: Army Air Force Exchange System.

FIGURE 12-9   Among larger companies the "company magazine" is a popular method for reaching employees with morale-raising news and information. This is particularly important when the company has as many widespread offices as does this well-known international advertising agency.

Credit: Doyle Dane Bernbach Inc.

KEY TERMS

Activities within the corporation
   New personnel, promotions
   Statements
   Procedures
   Plant openings
   Gifts
   Product development
   Civic activities
   Trade activities
   Advocacy advertising
Communications within the corporation
   Suggestion boxes
   Rumor "hot lines"
   Employee publications
   Pictures

   Employee friends and relatives
   Letters
   Displays
   Contingencies
   Labor relations
Community relations
   Good neighborliness
   Pollution and ecology
   Civic and political matters
   Education
   Photo exhibits
   Career literature
   Class time for employees
   Summer employment and internships
Corporate advertising

THE WAY IT HAPPENED

How would you like to be the president of a small-town electric supply company and suddenly find your name plastered all over the country?

In our neighborhood, slow-pitch softball is very popular. Men's and women's teams play in a Twilight League and draw enthusiastic crowds.

I was talking to some of our women employees at lunch one day and they said they'd like to have a company softball team. They had the name all picked out—Murphy Electric "Sparklets."

I figured it was good public relations, so we found the money for uniforms and equipment and they were on their way. I never dreamed how far they'd go.

They beat everyone in sight around here and then went to Atlanta and won the regionals. We had a shortstop who could throw standing on her head and a pitcher who baffled everyone, including our catcher.

We went to the nationals, and we won. Suddenly we were on every sports page. I turned on the TV and there's Murphy's Electric sliding in with the winning run in a cloud of dust.

Today when I go to a contractor's convention I wear a big button that says: Jack Murphy—Murphy's Electric—THE CHAMPS!

A PERSONAL PROJECT

One of the toughest assignments you may have to handle as a corporate public relations person is the *bad* news. It is those inevitable misfortunes that plague every company that are going to put you to your hardest test.

Let us do a little role playing. You are in the college's public relation's department. This morning, an explosion has occurred in the chemistry laboratory. Several students and a professor have been injured, and there has been considerable fire damage.

Now the press has descended on you (in the form of your classmates). They need to know all the details in order to write their stories.

How would you handle this?

Remember, newspapers and TV reporters are always on the lookout for suspicious stonewalling or evasion. Some of their questions are going to be sharp and penetrating.

READING TO BROADEN UNDERSTANDING

BARNUM, P. T. *The Life of P. T. Barnum Written by Himself* (New York: Redfield, 1855). The old master who understood it all.

BEARTON, PAUL. *Corporate Public Relations* (New York: Reinhold, 1966). Public relations from inside the corporation. Good on organization and management. Should give you some idea of what you are going to be involved in if your ambitions lie in the direction of a job in a corporate public relations department.

BERNAYS, EDWARD L. *Biography of an Idea: Memoirs of Public Relations Counsel Edward L. Bernays* (New York: Simon and Shuster, 1965). One of the founders of corporate public relations tells his fascinating story.

BILLINGTON, RAY A. *Words That Won the West* (New York: Foundation for Public Relations Education and Research, 1964). Billington is an interesting guy—a magnificent historian of America's development who really seems to understand the part played by publicity and advertising in that growth. See also his *Westward Expansion: A History of the American Frontier,* 3rd ed. (New York: Macmillan, 1967) pp. 706–708. See Chapter 5, "The Old West," for more on how immigrants were induced to come to America.

GARBETT, THOMAS F. *Corporate Advertising: The What, the Why, and the How* (New York: McGraw-Hill, 1981). Don't miss this—probably the best work on this specialized subject.

NADER, RALPH. *Unsafe at Any Speed* (New York: Grossman, 1965). This, and Rachel Carson's *Silent Spring,* are examples of publications that have shaken whole industries and created tremendous public relations problems for them.

REGIER, C. C. *The Era of the Muckrakers* (Chapel Hill: University of North Carolina Press, 1937). This interesting book will give you a good idea of how certain corporate practices, when revealed to the public, motivated the whole idea of corporate public relations.

TEDLOW, RICHARD S. *Keeping the Corporate Image: Public Relations and Business 1900–1950* (Greenwich, Conn.: Jai Press, 1979). Good history, Chapter I particularly.

SHOW BUSINESS

OVERVIEW AND GOALS

We are going to examine another kind of enterprise in which public relations and publicity have always played a spectacular part—"show biz." We will look at some of the ways shows—and this includes all kinds from tent shows to opera—are publicized. We will also see that the show itself can be used as a publicity vehicle. Public relations people often have an opportunity to cooperate with producers, and you will see how this happens. The chapter concludes with a look at that very specialized kind of "show biz"—the company-sponsored film. When you have finished this chapter, you should be able to

> ***Identify*** *the principal ingredients of the theatrical press book.*
>
> ***Recognize*** *how effective feature stories are written.*
>
> ***Enumerate*** *the other major vehicles by which entertainment publicity can be gained.*
>
> ***Understand*** *the technique of "spotting" products in production, the public relations firm's part in location shooting, and the uses of the company-sponsored film.*

The history of theatrical press agentry is a long and fascinating one. The Greeks had their masked tragedies and comedies. Throughout Italy and Southern France, the ruins of the great Roman stadiums and amphitheaters still stand. The roar of their crowds can almost be heard as they responded to circus, chariot race, wild animal baiting, and gladiatorial contests. They were advertised and publicized, of course.

There will be a Dedication or Formal Opening of Certain Baths. Those attending are Promised Slaughter of Wild Beasts, Athletic Games, Perfume Sprinkling, and Awnings to Keep Off the Sun.

In England and France, the plays of Molière and Shakespeare were widely discussed in the penny newspapers. In the nineteenth century, the actress Sarah Bernhardt's life filled newspaper columns.

In the United States, tent shows and circuses were "ballyhooed" (a word of American origin) by advance men with pockets full of cigars and complimentary tickets. Postermen plastered every available space with garish signs. P. T. Barnum, friend of kings and presidents, emerged as a master of public relations. He wrote a series of "biographies" with the almost irresistible title, "How To Make Money." If you should find that your career takes you into the public relations end of show business, you can be sure you have been preceded by a long line of illustrious and sometimes honest forebears.

Whether you are employed by a film studio, a broadcast network or station, a Little Theater or individual performer, a recording company or band, you are going to find your work pretty much what it was in the days of Shakespeare and Molière—to fill the house when the curtain goes up. You have certain special tools of the trade; we will look at some here.

The Press Book

You have already encountered the press book in the chapter on sports information. This is a compilation of all useful and significant material any news or broadcast writer might wish to have at hand when doing a piece on your client. The college football press book contains material about the university, the players and coaches, and past records. The show business press book contains much similar material.

Suppose you were putting together a press book for a new TV comedy series. You are working for the network's public relations department, but in cooperation with the p.r. people. The press book would contain:

> *1.* A detailed statement about the concept of the show. *This can be fascinating. What did the producers and authors want to do when they began putting together this show? What is the basic concept they hope will give them a smash hit? It took a lot of nerve to think up Archie*

FIGURE 13-1   Film studios and television networks have large staffs of professional publicists. But there are thousands of smaller show business enterprises that cannot afford whole public relations staffs. As in the case of Cross and Sword, it may be the general manager who handles publicity. Note that this local news release, announcing the monthly garage sale, is presented on a professionally designed release form. Though reproduced in black and white here, the actual color used in the promotion is a bright red.

Paul Green's
Cross and Sword
FLORIDA'S OFFICIAL STATE PLAY

CROSS AND SWORD GARAGE SALE THIS SATURDAY

THE MONTHLY AREAWIDE GARAGE SALE HELD BY CROSS AND SWORD WILL BE SATURDAY JANUARY 9 FROM 9:00 TO 5:00. NORMALLY, THE EVENT IS ON THE FIRST SATURDAY OF EACH MONTH (AND WILL RESUME THAT SCHEDULE ON FEBRUARY 6), BUT THE JANUARY SALE WAS POSTPONED FROM JANUARY 2 TO JANUARY 9 DUE TO THE HOLIDAYS.

SPACES ARE AVAILABLE FOR A $7.50 DONATION TO CROSS AND SWORD AND RESERVATIONS MAY BE MADE BY CALLING 471-1965 OR WRITING TO CROSS AND SWORD, P.O. BOX 1965, ST. AUGUSTINE, FLORIDA 32084.

THE GARAGE SALE IS ON THE PARKING LOT OF THE AMPHITHEATRE, TWO MILES SOUTH OF DOWNTOWN ST. AUGUSTINE, ON HIGHWAY A1A SOUTH.

THIS IS AN EXCELLENT OPPORTUNITY TO CLEAR OUT CLOSETS FOR THE NEW YEAR AND BENEFIT BOTH YOURSELF AND CROSS AND SWORD.

CONSTANCE HANSEN, GENERAL MANAGER

P.O. Box 1965, St. Augustine, Florida 32084 • (904) 471-1965
NEWS RELEASE

Credit: Cross and Sword.

Bunker, to say nothing of the nasty little man who runs the garage in "Taxi." But the idea of building a series on Archie, his wife, his daughter, and her husband—especially as they encounter social questions and are in conflict—was an interesting approach. You will want to explain the series concept in your press book.

2. The people involved. *You will wish to cover in detail the background of the important people involved in the show: producer, director, writers, actors, and perhaps others.*

3. Biographical sketches. *Each of the key people in the show will have a biographical sketch covering the usual facts of birth, education, experience, and so on. In addition, important credits will be mentioned—performances participated in and parts played, plays written, and so on.*

4. Appearances. *Talk show appearances, personal appearances, participation in charitable or "command" performances (such as a special evening of entertainment at the White House), and record albums will be included.*

5. Information sources. *You will also take care to give users of the kit full information on where and to whom to go for information. Sources of special information, personal interviews, and arrangements for "exclusives" should be noted. Both production executives and network executives in immediate control of the show should be listed.*

Feature Stories

One of your most important tasks will be preparing and getting exposure for feature stories regarding your show or client. These cannot be picked out of the air; they require careful interviewing and research, as well as lively writing understandable at the eighth-grade level.

What you are looking for is an angle—a fresh fact or idea that makes your piece newsworthy. Sometimes the reasons for these stories are earth-shaking—a star reveals a secret battle against alcoholism. This kind of story can get you in the feature position in any fan magazine. But all stories do not have to be "revelations." How about the concert pianist who discusses the problems of taking his instrument with him when he travels, and envies the violinists?

By-Line Stories and Filler Items

You may be called upon to ghostwrite a story for a client. "Mary-Jean Jones Tells How She Overcame Her Fear of Rattlesnakes," by Mary-Jean Jones. You should be a master of style when you attempt this sort of story. You have to sound like Mary-Jean Jones. You may get a request from an editor to do just this kind of story. The editor has clearly in mind just what is needed and will give you a strong push in the right direction.

FIGURE 13-2 Television's coverage of sports is pervasive and important. Often a television contract is the difference between a successful and an unsuccessful franchise. Here a television network announces the signing of a new contract with one of America's most famous sporting events. This contract is worth millions of dollars to both Churchill Downs and ABC. Observe that although it is released by ABC public relations, the announcement is attributed to both Roone Arledge, president of ABC Sports, and Lynn Stone, president of Churchill Downs, Inc.—a courteous touch. The last sentence regarding the 1980–1981 Emmy Award for Outstanding Live Sports Special is important. The battle for predominance in sports coverage among networks is a fierce one.

ABC Sports

ABC Public Relations
1330 Avenue of the Americas
New York, New York 10019
Telephone 212-887-7777

March 1, 1982

ABC SPORTS AND CHURCHILL DOWNS SIGN NEW SIX-YEAR CONTRACT FOR EXTENSION OF ABC'S
COVERAGE OF KENTUCKY DERBY AND ADDITION OF OTHER MAJOR CHURCHILL DOWNS EVENTS

ABC Sports and Churchill Downs have signed a new six-year contract, beginning in 1982, for the extension of ABC's coverage of the Kentucky Derby and the addition of other major Churchill Downs events, it was announced today by Roone Arledge, President of ABC Sports, and Lynn Stone, President of Churchill Downs, Inc.

Under the new contract, ABC Sports will continue to televise the Kentucky Derby, one of the world's classic sports events, through 1987. This year, ABC's live, exclusive coverage of the 108th Run for the Roses from historic Churchill Downs will air **SATURDAY, MAY 1** (4:30-6:00 p.m., EDT), on the ABC Television Network.

In addition, ABC Sports has acquired the rights to coverage of the Derby Trial and the Kentucky Oaks.

The $50,000-added, one mile Derby Trial for three-year-olds, which will be held a week prior to the Kentucky Derby, will air live on "ABC's Wide World of Sports" on **SATURDAY, APRIL 24**.

The $150,000-added Kentucky Oaks, the 1 1/8 mile race for leading three-year-old fillies, which is held annually the day before the Derby, will air on "ABC's Wide World of Sports" preceding ABC's live Derby coverage on **MAY 1, 1982**.

Commenting on the new contract, Mr. Stone said, "All of us at Churchill Downs are extremely pleased with the extension of our agreement with ABC Sports. We've had a most satisfactory relationship in the past and we're looking forward to the future with enthusiasm."

Mr. Arledge said, "We are delighted that the Kentucky Derby will continue to be televised by ABC Sports as a result of this agreement. The Derby has provided our viewers with countless memorable moments during the past seven years. We also are looking forward to the addition of the Derby Trial and the Kentucky Oaks to our comprehensive horse racing coverage and to bringing these important events to the viewing public."

ABC Sports received the 1980-81 Emmy Award for Outstanding Live Sports Special for its coverage of the 1981 Kentucky Derby.

* * * * * * *

Credit: ABC Sports.

You may also supply editors with filler items—small nuggets of information about stars or personalities that are frequently used to "fill out" a column or page.

Use of Broadcast Media

Radio and television, especially the latter, will offer you excellent opportunities to get publicity coverage for your show and your people. The Johnny Carson Show parades a steady stream of personalities before the cameras. One of the nice things about this kind of "talk show" is that it gives your client, literally, plenty of exposures, closeups, shots of changing facial expressions, and so on. Often the guest's appearance will coincide with the opening of a show or the publication of a book. Thus the guest can present interesting anecdotes about his or her favorite subject of the moment. As publicist, you will provide the show director with pertinent information on which to base remarks to the guest. Single interviews are very much like the panels, but are more difficult to arrange, and call for great effort on the part of the interviewer (the segment may last for 30 minutes). These spots are usually reserved for outstanding people whose views on a particular subject may carry some weight.

An inexpensive spinoff from a filming may be a *segment* shot on location with the star discussing the picture. These segments are often picked up by producers of variety entertainment shows featuring free footage from promotors of products, resorts, travel, and so on. Game shows may feature a visiting celebrity from time to time, but their panels of experts tend to be more permanent.

Community Events and Tours

There never was a ribbon-cutting yet that could not be enhanced by the presence of a visiting star. Is your client's old school having a big game, or is your client's home town opening a new auditorium? Get him or her out there, and be sure the picture and performance get on the wire services. A sad little story appeared recently about a small Georgia town that was planning its annual celebration for something or other. Try as they might, officials could not get a featured guest. Everyone from the governor on down was busy and could not make it. (They had to call the celebration off.)

Tours are put together to get the stars into key markets for personal appearances, interviews, and so on to coincide with the opening of the show. The problem here is that, in the case of motion pictures, shooting has been over for some time, and the cast is dispersed and often under other contractual obligations.

Motion Pictures as Publicity Vehicles

Let us reverse the roles now. Rather than publicizing a show, you are going to use the show to publicize something of your own. Making movies is a far different game today than it was when major studios dominated the market. Fewer pictures are being made by a wide variety of producers using a number of different financing and distribution methods—for example, the "twin" or "quad" cinemas instead of single large houses. The motion picture made for TV is common, but the movie theater has not died.

Many years ago someone discovered that it was possible to slip a product onto the set, get it photographed as part of the picture, and thus get a million dollars worth of free exposure. The days of such hankypanky seem to be gone. Today's directors know everything that is on the set and why it is there. Many prefer the "real thing" as contributing to the naturalness of the scene. They would not shoot a scene in a kitchen in which refrigerator, stove, and electric blender had been altered so as to not be readily identifiable.

If you talk to a professional store or window dresser, you would discover that an important part of this business is *knowing where to find things*. If he or she needs coconuts for a projected window display, the dresser cannot spend time tramping all over town looking for coconuts—or for an authentic eighteenth-century wig. It is the same with set dressers, the people who are responsible for obtaining and putting in place all the articles specified by the set designer. They too, as professionals, know exactly where to lay their hands on a variety of needed items—often with the help of people like you. It is up to you to put yourself in touch with these people and to let them know how you can help them. Believe me, they will appreciate it.

Often the process is a little more involved than simply getting your product on camera. If someone is going to be forever reaching into the refrigerator for a cold beer, it might as well be *your* beer. Often too, the set

---→

FIGURE 13-3   This release from CBS gives you a great chance to see how show business public relations people, working with the programming department, can put things together for the benefit of a lot of people. Let us see how it works. The Macy's Thanksgiving Day Parade in New York City is probably one of the greatest department store public relations events of all time. Millions view it in person and on TV each year. There are others, and remember that they are public relation *promotions*. CBS has taken five of them, arranged for three-hour coverage, and called it the "CBS All-American Thanksgiving Day Parade." Each parade will be "covered" by one or more stars from CBS shows. Everybody wins. CBS has a great spectacular for Thanksgiving morning. The parades and their sponsors get a national audience of millions, with the chance to have all kinds of nice things said about them. And CBS, of course, gets a golden opportunity to exploit its stars and give all kinds of interesting plugs for "Knots Landing," "The Dukes of Hazzard," "Dallas," and many of its other shows. In the classic public relations "happening," *everyone* goes home happy, including the public.

PROGRAM NOTES

CBS ALL-AMERICAN THANKSGIVING DAY PARADE

Thursday, November 26, 1981, 9:00 AM - 12:00 NOON, CNYT

The holiday season kicks off with the CBS ALL-AMERICAN THANKSGIVING DAY
PARADE, an array of CBS stars highlighting the traditional parades in
five major cities. The colorful, three-hour special will air Thanksgiving Day, Thursday, November 26th, from 9:00 AM to 12:00 Noon, CNYT
on the CBS Television Network.

For the tenth straight year, William Conrad will host the festivities
from New York. He will be joined by Joan Van Ark of "Knots Landing" and
Robert Reed of "Nurse" as they host the 55th annual Macy's Parade, com-
plete with floats, marching bands, ballooned characters and Santa Claus.
In Toronto, Canada, Donna Mills of "Knots Landing" and Daryl Anderson of
"Lou Grant" share the hosting chores at the 77th annual Eaton's Santa
Claus Parade. Patrick Duffy, Bobby Ewing on "Dallas" and Beth Howland
who plays Vera on "Alice" join in the celebration of the Aloha Floral
Parade in Hawaii by performing a special hula dance. The 61st annual
Gimbel's Thanksgiving Day Parade in Philadelphia will be covered by
Sorrell Booke from "The Dukes Of Hazzard" and Danielle Brisebois of
"Archie Bunker's Place". "M*A*S*H"'s Jaime Farr and Susan Howard, the

® CBS 1981-82 REACH FOR THE STARS

Credit: Courtesy CBS.

dresser is faced with technical and authenticity problems. Let us say you are working in the public relations department of an airline. Because of your demonstrated willingness to cooperate, a motion picture production unit staff has gotten in touch with you. They need to get a shot of a couple being served dinner on board a plane. No problem, you tell the director. "That's great," the director answers, and then adds, "By the way, the picture takes place in 1946." Your problem now becomes somewhat more complicated. Can you put your hands on a DC-7 with your company's insignia on it? Can you dig out a flight attendant's uniform of that era? They are counting on you, and it must be right. But your ability to come through for them is going to pay off down the road.

Sometimes you may be called upon to provide not only a product, but also information on how to handle the product. You and your company may be the very ones to show them how to get it right. Your client is a California vineyard. A bottle of your client's wine (thanks to you) is being served to a couple in a nice restaurant. The wine steward (a professional actor who knows and cares nothing about wine) approaches the table and goes through the little rigamarole wine stewards go through in the better restaurants. But what *is* that rigamarole? You, or someone from your client's vineyard, is going to have to show him every move.

I saw a commercial not long ago in which an actor was preparing a clam chowder. A shot showed him at a cutting board slicing tomatoes, onions, and potatoes. Then the camera came in close to his hands as he sliced, fingers curled under, and swept the pieces aside with a broad-bladed knife. It was done with such dispatch and expertise that you could not help but be impressed. Later, I realized what had probably happened. The camera cut away from the actor just as he was beginning to slice the vegetables. But the hands in the closeup were not his. They probably belonged to some sous-chef who had been doing this kind of thing since age twelve. Directors, you see, will spare nothing to get it right. They will appreciate any help you can give them. Look closely at the credit list that often follows a motion picture or TV show. Often thanks for help is given—a nice little plug for you and your product. "Alfred Jones' polo pony courtesy of Roundtree Farm Stable," and so on.

Location shooting differs from studio shooting in that the latter is done inside on the set whereas the location shot is done in the actual place. This is often, but not always, outdoors. It can be, literally, anyplace: a beach, up in a balloon, a city street. As Hollywood demonstrated a long time ago, it can do pretty well at re-creating "locations" right on the lot—a city street, a Western town, or a suburban front porch of the early 1900s. But with the trend toward naturalism, many directors prefer to get as close to the real thing as possible. You and your organization can be helpful here, too. Cities and states are very conscious of the benefits that go with a location shooting. Florida, for example, is breaking its neck to attract TV and motion picture producers. Houston, Texas, has made great strides in this direction. That soft drink commercial with all the kids jumping around on the beach was shot last December in Florida or Baja California. About five miles from where I live is the Sahara Desert. That's right—Sahara. It is about forty acres of denuded land left behind by a mining company; nothing but white sand and rolling dunes. The moviemakers love it. It has many advantages over Timbuktu, including a nearby Howard Johnson's. Every now and then, passing motorists will see someone in a Foreign Legionnaire's uniform come staggering over the sands, gasping for water.

Tie-Ins

The word "reciprocity," which you will often encounter in business, means "I'll help you if you'll help me." *Tie-ins* are reciprocal aids in action: I need a travel poster to decorate my window. So I go to see you, a representative of a vacation-land tourist bureau. Of course, you let me have all the posters I want. You are delighted to have them in my window where thousands of passing shoppers—and potential travelers—may see them.

Mutual aid tie-ins come in all kinds of forms and sometimes include as many as four different cooperators. A hamburger franchise did a nice three-way tie-in recently when it offered a hamburger and soft drink at a special price. If you ordered the soft drink "special," you got to keep the glass. The glass was decorated with pictures of clowns from the Barnum and Bailey Circus, which was about to come to town.

One of the most popular forms of tie-ins in show business is with the circus. Tie-ins with the circus offer almost unlimited possibilities. Any sale involving children can take advantage of the great fascination of the circus for them and their parents.

The influence of show business on our life styles is sometimes astonishing. It is a force that should not be overlooked by any public relations person. Popular dress designers, of course, want to dress the stars and receive a credit line for doing so. But a "period piece" like Bonnie and Clyde can set off a whole new trend to box-toed shoes and snap brim hats. It can work the other way, too. A generation ago, it became popular for matinee idols to go around hatless, with their coats tossed carelessly around their shoulders. It was considered very "continental." It was so continental it put a terrible crimp in the U.S. hat business. Yet take a look at any crowd scene of a slightly earlier era, and you will see that most men would no more dream of going hatless than pantless. How many men in your class own hats? Caps don't count.

Company-Sponsored Films

These may be short motion pictures or slide film presentations. A remarkable number of firms do "shorts" on their products or themselves. They find many outlets. One of the most productive, and useful, is schools and colleges. If you look through the index of your college's audiovisual collection, you will see that a great number of offerings were produced under the sponsorship of a commercial organization. If a teacher in a nursing program is giving a lecture on medication, what better learning aid could she or he have than a film short produced by one of America's leading pharmaceutical houses? Remember, if you work for a corporate public relations department, your company is an expert at *something*. People may not listen to you every time you open your mouth. But they will if you are United States Steel and have produced a film entitled "Proper Safety Procedures in Rod Mills."

Not all film shorts are designed for educational audiences. Any special interest group from the Sierra Club to the Veterans of Foreign Wars will welcome the opportunity to show a film if it is of interest to them. Scuba divers are always interested in what other scuba divers are up to (or down to). If your company manufactures diving equipment, you should be glad to provide them with a film for the next club meeting.

Your own college or university undoubtedly has at least a slide film presentation about itself, probably utilized in recruitment. Many institutions have much longer ones that are shown at alumni meetings and fund-raising events. Of course "game films," which the athletic department shoots anyway, make wonderful features at alumni meetings and pep rallies. You have seen brief examples of university promotion films during the brief time of NCAA football games on TV. These may be made especially for the occasion (the segment seldom lasts longer than two minutes), but they may also have been cut from a longer film.

The travel industry is a natural for the sponsored film with wide distribution possibilities. These are direct descendants of the travelogues of years ago. They were almost a standard "short" in movie houses. The emphasis in those days was on exploration and adventure, including encounters with crocodiles and exotic tribal groups. Today, a thousand sun-drenched beaches or snow-covered mountains compete for the vacationer's dollar, franc, lira, or pound. The crocodiles and the tribes are gone, replaced by the whitest sun or sand, the most beautiful people, and the most deliciously prepared food or drink in the world. When you have been subjected to about 15 minutes of this lotus treatment, about all you can do is sigh and say to yourself, "Boy, would I ever love to visit *that* spot sometime!" And that's the way the island's tourist bureau wants it.

SUMMARY

Since ancient times it has been necessary to publicize "shows" of various kinds. The Romans did it, and each spring the circuses do it. One of the major vehicles for conveying entertainment publicity is the press book, which carries all the basic information regarding the show and its participants.

Feature stories are widely used to publicize shows and show people. The television insert in the newspaper always carries this kind of story. Filler items are smaller bits of publicity designed for publication.

The use of broadcast media offers great opportunities for the publicist. Objects can be put where millions see them—the sponsored scoreboard, for example. Interviews and personal appearances are invaluable vehicles. The technique of spotting products in motion picture production involves getting your product into any natural or realistic scene. Location shooting involves naturalistic, rather than studio or "set" locations, and offers opportunities for cooperative public relations people. Company-sponsored films, often full length, are used for educational or entertainment purposes, with the goal of enhancing the company's image.

KEY TERMS

Press agentry

Press book

Biographical sketch

Feature story

By-line story

Filler item

Segment, insert

Tour

Spotting a product

Tie-in

Company-sponsored film

THE WAY IT HAPPENED

To most of us, P. T. Barnum is the epitome of the showman. He has come down to us as the flamboyant entrepreneur who roped in yokels with his two-headed calf and the Wild Man of Borneo.

Barnum was his own best publicist, and he seems to have been born with an instinct for public relations.

When he decided to give up drinking and become a teetotaler, he didn't do it quietly. He became one of the greatest enemies Demon Rum ever had and held a public smashing of all the bottles in his wine cellar.

When recruitment lagged in the early days of the Civil War, Barnum was inspired to raise an entire regiment from his home county—Fairfield, Connecticut. He promoted recruitment, helped finance it, and even supplied a band. It was the only one-county regiment in the entire country.

His p.r. instincts never died. During the war, he would appear at the encampment of "his" regiment—the 17th Connecticut—and deliver speeches on a variety of subjects, including how to win the war.

A PERSONAL PROJECT

Just how much of the "showman" instinct do you have?

Each year, representatives of educational institutions appear at high schools. Their purpose is to attract students to their schools or to their particular program. Often it involves someone seated at a table with some free literature. There is not much "show business" about it. Offhand, you would probably say there is nothing very dramatic or terribly interesting about your department of business education. But it might be *made* so for a group of high school seniors.

Do you think you could make a presentation for the business department that would keep the audience on the edge of their chairs, and cheering for more at the end? P. T. Barnum could have done it. How about you?

READING TO BROADEN UNDERSTANDING

The following books will give you an excellent perspective of the point of view and problems of the person who receives your news releases:

HALL, MARK W.   *Broadcast Journalism: An Introduction to News Writing* (New York: Hastings House, 1971).

YORKE, IVOR.   *The Technique of Television News* (New York: Hastings House, 1978).

The following publications will be very helpful to you in understanding the field.

Variety (Variety, Inc., 154 West 46th Street, New York, N.Y. 10036). This is the Bible of show business.

Billboard (Billboard Publications, 1515 Broadway, New York, N.Y. 10036). More emphasis on records and bands.

14

COLLEGE PUBLIC RELATIONS

OVERVIEW AND GOALS

Educational public relations is an interesting and growing field. In this chapter, we will look at it from the point of view of your college. We will examine some of the handicaps under which the college public relations director works. We will identify the major publics to whom messages are directed. We will also look at some of the tactical methods employed in creating the perceptions and images of the college. When you have completed this chapter, you should be able to

> **Understand** *the nature of the changing face of educational institutions.*
>
> **Appreciate** *the reasons for the lagging attitudes of faculty and administrators toward public relations.*
>
> **Understand** *the basics of the Greenbrier Program.*
>
> **List** *the principal publics toward which college public relations are directed.*
>
> **Command** *a working knowledge of the major devices used by college public relations directors in reaching their publics.*

As you are no doubt aware, your college has a public relations department, though it may not go by that name (information services and community relations are often used). You may have even seen evidence of some of its efforts: a faculty letter, bulletin board messages to the student body, or a guided tour for a delegation of legislators.

When you graduate, you will become even more aware that someone back there on the campus wants to talk to you. The alumni office and public relations are often closely associated. As you might expect, the support of growing numbers of alumni is vital to the very existence of the college. You will be on the mailing list, count on it.

What fun it would be to have an office of your own over there at Old Main. Wouldn't it be nice to just shift gears a little and begin your new career in the atmosphere you know and love so well? After all, a college town, with its exuberance, excitement, and cultural opportunities is a great place to live. (They call State College, Pennsylvania, "Happy Valley.")

Before you get carried away with the prospect, let me warn you: *It can be one of the most difficult, complicated, frustrating experiences in all of public relations.* Some public relations departments in some of the larger universities have things pretty much under control. After all, they have been at it for quite some time on a big-budget basis. But for hundreds and hundreds of smaller universities and colleges, the going can be—and is—very tough. Their problems are usually unique to themselves and are seldom encountered by people in industrial public relations or on the staffs of the big-time public relations firms. Let us look at a variety of college public relations and see why they are so different.

The Changing Face of Education

We've come a long way since the days when 95 percent of a nation could be illiterate—though certain Central American countries cling tenaciously to the custom. It took a lot of effort by liberals to pry some of the 6-to-12 year olds out of the mines, mills, and factories and into the classrooms. Thomas Jefferson fought all his life for the concept of universal education. The Morrill Land Grant Act of 1862 set aside public lands for institutions designed primarily for rural, middle-class students.

Your mothers and fathers and certainly your grandparents had nowhere near the educational opportunities available to you today. Only a couple of generations ago, most of you sitting in this classroom would have been destined for the mill or factory on completion of the eighth grade. The point, of course, is this: The face of education is changing rapidly and will continue to do so. With these changes come, inevitably, new problems that often demand the services of someone skilled in public relations.

The New Student

Sometimes I have a daydream. I am teaching a class of 20 carefully selected freshmen. They are all of the same age, well-dressed and well-scrubbed, alert, and with astronomical SAT scores. "Boy," I dream to myself, "wouldn't it be fun to teach a class like that!" Then I come to and realize that it would not. As a matter of fact, it would be duller than hell—no excitement.

But it was not too many years ago when college classrooms did look like that. Aside from the land-grant colleges, higher education was reserved for the privileged few—the sons (and an occasional daughter) of the well-to-do. Look around you. It sure is not that way today. The average college classroom has the broadest spectrum of students, geographically, racially, and culturally. And the spectrum is getting broader all the time.

These students are, literally, a new breed. They don't even look the same. They are older, more mature, more realistic in their outlooks, and in many cases, far more motivated. Many of them are making tough financial sacrifices to stay in school. Many of them are spreading their education thin between hours of work. The routine of four years of high school, four years of college no longer applies to many students.

The growth of the community college concept has changed the face of higher education dramatically. Thomas Jefferson would have been delighted with them, for they are really bringing education to the masses. In addition to the traditional students doing the first two years of a four-year career at great financial saving while living at home and quite possibly working part-time, there are a variety of other kinds of students. They range from young people acquiring a salable mechanical or industrial skill to grandmothers honing their office machine knowledge and preparing to reenter the job market.

Numbers

Despite some dire predictions college enrollment is holding up. However, as this is being written, the impact of cuts in student loans and the effect of the economic crunch have yet to be felt. Overall, college enrollment has increased by 5 million students during the past 15 years. But this figure can be misleading, for much of it is attributable to community college enrollments, which include many of the "nontraditional" students.

One of the most interesting and potentially explosive situations for public relations people is the very size of this alumni body. Many community colleges have enrollments greater than some well-known state universities. Being younger, the community colleges do not have the numbers of alumni the universities have, but they have a far greater concentration of young alumni right out there in the community. That is the potentially explosive situation you, as a college public relations person, may have to face.

Think of it—thousands and thousands of ex-students out there ready, willing, and able to express their opinions about the college, its teachers, and its administration. Have you ever counted the numbers of community college parking decals on the cars in your community? These people often talk about the college to their friends and at their dinner tables. They can be a tremendous force for good or ill.

Money

The traditional universities have suffered particularly from inflation and its accompanying effects. Many of the big state universities, dependent on state and federal grants for part of their financial support, have been hurt badly by economy-minded legislatures. Many of the great old private Ivy League institutions, dependent on the income from endowments, are in the position of the well-to-do retiree who suddenly finds himself caught in the cost-of-living inflation spiral.

Many of these institutions have had to raise tuition year after year. We hear more frequently that we are returning to the situation when the prestige university was the exclusive preserve of the sons and daughters of the rich. These bright university-bound siblings can drive a reasonably well-to-do family, which is not eligible for financial aid, right into debtor's prison. Many universities are putting a cap on enrollment and reducing staff. Many tenured professors across the country are out of work.

The results of the squeeze are not entirely bad. Many a college, grown flabby with useless bureaucracy, has been forced to tighten its belt and apply modern management principles (a proportion of 4.5 faculty to 1 administrator is not unusual). In many cases, colleges have called in management consultant firms to help them clean house.

The colleges and universities deserve our sympathy. As we pointed out, the face of the college is changing rapidly. Many college administrations find themselves trying to cope with a world for which they never were quite equipped. Their Ph.D. curriculum in education contained many interesting courses. But few of them have ever seen the inside of a textbook in public relations, marketing, advertising and promotion, or for that matter sales.

Traditional Attitudes

Together with medicine, there are probably more idealists in education than any other profession. Many of us, perhaps subconsciously, long for the return of the day when the campus was a placid, undisturbed place, far removed from the outside world. That day was not too long ago. In fact, there are a few small, private institutions that still cling to that ideal.

FIGURE 14-1   Here is an example of how colleges keep in touch with the "internal family." Weekly and biweekly publications such as this can keep staff, faculty, and administrators up to date on what is going on around the campus. Many, such as this one, contain a job opportunities section in which the news of openings is brought directly to those in the college. Note the number of activities listed for a relatively short period.

Florida Junior College at Jacksonville

VOL. 15, NO. 9   OCTOBER 29, 1982

FACC convention Nov. 17–20 in Jax.

The 33rd annual convention of the Florida Association of Community Colleges (FACC), billed as an "Education Celebration," promises to be more than an opportunity to congratulate ourselves on a 25-year job well done.

During this the Silver Anniversary Year of community colleges in Florida, the November 17-20 FACC convention also will provide solid, professional programs for every community college employee, and to the benefit of every community college student.

FACC executive director Frank Casey calls the annual meet "the heartbeat of the FACC," and in practical terms, the scheduled activities bring to life the notion that the FACC is *the* professional organization for all Florida community college employees.

The convention will headquarter in Jacksonville's Sheraton at St. Johns Place, "one of the finest sites we've visited to date," says Casey. "The annual FACC convention has never before met in Jacksonville."

Conventioneers will hear what the FACC's Casey hears in Tallahassee: namely, discussion and analysis of mission change, admission standards, program based funding, restructuring colleges, expanding programs in high technology, governance changes, preservation of local autonomy, and increase of statewide coordination.

In addition to informative education sessions, statewide FACC elections, awards, exhibits, musical entertainment, and a gala banquet, the convention will feature guest speakers, including Dr. Dale Parnell, president, American Association of Community and Junior Colleges (AACJC), who also will address FJC Trustees at their November 17 meeting. Jesse Burt, director of Industry Services, State of Florida, will keynote the convention awards luncheon, an occasion for honoring those who have provided major contributions to the quality of community colleges in Florida, among them, Representative Steve Pajcic, tapped to receive one of 10 statewide FACC Legislative Service Awards, and Dr. Lee G. Henderson, retiring director of the Division of Community Colleges, who will be presented an FACC Honorary Life Membership.

"FJC's FACC membership is at an all time high of 351 members," says Dr. H. D. "Bo" Cotton, FJC North Campus dean of Student Development, candidate for FACC president-elect, and general chairman of the FACC Convention Assistance Team. "FJC will be represented by Dr. Benjamin Wygal, 34 delegates, and 36 commissioners. Those FJC employees who were not elected delegates or commissioners are urged to attend the convention; all general sessions and commission meetings are open to anyone who has paid a convention registration fee."

"The Cabinet encourages all other FACC members to attend those activities appropriate to their College responsibilities," says FJC President Wygal. "The cost of a single day's registration is $15 and may be shared by more than one person by attendance at alternate times."

SAVE THE DATES

November 1-19, 10 a.m.-6 p.m. Mondays-Thursdays, 10 a.m.-5 p.m. Fridays. The works of Helene Baker, Kent Gallery, Kent Campus.

November 4, 7:30 a.m.-3 p.m. FJC Admissions Services workshop, "Counseling High School Seniors Entering Public Universities & Colleges in the State of Florida in the 80s." Downtown Campus. For info: 632-3211.

November 5, 6, 12, 13, 8:15 p.m. FJC Players present *Travesties,* South Campus Main Auditorium.

November 8, 3:30 p.m. FJC chapter ACE/NIP (American Council of Education's National Identification Program for the Advancement of Women Administrators in Higher Education) meeting. College Administration Building. For info.: 632-3221.

November 8-12, 4-5 p.m. Steve Grad's WJCT-FM program, *Metro,* features FJC "Beyond Stress" seminar speakers Monday-Thursday, and nutrition writer Jane Brody on Friday.

November 8, 22, 7:30 p.m. Kalliope Fiction Collective meeting. Downtown Campus room 1196. For info 387-8211.

November 9, 11 a.m. North Campus Lyceum Series features Dr. Peter Lipkovic, chief medical examiner, Duval County, on "Interesting Cases." North Campus Auditorium.

November 9, 7:30 p.m. Film Institute of Jacksonville (FIJ) presents Werner Herzog's 1979 film, *Nosferatu,* Kent Campus Main Auditorium.

November 9, 8:15 p.m. FJC Jazz Ensemble in concert Downtown Campus Large Auditorium.

November 11, College holiday.

November 12, 13, 18, 19, 20, 8:15 p.m.; **November 14,** 2:30 p.m. FJC's Troupe de Kent presents *Thank Zeus, It's Friday* Kent Campus Main Auditorium.

November 13, 8 a.m.-4:30 p.m. FJC seminar "Beyond Stress: New Dimensions of Wellness" Downtown Campus. For info Marti Davis, 633-8321.

November 13, 9 a.m. FJC Auction Phillips Mall.

November 15, 29, 7:30 p.m. Kalliope Poetry Collective meeting, Downtown Campus room 1196.

"Happenings"

FIGURE 14-1   continued

New York Times' Brody to headline wellness seminar

Jane Brody, *New York Times* syndicated health columnist, will headline the seminar, "Beyond Stress: New Dimensions of Wellness" (see SAVE THE DATES).

Also keynoting the 15-session seminar will be Dr. Yank Coble, medical practitioner of endocrinology, metabolism, and nutrition, Fellow of the College of Physicians and American College of Nutrition, and consultant to the Food & Drug Administration; and Dr. David Munz, associate director of St. Louis University Hospitals and St. Louis University Medical Center, psychology professor at St. Louis University, and consultant to business, industry, government, and health care systems.

Brody, whose health column appears weekly in over 100 newspapers nationwide, is the author of *Jane Brody's Nutrition Book* and the recently published *Jane Brody's New York Times Guide to Personal Health.* Her far-ranging articles on other aspects of science and medicine appear frequently throughout *The Times.* Brody holds a bachelor's degree in agriculture and life science and a master's degree in science writing.

The seminar, sponsored by FJC with assistance from Riverside Hospital's Center for Health Promotion, will address the management of stress in both personal and professional life. It's designed for medical and business professionals, dieticians, human resource managers, and others involved in stressful situations.

"Beyond Stress" general sessions will feature Brody on "New Dimensions of Wellness"; Coble on "The Whole Person"; and Munz on "Health and Productivity."

The registration fee of $35 covers admission to the seminar, attendance at three of the 15 special sessions, workshop materials, refreshment breaks, and lunch.

Continuing education credits will be offered for nurses, dieticians, psychologists, and physicians.

While Brody is in Jacksonville she will appear on the FJC "Worth Quoting" cablevision series which will be taped in an audience participation/interview format in FJC's Downtown Campus television studio.

Winter scholar dollars

High school graduates who intend to enter college for the first time in January, 1983 may apply now through December 1 for FJC General Academic Scholarships. Applicants must be entering college students who intend to enroll at FJC full-time in college credit Certificate, Associate in Arts degree, Associate in Science degree, or Associate in Applied Science degree seeking programs. Applicants also must have maintained a minimum overall 2.75 high school grade point average. Each applicant must submit a 1983-84 scholarship application, a high school transcript, and two letters of recommendation. Applicants also must submit an application for admission to the college. Each scholarship provides $250. Scholarship recipients may renew for additional

terms according to established criteria. "We emphasize that there is no age limit for applicants. This is an opportunity for persons of all ages to become degree seeking or certificate seeking college credit students," says FJC Financial Aid director Guy Kerby. General Academic Scholarship program areas include Metal Trades Technology, Food Service Technology, Data Processing, Respiratory Therapy, Secretarial Science, Sales Marketing and Retailing, Air Traffic Management, Science, Road Vehicle and Small Gasoline Engine Technology, Printing and Graphic Arts, General Business, and many others. Additional information may be obtained by contacting Charlotte Minter, FJC director of Admissions Services, at 632-3211.

Gallery features Helene Baker

The works of artist Helene Baker are on view in FJC's Kent Gallery (see SAVE THE DATES). Critics have acclaimed Baker's drawings as being "fine and intelligent," "carefully thought out" renderings that make it "obvious that she is knowledgeable about traditions in art," though not "sterile and academic." Baker's "Plant Burst Series" reflects that studious sensitivity and is showcased at the Kent Gallery. "While enlarging a photo of a favorite plant, the image began to take on monumental proportions," she says. "As it was blown up, it seemed imbued with energetic qualities and appeared to escape the picture plane. Hence, the chal-

lenge began to wed a realistic plant form with the smooth surface of the paper." Prisma color pencils, gold and silver spray paint, and various handmade stencils in hand, Baker delicately used positive and negative shapes, hard and soft edges, plus contrasting levels of spatial depth, "all employed as tools" she says, "in order to transform an ordinary house plant into an archetypal image of all house plants." Baker graduated magna cum laude from UNF where she majored in painting and art history. She also studied art history at the Boston Museum School of Fine Arts, and at FJC. She has been represented in juried shows of the Boston Museum, Group Gallery, the University of South Florida, the Jacksonville Art Museum, the Jacksonville Arts Festival, the University of North Florida, the New Orleans Biennial National Art Show, among many others. She also has exhibited her works at Ringling Museum, Jacksonville University, Imagery Gallery, and Gallery Contemporanea.

Job lines

Open Positions Deadline Dates

Administrative
    Assistant I, SC   11/3
Professor of Engineering
    Technology
    (two positions), DC   Open
Professor of
    Criminal Justice/
    Corrections, SC   Open
Professor of
    Chemistry/Physical
    Science, SC   Open
Professor of English, SC   Open
Professor of Nursing, NC Open
Professor of
    Accounting, KC   Open

FJC SCAPE is published every two weeks. If you'd like to contribute, call Joanna Moore in News & Media Services, College Relations and Development. 632-3254.
FJC/AN EQUAL OPPORTUNITY COLLEGE

Credit: Florida Junior College at Jacksonville.

FIGURE 14-2 **The sports broadcast tie-in is very important to all university public relations programs. Televised games are important not only financially, but as a means of enhancing the image of the college. This ad for WHO, Des Moines, Iowa, shows the remarkable radio coverage achieved by Iowa football. From a pregame broadcast at 12:30 P.M. to a wrapup conference at 6:10 P.M. there is complete coverage sponsored by a variety of businesses. The talent is outstanding, too. Jim Zabel, WHO sports director, must be gratified to have such outstanding sports people as Forest Evashevaski, Hayden Fry, and Bump Elliott working beside him.**

The ⟨50⟩Fiftieth Season

Fifty seasons ago the hallmark of University of Iowa football broadcasts began when a young sports announcer — Ronald Reagan — teamed with WHO-Radio for the station's first season of Hawkeye football.

WHO Sportsradio proudly continues to present the exciting drumbeat of Iowa football... with Jim Zabel, Forest Evashevski, Hayden Fry and Bump Elliott broadcasting six big hours of Hawkeye action.

JIM ZABEL
WHO Sports Director

FOREST EVASHEVSKI
Former Hawkeye Coach

HAYDEN FRY
Hawkeye Coach

BUMP ELLIOTT
Athletic Director

12:30 pm HAYDEN FRY SHOW
Amana Dealers of Iowa
Ottilie Seeds

12:45 pm HAWKEYE PREVIEW
Iowa Ford Dealers

12:55 pm PLAY-BY-PLAY with
ZABEL & FOREST
EVASHEVSKI
Pester Stations
Northwestern Bell
Associated Grocers of Iowa
American Federal Savings
Blue Flame Gas
Association

3:30 pm WHO NEWSRADIO
Viking Window Specialists

3:45 pm EVY'S WRAP-UP
Life Investors

4:00 pm SCORE PARADE
The Leather Shoe
Triple 'F' Feeds

4:55 pm WHO NEWSRADIO
Betts Cadillac

5:00 pm LOCKER ROOM
REVIEW
Continental Western
Insurance Co.

5:20 pm SCORE PARADE II
Triple 'F' Feeds
The Leather Shoe

5:45 pm PRESS BOX
REPORTS with JIM
ZABEL and BUMP
ELLIOTT
Hamm's Beer

6:00 pm WHO NEWSRADIO
The Lamplighter

6:10 pm HAYDEN FRY'S NEWS
CONFERENCE
Capitol Carpet Dealers
of Iowa

Before leaving for the game listen to WHO Newsradio's exclusive Accu-Weather football game forecasts Fridays and Saturdays.

WHO SPORTSRADIO
1040 DES MOINES

Credit: WHO Sportsradio, 1040 Des Moines.

In the old days there were far fewer Ph.D.s around. The college president had one, probably from a German university—the very best kind to have in those days. He would have been astonished at the need for so many "administrators." When he had a problem, he simply called together an ad hoc committee of the faculty and had them solve it for him. Aside from the more prominent alumni and a few generous endowment givers, the college had little to do with people on the "outside." The whole idea of relations with various "publics"—with positioning the school in their minds—would have seemed preposterous as well as vulgar.

That attitude hangs on in many colleges today. To some of them, "public relations" is a dirty word. Calling it "community relations" or "information service" takes some of the onus out of it. To many faculty and administration members, whose training and experience has been almost entirely in the educational field, anything that smacks of "commercialization" is downright repugnant. All of this, of course, makes the college public relations officer's job more difficult. Fortunately, during the past few years, the American College Public Relations Association and the American Alumni Council have bent every effort to improve understanding and cooperation among the college "family."

Institutional Advancement

The phrase used today for the college or university structure that corresponds to an industrial public relations department is *advancement program.*[1]

The American College Public Relations Association and American Alumni Council, meeting at The Greenbrier at White Sulfur Springs, West Virginia, in 1958 set down certain specifics concerning the carrying out of the public relations function by colleges and universities.

As a basic requirement to the carrying out of a successful program, they saw the need for:

1. *A clear statement of institutional purposes.*
2. *A "sound product."*
3. *An adequate budget.*
4. *Adequate personnel.*[2]

---

[1] The author is indebted for much of the material that follows to Michael Radock, at that time vice-president for university relations and development and professor of journalism at the University of Michigan. His definitive article, "Public Relations for Educational Institutions," appears in *Lesly's Public Relations Handbook,* Philip Lesly, ed. (Englewood Cliffs, N.J.: Prentice-Hall, 1978).

[2] Ibid., p. 288.

FIGURE 14-3   The complex world of a university contains all kinds of interesting people doing all kinds of interesting things. Here Washington University in St. Louis's feature service (a part of its public relations department) sends out the facts and accompanying illustrations from which a very interesting feature story could be prepared by a magazine or newspaper. Note the number of items in this short release you might use if you were a feature writer. Try writing a headline based on any one of them. This is what makes a release of this kind effective.

	Feature Service	Charles Koltz
WASHINGTON UNIVERSITY IN ST LOUIS	Campus Box 1142 Washington University St Louis. Mo , 63130	Feature Editor 314-889-5408

A Feature Story for Lincoln's Birthday (February 12)

Lincoln Gets a Face-Lift

For the past few months a group of "conservators" has been rejuvenating Abe Lincoln. Honest Abe's likenesses, as depicted in bronze by the famous statues and busts at Lincoln's Tomb State Histor- ical Site in Springfield, Ill., are all showing their age, thanks to the harsh effects of weather and air pollution. The conservators -- who have been polishing up Abe's complexion and smoothing out the pitted surfaces caused by 108 years of wear and tear -- all work for a center that has been variously described as a monument hospital and a health spa for statues. One more intriguing fact: They conserve these historical figures by using space-age techniques recently developed by chemists and physicists for cleaning jet engines.

A photo proof sheet is included. This proof sheet shows you four available photos depicting the work of the above statue conservators.

To order 8x10 glossy prints or to obtain further information, please call Feature Editor Charles Koltz at (314) 889-5408.

FIGURE 14-3   *continued*

Weil Touches Up Abe

Before

After

Reviving Saint Louis

Available Photos for article about
"Lincoln Gets a Face-Lift." <u>Not
Reproduction Quality</u> -- Order 8x10
glossy prints from Feature Editor
Charles Koltz at (314)889-5408.

Credit: Washington University in St. Louis.

FIGURE 14-4   Sometimes an institution will use a publication to reach far beyond its own immediate family. As universities grow in complexity, public relations efforts are made by departments within the college. Here is a publication by the National Institute for Staff and Organizational Development at the University of Texas at Austin, a part of the College of Education primarily involved in community college education. Its message is carried to institutions of this kind all over the country.

LINKAGES/

National Institute for Staff and Organizational Development/Kellogg Foundation Project
University of Texas, EDB 348, Austin, Texas 78712

Presidents attend NISOD breakfast at AACJC

Over 100 college presidents gathered for breakfast and the fourth annual NISOD Presidents' Meeting on April 5 in St. Louis. As in the past, the meeting coincided with the annual AACJC Convention.

Dr. John Roueche, Director of the Program in Community College Education at the University of Texas at Austin, was featured speaker at the breakfast meeting. His presentation, "Literacy: New Realities in the 80's," addressed two key issues facing community college leaders in the next decade: how best to respond institutionally to the underprepared learner and how to engender commitment to quality teaching.

Stating that 40 million Americans are below functional literacy levels, Roueche advised that dealing with these students requires "tough entry-level placement" that is based on "the reality of the situation that surrounds students' enrollment."

Tracing a relationship between dealing with underprepared learners and developing teaching excellence, Roueche observed, "These students need extensive experience with quality teaching," which he defined as a blend of nurturing and tasking.

Concluding his presentation with the observation that sometimes "those of us who lead obviate all we would know," Roueche challenged college presidents of the 80's to establish standards and set examples and then "expect, demand, and insist" on quality performance from people in their institutions.

Keynote speaker John Roueche, The University of Texas at Austin

New
NISOD members

Two more colleges have recently joined the NISOD consortium:

Niagara County Community College in Western New York at 3111 Saunders Settlement Road, Sanborn, NY 14132, (716) 731-3271. Dr. Donald Donato is president of NCCC and Judith Blackley is the staff-development contact person.

San Antonio College in South Central Texas at 1300 San Pedro Ave., San Antonio, TX 78284, (512) 734-7311. Dr. Truett Chance is SAC's president and Dr. Max Jabs is the staff-development contact person.

NISOD is pleased to welcome these colleges into the consortium.

C. C. Colvert, The University of Texas at Austin and B. Lamar Johnson, Pepperdine University

Other NISOD-member college administrators enjoy the fourth annual Presidents' meeting

New Creative Teaching modules available

Four new modules in The Media Systems *Series in Creative Teaching* have been published recently and are now available. Titles are *Showing and Telling: The Demonstration as an Effective Teaching Tool,* by James K. Archer; *Stress Management: Self-Help for the Helping Professional,* by George A. Baker III and Frank Renz; *Tying It Together: Designing a Preregistration Assessment Program for New Students,* by Anne Hammond; and

Nonverbal Communication and Classroom Climate, by Alberta Goodman and Patricia F. Archer.

Requests for further information may be directed to Media Systems or to the NISOD office at The University of Texas at Austin. Orders may be placed directly with HBJ Media Systems Corporation, 757 Third Ave., New York, NY 10017, 800-221-4681.

April/May 1982, Volume 5, Number 2

FIGURE 14-4   continued

The Environment for Great Teaching: Professionals Offer Comments

●

Editor's note: Pursuing the theme for the 1982 Institute on Staff Development and Conference of Presidents, "Promoting Great Teaching: A Professional Development Imperative," raises a multitude of related issues. One of them is the relationship between the environment and great teaching. We asked five professionals in NISOD colleges to comment about this relationship. Specifically, these people were asked to draw upon their personal and professional experiences and training in order to describe the kind of environment in which great teaching occurs. Their highly thoughtful, perceptive, and individual comments are printed in Linkages so that readers can share in a topic that touches us all. Thanks to these five people for offering their responses.

Paul Keating is Associate Professor of Communications/Media at *Brookdale Community College* in Lincroft, NJ, where he has taught for twelve years. Keating's degrees are a BA from Montclair State and an MAT from Teachers College, Columbia University.

What is it that makes the difference? Could the most memorable classes be great teaching? Mine occurred . . .

. . . at night in a thatch-roofed house on stilts in the jungle of Malaysia, showing slides with a projector made from a flashlight, tin cans, and a magnifying glass, while the children of the village, who had memorized my narration, *shared my wonder of their world* with people who had walked miles to visit the white man who lived like them.

. . . in the basement of a church on the upper West Side of New York City, teaching English, learning Spanish, and sharing culture with a half dozen Latin American adults trying to *improve themselves* rather than trying to get a grade.

. . . in a round room with no windows in an "open space" college in a country club setting, providing students from seventeen to seventy with the opportunity and encouragement to "see" the world and themselves differently with the help of readings, films, activities, and *each other.*

These varied experiences indicate I cannot give credit for great teaching to the design of the space, the time of the day, or the newest technology or technique. What

works is an atmosphere, a relationship, a rapport. What the experiences tell me is that the teacher must bring a sense of discovery to the process, maintain a willingness to learn from the student, value the student's world, encourage students to learn from one another, develop the ability to adapt technique to situation, and most of all, master the skill of listening.

Herb Bryant is Personnel and Instructional Development Officer at *New Mexico Junior College* in Hobbs, NM, a position he has held for a year and a half. Bryant holds BS and MA degrees, both from Eastern New Mexico University.

Education continues to face the challenge of preparing people to live comfortably in an environment of accelerating technological and sociological changes. If an aim of education is to develop individuals who are open to change, then educators themselves must be open, flexible, and involved in the process of change.

To be effective, a teacher must
1. be less protective of personal constructs and beliefs, and able to more accurately listen to others;
2. be open, willing to experiment, and exhibit a capacity for growth;
3. be able to decide issues on merit, not always according to bureaucratic rules;
4. be able to pay as much attention to relationships with students as to the content material of a course;
5. separate research and teaching functions;
6. be interested and enthusiastic about subject matter; and
7. develop an atmosphere in the classroom conducive to spontaneity, to creative thinking, and to independent and self-directed work (teaching should communicate an experience as well as facts). This is by no means, however, all that makes one an effective teacher or that creates an environment for great teaching.

No one person can possess the sum total of the qualities that contribute to great teaching. However, all teachers can be effective by being enthusiastic, dedicated, and genuinely interested in students as people. Education requires a comradeship of sharing and exchanging of experiences.

It also requires an excitement that grows from common interests and hopes between teacher and student, since both are involved in the process of change in an environment that permits growth.

Louise Skellings is Professor of Communications at *Miami-Dade Community College—North Campus*, where she has taught for fourteen years. Her degrees are a BA and an MA from the University of Iowa, and an EdD from Nova University.

In one old and famous definition, the best environment for great teaching was a log with the teacher on one end and the student on the other. In the near future, it may be a womblike cubicle with the student working in harmony with a computer. Meanwhile, I have 140 students, no logs, and only indirect computer assistance. All I can require of the physical environment is that it allow concentration. If that environment is too hot or cold or noisy or ugly, it will not promote great teaching.

The mental environment needs to be reinforced with a constant positive attitude. Students and teachers need to know that parents, peers, administrators, media and community view education as important and valuable for both the individual and society. Especially, the students need to know that education offers something for them and that they deserve access to it. Once students have enough of a positive attitude to get to the classroom which allows them to concentrate on learning, the most important aspect of the environment for great teaching becomes what the students and teachers create for themselves. **(continued on p. 4)**

Students at Spokane Community College involve themselves in active learning as they identify points made in U.S. Supreme Court rulings.

FIGURE 14-4   continued

Field gems

New learning center reaches out to community

The Learning Shop, a new outreach learning center at **Niagara County Community College,** New York, has been located in Summit Park Mall in order to more effectively serve the community. "Locating the Learning Shop at the mall offers mall employees and others in the area the chance to take classes or obtain career and educational counseling close to their homes or places of employment at hours convenient to them," stated Carol Henschel, Learning Shop Coordinator.

A unique feature of the Learning Shop is that it is the permanent home of SIGI (Systems of Interactive and Guidance Information), the college's new computerized career information center. Locating SIGI in the mall site offers any community member, whether a student at NCCC or not, easier access to career-planning aids. Those who visit the Learning Shop receive further assistance by scheduling on-site appointments with counselors. In addition, visitors to the shop can obtain information about NCCC programs, financial aid, and campus events.

Visitors to the Learning Shop, which opened in March of this year, can become NCCC students by selecting from a variety of credit courses taught at the site. Among them are *Introduction to Psychology, Macro-Economics,* and *Business Organization and Management.* Rounding out the comprehensive offerings of the Learning Shop are non-credit courses such as *Writing Improvement, Back-to-Basics Math,* and *Investment Fundamentals.* Enrollment in credit and non-credit courses has totaled approximately 150 for the first term.

For further information, contact Carol Henschel, Learning Shop Coordinator, Niagara County Community College, 3111 Saunders Settlement Rd., Sanborn, NY 14132, (716) 297-6640.

College values adjunct faculty

Each semester, **Anchorage Community College** in Anchorage, Alaska, employs between 250-350 adjunct faculty who teach on the campus, at several satellite locations throughout the city, and at extension centers in urban areas. Because of the difficulty in communicating with the adjunct faculty, it became important to give them a reference tool that would assist them in their teaching assignments. Thus, when the Career Development Committee was established two years ago at the college, its first task was to prepare and publish a handbook especially for these faculty members.

Aiming to address regulations and services that pertain to adjunct faculty, the handbook touches on many concerns of this group. Content, for example, includes a welcome letter and classroom teaching tips from the campus president, Dr. Ron Smith. Also included are a campus map, the college mission and philosophy statements, and information about instructional support services and student personnel services.

For further information, contact Doris Simmons, Director of Personnel, Anchorage Community College, 2533 Providence Ave., Anchorage, AK 99504, (907) 263-1200.

Students learn by "living" language

Convinced that foreign language instructors need to inject life and enthusiasm into the language acquisition process, Norman Damerau, French and Spanish instructor at **Bee County College** in Beeville, Texas, engages his students in "living" language. The result is that students learn language by physically responding to command sequences as they focus on meaning rather than on form.

The hypothesis of this process, based on the work of James Asher, psychologist, states that language understanding comes in learning commands before speaking. This sophisticated developmental process is always more advanced than speaking, and when enough of the internalized language is perceptually ready, speech will appear spontaneously.

After viewing a live demonstration of the approach presented by Dr. David Wolfe of Temple University in October, 1981, Damerau returned to his classroom and began introducing planned command segments of twenty and thirty minutes to complement regular textbook units.

Both Damerau and his students are convinced that these "living" lessons are the most meaningful form of class instruction. Because motivation, interest, enthusiasm, and learning have increased significantly for students of all ages who are engaged in the process, Damerau plans to expand its use. He is currently considering combining computer-assisted instruction with the process.

For further information, contact Norman Damerau, Bee County College, 3800 Charco Road, Beeville, TX 78102, (512) 358-7030.

College, civic efforts result in new building for program

Efforts of students and faculty, combined with efforts of groups and businesses in the community, are resulting in a new aquaculture building for part of the Fisheries and Wildlife Program at **Grays Harbor College** in Aberdeen, Washington. "No state funds whatsoever have been or will be contributed to the building effort," stated Don Samuelson, fisheries instructor.

The fund-raising effort began in 1980, after the college determined that state budget cutbacks precluded obtaining state funds for the construction. Students, supervised by faculty, have raised most of the cash used for clearing, filling, and site preparation by sponsoring projects such as documentary films of marine life. Joining in the spirit of the project, industries, businesses, organizations, and individuals in the community have contributed to different phases of the project with donated cash and materials.

The facility, located near a man-made lake on the college campus, is being constructed by the college's vocational training carpentry class. One advantage of the facility is that it will allow the college to replace outmoded fish-rearing equipment located outdoors with current technology used in the trade that must be housed indoors.

For further information, contact Don Samuelson, Fisheries and Wildlife Program, Grays Harbor College, Aberdeen, WA 98520, (206) 532-9020.

3

FIGURE 14-4 continued

LINKINGS...

Environment (from p. 2)

Pikes Peak Community College, Colorado Springs, CO, will develop a scholarship fund with $200,000 it will receive from the George Lum will. An estimated 200 students per quarter may be able to receive tuition from the interest the investment will bring.

The chemistry department at **Laney College,** Oakland, CA, has added a $4,400 Vreeland Spectroscope to its growing supply of sophisticated scientific devices. The instrument is particularly useful at Laney because it can be used not only in chemistry, but also in physics, geology, metallurgy, welding, and astronomy. The spectroscope was purchased with funds from a $200,000 grant from the National Science Foundation's minority institutions science improvement program.

Free copies of two publications that may be of interest to *Linkages* readers are now available through the U.S. Department of Education. One, *Vocational Education for Older Persons,* a three-document set prepared by Conserva, Inc., offers a state-of-the-art analysis and serves as a resource for planners and administrators concerned with the future educational and training opportunities for older people. The second publication, *Competency Measurement in Vocational Education: A Review of the State-of-the-Art,* summarizes the major milestones in the history of competency measurement in vocational education and presents an overview of the current status. Contact Steven Zwillinger, Office of Vocational and Adult Education, Room 5026, ROB 3, Washington, DC 20202.

Lynn B. Burnham, Editor

Linkages is a bi-monthly publication of the National Institute for Staff and Organizational Development, EDB 348, University of Texas, Austin, Texas 78712, (512) 471-7545. April/May 1982, Vol. 5, No. 2. Subscriptions are available to nonconsortium members for $6 per year. Bulk copies of the newsletter are available to consortium members for $15 per 100 copies. Funding in part by the W. K. Kellogg Foundation. Second class postage paid at Austin, Texas. ISSN 0195-0266.

My current students range in age from 16 to 60, in nationality from Chinese to German to Haitian to Peruvian, and in writing ability from near illiterate to professional. When I asked them to write about their best learning experiences, they expressed remarkable similarity in what they want in the learning environment. They want respect, enthusiasm, challenges that can be met, encouragement and fairness. That is what teachers and students must supply themselves in every successful learning experience.

Mary Stubbs **is Assistant Academic Dean for Learning Resources at** *Westmoreland Community College* **in Youngwood, PA. She has been at Westmoreland for eleven years. Stubbs' degrees are a BS from Carnegie-Mellon University and an MLS from the University of Pittsburgh, where she is currently a doctoral student in higher education administration.**

The environment in which great teaching occurs is an active, participative, human environment. To borrow from Martin Buber, it is an environment in which the I-Thou (or I-You) relationship occurs. The great teacher creates this environment by knowing and understanding the subject, but not teaching "it." Instead, this teacher uses the subject in a reciprocal I-You relationship with students. The I-You relationship in teaching occurs when the teacher speaks not *about* something but *to* someone, and when there is an expectation and anticipation that students will reciprocate.

As an undergraduate, I encountered an instructor who created an I-You relationship. Together, he suggested, we would work through James Joyce's formidable novel, *Ulysses.* He did not propose to teach "it," but rather to engage us in a process with him. I still reread *Ulysses* from time to time, not only because this is a pleasurable experience, but because rereading it allows me to recall the excitement and energy of that first encounter.

Some may say that not all subjects lend themselves to an I-You relationship, that accounting, for example, creates an I-It relationship. Yet, I know of an accounting instructor who engages his students in intense and personal conversation about the subject, creates an I-You relationship, and exemplifies great teaching to me by creating an active, human environment.

Administrators can enhance the environment for great teaching if, in an I-You relationship, they view what happens in the classroom as the development of human resources, rather than, in an I-It relationship, as the development of a product.

Jim Pollard **is Instructional Specialist and an instructor in police science at** *Spokane Community College,* **Spokane, WA, where he has taught for fifteen years. Pollard's degrees are a BA from UCLA and an MA from Eastern Washington State University.**

As facilitator of learning, the effective learning manager strives to create an environment in which students are actively involved in the learning process through exposure to a variety of realistic activities and alternative delivery systems. Without such activities and delivery systems, the environment remains stale, non-productive, non-conducive to learning. It is difficult, for example, to imagine that an individual could develop skills necessary to play the piano without ever touching one.

The same principle is equally applicable to mathematics, history, music appreciation, photography, sociology, engineering, carpentry, and other subjects. Operating on this principle, the learning manager strives first for a realistic conceptualization of the external environment. Then, understanding the limitations of passive learning activities, the manager designs and/or chooses realistic simulations controlled by objectives designed to bring the learner face-to-face with issues that are as realistic as the constraints permit. The learner is thus offered first-hand experience through on-job simulations and manipulation of real objects, and through demonstrations, games, and role playing.

A student who must learn in an environment that does not simulate reality remains passive, perhaps only looking, only hearing, only writing. In contrast, a student who learns in a realistic environment becomes an active learner, engaged in listening, identifying, reading, receiving and giving feedback, seeing, analyzing, speaking, choosing, prioritizing, researching, writing, and evaluating.

4

Credit: National Institute for Staff and Organizational Development, The University of Texas at Austin, Austin, Texas.

As any student of management will point out, the first of these qualifications is essential. The statement of institutional purpose must come from the institution's top management people. It is thus implied that they know exactly where they wish to go, and that they are enthusiastically committed to getting there. As you may realize, this may take some doing.

Most of us would probably have no trouble accepting conditions 3 and 4. Certainly an adequate staff and money to support it are essential to any project. It is 2 which often poses some problems. Certainly all of us want a "sound product" to publicize. The more outstanding the product, the easier and more effective the job. Just one bad apple in the faculty, just one foot-in-the-mouth type in the administration, can negate a lot of careful work.

But it is not your job to point this out. You probably have competent people running your institution who may be more aware than you realize of its shortcomings. They are probably bending every effort to make the changes that seem to be so obviously needed. They probably do not want help or advice from you. Just about the worst thing that can happen to your department is for word to get around that you "have the executive vice-president's ear."

An ACPRA study has shown that there are two basic organizations, depending on the size of the institution. Both see the "advancement program" as three-pronged: alumni relations, fund-raising, and information services. In the smaller institutions, these three report directly to the president. In the larger universities, an office of manager of advancement programs controls the functions of the three and is immediately responsible to the president. Within this structure, the ACPRA sees the "advancement program" as functioning in several different areas:

1. *Fund-raising and government liaison.*

2. *Information services, which would include news releases and radio-TV script preparation and distribution.*

3. *Publication services, which would include the preparation of the great variety of printed materials—alumni magazines, informational brochures—destined for a variety of publics.*

4. *Participation in the creation and funding of certain events, such as commencements, homecomings, dedications.*

5. *The organization of a research and evaluation service so planning and evaluation of the advancement program can be done on a scientific basis.*

6. *The setting up and administration of an efficient office staff with its various support services, such as printing, recordkeeping, personnel.*

These functions will be directed toward a number of constituencies or publics:

1. *Alumni*
2. *Business and industry*
3. *Communications media*
4. *Faculty and staff*
5. *Foundations*
6. *Governing boards*
7. *Particular individuals, such as big donors and outstanding alumni*
8. *Parents and students*

Audit of Resources

An essential part of any planning or problem-solving process is the review of the environment—where are we, who we are, and what we have. The review of the environment or audit of resources must take place prior to the setting up of a successful public relations program. This inventory has been put in the form of a series of questions which the public relations director or manager of the advancement program might ask himself or herself.[3] Here are some of them:

1. *What category does your university fall into? Church-related, community college, traditional university?*
2. *Have you and the administration reached an understanding as to your specific responsibilities?*
3. *What is the character of your present public relations department? Does it correspond to the broad concept, including fund-raising and alumni relations, preferred today?*
4. *What constraints will be put on your operation? Where do you stand in the management hierarchy?*
5. *What is the "total environment"—political, social, economic?*
6. *What are the present strengths and weaknesses of your department? What effort will be needed to bring it to efficient working order?*
7. *Do you have a self-evaluating feedback system in place that will monitor your performance?*

These seven questions are excellent ones for the college or university public relations director (or whatever other name you happen to go by) to ask. Asking them and accepting realistic answers can avoid a lot of grief. Take item 1. The problems of a Jesuit school in the Boston area and a West Coast community college are very different. The constraints (4) are always good to know about, too. You might find yourself so constrained by a dominant board of trustees or a powerful executive vice-president that you would be walking right into a Catch-22 situation.

---

[3]Adapted from *Lesly's Public Relations Handbook,* pp. 289–90.

Inside Constituencies

We listed above nine broad groups that might be considered as publics or "constituencies" for the college public relations director. These categories can be further broken down into *inside* and *outside* constituencies—or, if you will, the immediate family and all the relatives. Our immediate family is the one we are associated with on campus—staff, students, and faculty. Since staff can include both the people who keep the blackboards clean and the dean of the history department, perhaps we should regard our family as four distinct groups, each with its own particular interests.

Your goals in communication with these groups will be to maintain, or improve, morale; to provide accurate information (and to counter inaccurate information); and to aid in coordinating the efforts of these various groups in collegewide projects. Let us look at some examples.

You might prepare a poster safety campaign for the maintenance crew, encouraging care on the job and the avoidance of hazards, including fire. A weekly college newsletter to family and staff could be a newsy, up-to-date communication of a general nature, including personal accomplishments and honors, retirements, job opportunities, and general activites of the college. Regular information letters from the top administrator to all levels of administration within the university could be used to help acquaint administrators with the background of policy decisions, and to gain their understanding and support.

You might also provide letters, brochures, and support materials for fund drives, insurance coverage, and other college-supported projects. The college's encouragement of participation in the United Fund drive would be an example. A letter from the president could explain controversies and squelch rumors. The problem of the grapevine rumor is ever-present for public relations people. This is particularly true in a close-knit college community. One of the best ways to deal with these rumors, particularly if they are completely off-base, is to let the president, or appropriate official, come forth with a direct, candid statement.

The college public relations department that finds itself with a labor dispute on its hands is not a happy one. Perhaps if things had been handled properly by faculty, staff, and administration in the first place, the dispute would not have gotten to the showdown stage. On the other hand, many colleges, particularly smaller private universities, find themselves pushed into confrontation situations by adamant anti-union trustees and big business supporters who view any encroachment by the NEA, AFT, or AAUP as a fate worse than death.

Fortunately for you, many colleges today rely on specialists (management consultant firms), who take over the entire process of union activity with a well-organized program of letters, speeches, and other activities. "What to do when the union comes" is a specialized business today for those who

FIGURE 14-5   In today's world of ever-tightening budgets, financial support from alumni is vital. Here is an excellent example of a letter produced by a college public relations department and designed to raise funds. As marketing people know, a letter of this nature is probably the most difficult kind of selling communication to create. You do not just sit down and bang out a letter asking for help. This letter is quite professionally done; note particularly the opening. Penn State also uses personable students to "jog" alumni by phone if there has been no response to the appeal after a certain period of time.

THE PENNSYLVANIA STATE UNIVERSITY
III ARTS
UNIVERSITY PARK, PENNSYLVANIA 16802

College of Arts and Architecture
Office of the Dean

Area Code 814
865-2591

October 1981

Dear Penn Stater:

In 25 words or less, describe the Mona Lisa, or Death of a Salesman, or Frank Lloyd Wright's Falling Water. Pretty tough?

It's true: talking about the arts poses real problems and I wish, instead of talking to you about the arts at Penn State, I could take you on a tour of the campus.

On our tour you'd encounter many familiar faces. For example, that grand old lady of campus halls, Schwab Auditorium, has never looked better, thanks to a recent face lift. And inside on stage, you'll still find the Thespians, singing and dancing with the same enthusiasm you remember from your college days. Old Main continues to house those wonderful Henry Varum Poor murals on the Land Grant theme. And would you believe it?--Professor Harold Dickson, who gave so many of you your first introduction to art history in his 41 years on our faculty, recently marked his 81st birthday with a new publication on the Poor frescoes.

While much of what I would show you would be familiar, there is also much here that is new. Our facilities are our most obvious additions. In recent years we've added a Museum of Art, the 2,600 seat Eisenhower Auditorium, new music and visual arts and theatre facilities and newly renovated quarters for architecture and landscape architecture.

Of course, buildings don't make programs: people do. You should meet ours. Each of you, I hope, harbors special memories of faculty members whose influence truly made a difference in your life. That tradition persists: teaching is still a major commitment.

Most of all, I'd like you to meet our students. I think you'd find them to be an exciting and dedicated group who deserve our interest and support. That's why for the first annual fund drive of the College of Arts and Architecture Society, I'm asking you to help in establishing a Society Student Assistance Fund. Our Fund will provide student aid to students in three areas: (1) scholarships; (2) special projects, such as off-campus field study; and (3) research.

AN EQUAL OPPORTUNITY UNIVERSITY

FIGURE 14-5   *continued*

Undergraduate and graduate students will be eligible to
apply, as will students from both the College and performing
arts organizations. The amount of individual grants will
vary, but none will exceed the cost of one term's tuition--
about $600 currently. We hope to raise $10,000 for this
project this year. This would provide aid for a lot of
deserving students.

Our Society Student Assistance Fund is a society-wide appeal.
Many of our academic units and performing arts organizations
also have worthy projects for which they hope to attract
your support. That's why you are finding other appeals
enclosed with this one. I urge you to study them carefully
and to make your decisions about how to give based on your
own particular interests and priorities. I can assure you
that every one of these appeals represents a real need for
the arts at Penn State.

Allow me a few personal observations in closing. This is my
last year as Dean of the College of Arts and Architecture at
Penn State; I will be retiring at the end of December. One
of the tasks that I regard to be the most vital in my long
tenure with the University has been the encouragement of
private support for the arts at Penn State. I don't need to
tell you, I'm sure, that never before in this country has
private giving been so necessary for the arts. In many ways
your decision to support us is as important to the future of
the arts at Penn State as any being made here on campus.

I leave you with my good wishes and heartfelt thanks for
your caring.

                         Sincerely,

                         Walter H. Walters

                         Walter H. Walters, Dean

Credit: The Pennsylvania State University.

FIGURE 14-6 **The alumni magazine is one of the most important vehicles for maintaining contact with the "family"—in this case (box, lower right) alumni, parents of students, and friends of the university. The "message from the president" is almost always a part of these publications. Note that President Frances Bartlett Kinne has used her opportunity well. In addition to stories of interest to alumni and friends, these magazines also usually include obituaries, wedding announcements, and news of outstanding alumni activities.**

FIGURE 14-6   *continued*

From The President's Desk

by Frances Bartlett Kinne

Governor Bob Graham has proclaimed January as Independent Higher Education Month in Florida noting that "Independent colleges and universities in Florida have long provided educational, cultural, scholarly, and scientific enrichment to the people of this State." This commemoration gives cause to reflect on the role of Jacksonville University and her sister institutions in the overall system of higher education. While my column will focus on JU and Florida, its application is suitable to private universities throughout the nation.

Because independent institutions are free to experiment, innovate, and specialize, they give a richness and diversity to the higher educational structure. True academic freedom flourishes, unhindered by the whims and pressures of politics. Because of its diversity, independent higher education allows for specialization, preserves cultures and traditions, embraces values, encourages research, and ultimately, through this diversity, it fosters freedom in the true American tradition.

As a free enterprise, Jacksonville University receives no tax revenues for operating expenses from any local, state or Federal government. We are not subsidized by the taxpayers for the excess cost of providing education above what is covered by student tuition.

In 1972, far-sighted Florida Legislators saw fit to narrow the tuition gap between public and private institutions while providing savings to the taxpayers through the provisions of the Florida Student Assistance Grants. Again in 1979, the Legislature responded to an appeal to common sense and created the Tuition Voucher grant, making $750 per year available to every Florida resident who chose an independent institution. With the cost of educating an undergraduate in a state institution exceeding $3,600 per year, and tuition covering less than 20% of that cost, the advantages of shifting a portion of that burden to the private sector should be obvious.

It is ironic that more state funds go to support out-of-state and foreign students in our state-supported system than are invested to help Floridians attend an independent college or university in Florida. The amount of the Tuition Voucher grant is less than one-fourth of the cost to the Florida taxpayers of educating a student in a four-year State University. The savings at JU alone with its 1,598 Florida students is over $4.6 million, and that figure is multiplied many times by the 20 other independent institutions in the state.

Even without the diversity and freedom provided by independent higher education, it's just good business for the taxpayers to shift part of the expense of educating our young people to the private sector. We should recognize these advantages and promote independent higher education.

If you share our belief in the importance of independent higher education and recognize the tremendous savings to you, the taxpayers, please use your personal influence to urge that these programs be strengthened and fully funded. Your legislators will listen to you, but you must speak out now. None of us who believes in the free enterprise system should have any problem supporting the independent sector which has proven so many times its ability to provide quality higher education in the most efficient manner possible.

On the Cover . . .

Old brochures remind us that Homecoming is a time for looking back to all the good times we had as students at JU. The logo for Homecoming '82, "A Dolphin Tribute to Walt Disney World," also reminds us that now is the time to look ahead and make plans to attend this year's reunion of Jacksonville University alumni. This issue contains a full schedule of the week's events and a return envelope (in Alumni copies) for voting for your Alumni Association Board of Governors and ordering tickets to the gala Alumni Banquet and Annual Meeting. Don't put down this issue of **COMPASS** until you have filled out your ballot and order form.

JACKSONVILLE UNIVERSITY
WINTER 1982

COMPASS
VOLUME XV, NO. 1

Jerry L. Gantt, Editor
Mary Anne Rogers, Associate Editor
John Iamarino, Sports Editor

Published three times per year by the Office of University Publications, Howard Administration Building, Jacksonville University, Jacksonville, Florida 32211. Printed by Hartley Press, Inc.

Alumni and parents send change of address to the Alumni Office. All others send change of address to the Office of Development and Community Relations.

Distributed to alumni, parents of currently enrolled students, and friends of Jacksonville University. Statements and opinions published herein do not necessarily represent official policies of Jacksonville University.

Jacksonville University is an affirmative action/equal employment institution.

Credit: Jacksonville University Office of University Publications.

wish to play it that way. Not everyone does. Many educational institutions have achieved good working relationships with the unions representing their people.

The Outside Constituency

A recent survey purports to demonstrate that only about 5 percent of any given total population can be classed as "important" as far as college public relations are concerned. That is, only 5 percent are "thought leaders:" concerned, participating, and likely "supporters" in a variety of ways. Though I have not seen the methodology used in this survey, nor the data derived from it, it seems to me that we should approach that 5 percent figure with some care.

The impact of a community college with its sizable attendance figure (some colleges you never heard of have student bodies almost as large as Ohio State) can be tremendous. Multiply the number graduating over a period of time by each individual's immediate family and friends, and you have a sizable *concentration* of people in one community. In much the same way, large state universities tend to accumulate, over a period of time, large concentrations of alumni within the state—alumni *and* people who have adopted the university as their own. The howling mobs that fill many large state university football stadiums every Saturday afternoon in the fall are but a small sample of the university's "following."

It is easy to lose sight of the changed face of the college or university constituency. No longer is it simply the nostalgic, banner-waving Old Grad who could be counted on for larger gifts as his or her hair grew grayer. If we may define our public out there as all those who are "interested" in our institution, then we encompass a great many different kinds of people: high school students' parents and relatives of future and present students; employed persons intent on upgrading their skills; those who are interested in developing a specialized skill, such as a foreign language; employers and personnel departments; dropouts who may drop back in; people beginning new careers (women with grown children returning to the work force, for example). The list could go on.

Note that all these people have *special* interests in you and your educational institution. Therefore, it is to your advantage to shape all your communications with these disparate groups in mind. In many cases, of course, your efforts will be general. But it is obvious that the focus of interest of a high school senior is somewhat different from that of a 30-year-old salesperson seeking to upgrade job skills. The manner in which one goes about reaching these outside publics often comes under the heading of "recruitment." These activities are usually the responsibility of the admissions dean or student development office. The tactics include visits to schools, media advertising, distribution of brochures and booklets, personal letters, and "consultants"

FIGURE 14-7 The weekly "football letter" during the season is an important and effective way of keeping in touch with alumni, particularly the sports-minded ones. Observe how the writer of this letter, while reporting on the game, has tied the alumni and their activities to it in a number of different ways.

THE FOOTBALL LETTER

OF THE PENN STATE ALUMNI ASSOCIATION   **NOVEMBER 30, 1981**   **VOL. 44, NO. 12**

PENN STATE	0	14	17	17 — 48	
PITTSBURGH	14	0	0	0 — 14	

1st Quarter
PT — Collins 28-yd pass from Marino capping 5-pl 53-yd drive. (Everett kick) 4:03
PT — Collins 9-yd pass from Marino capping 10-pl 64-yd drive highlighted by 33-yd Marino pass to Brown. (Everett kick) 10:13
2nd Quarter
PS — Meade 2-yd run capping 8-pl 80-yd drive after Jackson's interception highlighted by 28-yd pass to McCloskey. (Franco kick) 3:05
PS — Blackledge 8-yd run capping 6-pl 80-yd drive highlighted by 52-yd pass to Jackson. (Franco kick) 12:18
3rd Quarter
PS — Jackson 42-yd pass from Blackledge capping 3-pl 56-yd drive after fumble recovery by Parlavecchio. (Franco kick) 3:06
PS — Jackson 45-yd pass from Blackledge capping 4-pl 56-yd drive. (Franco kick) 5:53
PS — Franco 39-yd FG after 9-pl 57-yd drive highlighted by 44-yd pass to McCloskey. 15:00
4th Quarter
PS — Franco 38-yd FG after 6-pl 23-yd drive highlighted by roughing the kicker penalty on Pelusi 3:50
PS — Farrell recovers Warner's fumble in end zone capping 4-pl 51-yd drive highlighted by Warner & Meade's runs. (Franco kick) 6:14
PS — Robinson 91-yd interception return. (Franco kick) 9:30
Attendance — 60,260 (capacity)

Photo by Dick Brown

TURNING POINT — This spectacular interception by Roger Jackson (49) marked the end of the first game — a 15-minute encounter won by Pitt, 14-0 — and the beginning of the second — a 45-minute encounter won by Penn State, 48-0. Mark Robinson (32) also had two interceptions later. One he returned for a 91-yard TD.

With fire in his voice, Joe Paterno told 475 Penn Staters at a pre-game luncheon in Three Rivers Stadium last Friday, "You're going to see one great football team out there tomorrow — maybe two, but at least one."

But it is doubtful that even the most avid alumni bearing Joe's prediction at the Allegheny County Penn State Club gathering expected to see as great a Nittany Lion team as they saw in Pitt Stadium Saturday afternoon.

Vindicating themselves before another national television audience, the once first-ranked Nittany Lions devoured the team that succeeded them to the top of the heap four weeks ago and remained there longer than any other club.

In so doing, State broke Pitt's 17-game winning streak (longest in the nation), its 23-game streak at home (since the last time Penn State played there and beat them, 15-13, in 1977) and its 34-game streak on artificial turf. But most

important to State's seniors — they broke Pitt's two-game winning streak over the Lions.

Also in so doing, the Lions recaptured the Lambert Trophy, regained their self-respect, re-established themselves as one of the nation's premier teams and regaled the Fiesta Bowl with one of the best pairings of any of the post-season classics — two Top Ten teams with 9-2 records against difficult schedules, boasting two of the nation's most outstanding running backs and the best football traditions on the East and West coasts.

And the manner in which it was done only served to heighten the exhilaration of the Penn State fans, who seemed to be the only spectators left on Cardiac Hill by the middle of the fourth quarter.

Losers of 7 of their last 9 games on live television, the Lions scared the daylights out of the thousands of alumni watching at Penn State Club parties throughout the country by surrendering the first 14 points, as Pitt's All-American quarterback Dan Marino completed 9 of 10 passes for 121 yards, while Pitt's defense held the Lions to minus one yard throughout the first quarter.

Fiesta Bowl Tour

A festive tour to the Fiesta Bowl in Phoenix will be sponsored by the Penn State Alumni Association from Tuesday, Dec. 29, to Saturday, Jan. 2. A Pan-American jet charter will provide round-trip transportation from Philadelphia and Pittsburgh and accommodations will be available at the 5-star Arizona Biltmore or the luxurious Radisson Scottsdale Resort and Racquet Club.

The tour will also include a welcome cocktail party, a gala New Year's eve candlelight dinner and party with dancing, a pre-game brunch, souvenir stadium cushion, baggage handling and ground transportation. All-inclusive price from Pittsburgh is $725 per person for the Radisson Scottsdale and $825 for the Arizona Biltmore. Prices from Philadelphia are $775 and $875, respectively.

For reservations or information contact the Penn State Alumni Association, 105 Old Main, University Park, PA 16802, 814-865-6516. Space is limited and reservations will be handled on a first-come first-served basis.

West Coast alumni interested in land packages in Phoenix should contact Regional Coordinator Irv Segal, 213-889-2100.

FIGURE 14-7 *continued*

At that point, however, the Lions pulled the greatest turnaround for a northern team since the Battle of Gettysburg and won the last three quarters, 48-0.

Marino, who has been called a pro quarterback playing in college, could complete only 13 of his final 35 passes against a Penn State defense that rushed three men and dropped eight back to cover the passing zones.

Meanwhile, Todd Blackledge stole the spotlight from Marino. This was the same Todd Blackledge, who, on the second snap of the game, ran a busted play into the left side of the line, reinjured an ankle he had hurt against Notre Dame and limped to the sidelines, looking like he was through. He limped back in and completed just one of three passes for only five yards in the first quarter. But from there on he connected on 11 of 20 for 257 yards, including touchdown bombs of 42 and 45 yards to Kenny Jackson plus another 52-yard mortar to Jackson and 44 and 28-yard shots to Mike McCloskey in the face of a safety blitz to set up scores. For this he earned the James Coogan Award as the game's outstanding player, while Jackson won the TCS and Chevrolet awards for the TV networks.

The TCS defensive award went to "the entire Penn State defense" for shutting down the nation's third best scoring offense with its lowest point total of the year.

With Blackledge and Jackson playing pitch and catch and the offensive line opening holes for Curt Warner to register his 11th 100-yard plus rushing game, and join Lydell Mitchell, John Cappelletti and Lenny Moore in the 1,000-yard per season club, the Nittany Lions more than doubled the average number of yards given up by the nation's No. 1 total defense, more than tripled the average number of yards given up by the nation's No. 1 rushing defense and more than quintupled the number of points given up by the nation's No. 4 scoring defense.

For poetic justice, Sean Farrell, already named to three All-American teams, an Outland Trophy candidate, one of four finalists for the Lombardi Trophy, and the offensive guard who has opened so many holes for Warner, Williams, Meade and company to score, achieved the lineman's dream when he got his only Penn State TD in his final regular season game by recovering Warner's fumble in the end zone.

"You know I wanted to spike that ball," he admitted to reporters after the game. "This was the biggest and best win of the season."

Other Lions agreed with him.

"This was the greatest win of my life," said Matt Bradley, who had an interception and was the Lion's leading tackler. "This was one of the best things ever to happen to this team," said Mike Munchak, who protected Blackledge and opened holes for Warner.

"We had to show the nation we could win on TV," said Kenny Jackson, who scored the go-ahead touchdown with a move that would make John Travolta jealous. Catching a pass along the left sideline, Jackson planted his foot within a whisker of the stripe, made a 270 degree reverse

pivot that left the defender flailing at empty air and angled inside the safetyman for the score. Three minutes later he made such a good fake on Tim Lewis he got 15 yards behind him to make the TD catch that tied him for the season record with Greg Edmunds and Scott Fitzkee at 6 and the career mark with Fitzkee at 11.

"We had our pride on the line today," said co-captain Leo Wisniewski, who teamed with Walker Ashley and Dave Opfar or Greg Gattuso to bottle up Pitt's running attack with just a three-man front. "Many people had counted us out, but we knew if we beat Pitt we could have a truly great season."

Co-captain Chet Parlavecchio said, "We went out to win against the No. 1 team in the country and prove we were a better team than a lot of people were giving us credit for being. We're on the verge of a really great season. If we beat Southern Cal we have to be close to the top."

The Pitt players were gracious in defeat.

"They were better than us. They deserved to win," said Marino. "Give Penn State the credit," said tight end John Brown. "They outplayed us. They deserved to win. They're a great team. But we're a great team, too."

"I didn't think anyone could score that many points on us," said All-American linebacker Sal Sunseri. "They're the best team we've played," said middle guard J.C. Pelusi. "That's evident."

Pitt Coach Jackie Sherrill, whose 38th birthday present from the Lions did not come giftwrapped, said: "When a locomotive gets out of control, there's nothing you can do to stop it."

As has been the case every year since Pitt's resurgence in the mid-70s, the interest in this clash intensified throughout the season. Saturday even the temporary bleachers erected to hold 6,000 extra witnesses and give Pitt its largest home crowd in 34 years couldn't meet the demand that brought scalpers payoffs of $35 and more on game day.

The media had billed the game as the true test of strength for the No. 1 team that had gone undefeated against a "suspect" schedule by a

Photos by Dick Brown

TYING TD is scored by QB Todd Blackledge, who is about to be hugged by Bill Contz (79), one of blockers who cleared his path *(top)*. **BOMBS AWAY** — Kenny Jackson scores first of two TDs on long passes from Blackledge *(middle)*. **ACROBATIC DEFENSE** by Matt Robinson (32) and Roger Jackson (49) were one key to victory *(bottom left)*. **SCARED PUNTER** Dave Hepler runs from Dan Biondi (39) before getting kick away *(bottom right)*. However, Hepler was injured on play and could not kick in second half.

FIGURE 14-7 continued

team that had fallen twice while playing a schedule rated by the NCAA as the toughest in the nation. Comparative scores showed State beating five common opponents by 60 points more than Pitt. Those who gave the edge to Pitt, did so because of Marino.

"Marino is probably the best quarterback in the country," said Blackledge after the game. "But I have confidence in my abilities, too, and all those articles comparing us just gave me extra motivation to play my best game ever."

What was the secret to stopping Marino?

"We played stable in the deep zones and disguised our coverage in the short zones," Paterno said. "I think our defensive coaches did a great job making a couple of adjustments and we took away a lot of his reads."

Paterno said Marino reminded him of Ohio State's Art Schlichter, who threw so well against the Lions in the first half of last year's Fiesta Bowl and then was shut down by a strong pass rush.

"Marino made some super passes on the touchdowns. You can't stop throws like that. But when we got used to a couple things, we played better. We played very alert, very smart football. We didn't panic. That is the only way to stop someone as good as Danny. We figured we had to contuse him at the line of scrimmage, maintain good position in the secondary and get about three interceptions to win."

The Lions got four interceptions — the bonus being returned for a touchdown by Matt Robinson, a hard-hitting tackler suddenly turned aerial thief. The only one who came close to stopping Robinson on his 91-yard runback was the Panther who tackled his left shoe. But Robby thumpty-thumped the last 65 yards on one set of cleats and a dirty white sock to raise the final tally to 48-14.

The Lions also got three fumble recoveries — two by Gattuso, who made the momentum-turning interception against Notre Dame last week, and one by Parlavecchio, who also had 8 tackles. Parlavecchio's recovery of a fumble knocked loose by Roger Jackson on the first series of the second half set the stage for the go-ahead drive. Gattuso's recoveries in the first half each stopped Pitt scoring threats.

The 7 turnovers along with 13 penalties for 110 yards, including several personal foul calls, led to the Panthers' downfall.

Hard hits by Jackson and Dan Biondi turned two potential touchdown receptions by Pitt receivers into an interception by Robinson and an incompletion.

"Our defense put the fear of God in their receivers," said co-captain Farrell.

Farrell and several other Lions also felt that being behind in tough games before aided the Lions. "Pitt never had to react to problems like that, but we had to," said Farrell.

"They haven't been in dogfights like we have," said Bradley. "They weren't used to it."

"I don't know if Pitt's been in a game with such intensity," said Kenny Jackson. "We've been in so many tough games this year that we know what it takes to win a game like this."

Jackson also said Pitt's aggressive secondary allowed State to capitalize on the long bomb. "They like to come up. They like to take chances. We just caught them," he said.

Pitt also made the mistake of putting single coverage on Jackson, according to Blackledge. "You can't play Kenny Jackson one-on-one," he said. "If you do, he'll break any game open."

In Pitt's blue and gold carpeted locker room, two signs were displayed prominently. One read: "I would rather beat Pitt than go to any bowl game." — Joe Paterno. The other: "We have better athletes with better character." — Joe Paterno.

They were meant to provide inspiration to the Panthers. They turned out to be nothing short of prophetic.

For the glory,

John Black

Photo by Bob Goerder

Notes from the cuff: Sean Farrell received the TCS/Westinghouse Player of the Year Award. He is the only offensive lineman among the final four for the Lombardi Trophy. The others are Notre Dame linebacker Bob Crable and defensive linemen Ken Sims of Texas and Billy Ray Smith of Arkansas. . . . Refusing to be drawn into comments about showing he can win the big ones, Paterno said simply, "This was a great win for the squad, which had been a bit maligned, but believed in itself." . . . Penn State now leads the series with Pitt, 40-38-3, but Pitt leads, 33-25-3, in Pitt Stadium. Paterno is 13-3 against the Panthers. Sherrill is 2-3.

Other Sports

Penn State's Alan Scharsu was the first American to cross the finish line in the NCAA cross-country championships last week as he led his team to a 14th place finish. All-American Scharsu placed sixth among the 191 finishers, covering the 10,000 meter course in 29:30.5. Other Nittany Lion finishers were Barry Enright (68th), Gary Black (79th), Dwight Stephens (104th) and Brad Althouse (124th). The University of Texas at El Paso captured the team crown.

The **Lady Lion harriers** finished 10th in their NCAA championships with Heather Carmichael (39th), Patty Murnane (41st), Doreen Startare (53rd), Monique Purcell (54th) and Carolyn Ihrig (62nd). Virginia won the team title.

The **men's basketball** team opened its season with a 49-48 victory over Bloomsburg and the **women's volleyball** team dropped its first match in a month to Northwestern 15-3, 15-4, 15-8. The season record now stands at 43-4.

The **wrestling** team placed second to LSU at the East Stroudsburg Open as Scott Lynch (126) John Manotti (134) and John Hanrahan (167) took individual titles. Eric Childs finished second at 150, Carl DeStefanis third at 118 and Eric Brugel third at 158.

FIGURE 14-7 continued

Seniors Not Pictured in Previous Issues

 Jeff Bergstrom

 Jim Brown

 Keith Brown

 Mike Cartwright

 Rich D Amico

 Brian Franco

 Jim Funk

 Vyto Kab

  Paul Lankford

  Stu McMunn

 Mike Meade

 Pat Monroe

Scott O'Donnell

Terry Rakowsky

Bill Rishell

 Frank Rocco

STATISTICS —	PSU	PITT
Total Plays — Yards	68-434	82-393
Rushes — Net Yards	45-172	37-126
Passing Yards	262	267
Passes (Att-Compl-Int)	23-12-1	45-22-4
Average Gain Per Play	6.4	4.8
First Downs	17	20
Yards Lost Rushing	15	12
Kickoff Returns — Yards	2-25	9-164
Interception Returns — Yds	4-111	1-15
Punt Returns — Yards	3-11	3-24
Punts — Average	6-41.8	8-35.5
Fumbles — Lost	2-1	4-3
Penalties — Yards	7-106	13-110
3rd Down Conversions	4 of 15	2 of 16
Time of Possession	31:15	28:45

Rushing — Warner 21/104 (14); Meade 6/35 (21); Blackledge 6/24 (13); Mumford 3/9 (3); Jackson 1/6; Barr 4/4 (4); Williams 2/3 (3); Sydnor 1/-1.

Passing	No.	Com.	Int.	Yds.	TD	Long.
Blackledge	23	12	1	262	2	52

Receiving — Jackson 5/158 (52); McCloskey 2/72 (44); Warner 2/16 (12); Williams 2/9 (7); Garrity 1/7.

Interceptions — Robinson 2/108 (91); Bradley 1/3; Jackson 1/0.

Passes Knocked Down — Jackson 3, Robinson 2, Pryts.

Fumbles Recovered — Gattuso 2, Parlavecchio.

Fumbles Caused — Jackson.

Punt Returns — Baugh 2/11 (9); Jackson 1/0.

Kickoff Returns — Hamilton 1/14; Baugh 1/11.

Tackles — Bradley 10; Jackson 9; Parlavecchio, Hamilton 8; D'Amico, Pryts 7; Wisniewski 6; Ashley 5; Harris 4.

Tackles for loss — Bradley 1/5; Wisniewski 1/4; Ashley 1.

Players — **TE:** Kab, McCloskey, Heller. **OT:** Contz, Speros, Laube, Brown, Funk. **OG:** Farrell, Munchak, Maginnis, Carraher. **C:** Romano, Battaglia, Rishell. **WR:** K. Jackson, Garrity, Baugh, T. Robinson, Monroe, Sydnor. **QB:** Blackledge, Rocco, Strang. **FB:** Meade, Barr. **TB:** Warner, J. Williams, Mumford. **DE:** D'Amico, Ashley, A. Harris, Bowman, Garrett. **DT:** Wisniewski, Opfar, Hines, Paffenroth, Gattuso. **LB:** Parlavecchio, Pryts, Bradley, Hamilton, Kelley, Walter, Masciantonio, Sefter, Radecic, Hochberg, Puz. **DHB:** Lankford, R. Jackson, Kraus, Fruehan. **Saf:** M. Robinson, Biondi, Suter. **KT:** S. O'Donnell, Bergstrom, R. Williams, McMunn, Giotto. **P:** Giacomarro. **K:** Franco.

The Football Letter (USPS 763-880)
Published monthly in August and weekly following a football game during the University's football season by The Pennsylvania State University, 104 Old Main, University Park, PA 16802. Second class postage paid at State College, PA 16801. POSTMASTER: Send address changes to The Football Letter, 104 Old Main, University Park, PA 16802

THE FOOTBALL LETTER

SECOND CLASS
Postage Paid
at
State College, Pa. 16801

Penn State 52	Cincinnati 0
Penn State 30	Nebraska 24
Penn State 30	Temple 0
Penn State 38	Boston College 7
Penn State 41	Syracuse 16
Penn State 30	West Virginia 7
Miami 17	Penn State 14
Penn State 22	N.C. State 15
Alabama 31	Penn State 16
Penn State 24	Notre Dame 21
Penn State 48	Pitt 14

Credit: The Pennsylvania State University Alumni Association.

positioned in high-traffic areas. As Kotler has pointed out,[4] there is an analogy between the marketing tactics developed by profit-making organizations and those available to educational institutions. Colleges need to develop their own "marketing mixes."

Position—The Bottom Line

Though the interests of our publics—and the publics themselves—may be fragmented, nevertheless there is one ultimate goal toward which everyone must be headed. That is the *position* of the institution in the mind of its publics. What are the perceptions? How do these people "see" us—the future student, the member of the state legislature, the "retread." What are their attitudes? What comes to mind when they see us or hear us?

Are we regarded as a hopeless goal, a bunch of snobs, wacky impractical dreamers? Or do they look upon us with pride, are they aware of our accomplishments, are we a credit to our community, our state, and our country? This is where it all comes out in the end. Yet, strangely enough, many college public relations departments wander from the main path. It is up to the administration of the college to set its specific "image" or "position" goals. It is up to you to help the college get there. There are ways, through attitudinal studies, to determine just exactly what people think of you. And methods are available to determine just what progress you are making. This is the "background" of much of your activity, and it is vital to you. Without the proper position, attitudes, and perceptions, all else you do loses much of its luster and effectiveness.

Few business firms neglect this aspect of the operation. You cannot spend millions of dollars on commercials telling the public how concerned you are about the environment or the ecology. But you can know just where you stand with your publics and what success you are having in closing the gap to the position you and your administration would like to reach.

SUMMARY

The face of education has changed and continues to change at a rapid pace. Students today are far different kinds of people than they were just a few years ago. Much of this is due to the growth of community colleges. As a result, college graduates—alumni—are an ever-growing segment of the public.

[4]Philip Kotler, *Marketing for Nonprofit Organizations* (Englewood Cliffs, N.J.: Prentice-Hall, 1979), p. 344.

College attitudes toward public relations change slowly. Many members of the faculty and administration are not comfortable with the idea of publicizing or "selling" the institution.

Colleges have constituencies: alumni, business, faculty and staff, parents and students, who need to be influenced. The college public relations director must first audit the "environment"—the present situation. There are inside and outside constituencies, and a number of means for reaching each.

The ultimate goal is to "position" the college—to get the publics to see an image that will reflect credit on the institution.

KEY TERMS

Information services	Audit of resources
Community relations	News information letter
Morrill Land Grant Act of 1862	Personal letters
Community college	Outside constituency
Advancement program	Inside constituency
American College Public Relations Association (ACPRA)	Marketing mix
	Position
Alumni magazine	
Homecoming	

THE WAY IT HAPPENED

Though Philip Kotler's original article about applying marketing principles to nonprofit organizations excited a great many people in education, there have been very few authenticated reports of actual successful performance.

When I was appointed to chair a marketing committee at my college, I began to understand why. It is strange, but true, that a great many college administrators who hold doctorates in education have very little knowledge of marketing. Even as undergraduates, few took a course in this subject. And since their careers have been on school campuses, few have had the opportunity to learn the practical side of marketing.

As a result, I discovered that most of them did not, literally, know what I was talking about. My first months in office became a struggle to induce some very well-placed Ph.D.s to go back to school and learn a new subject—or at least skim a textbook. It wasn't easy.

Few thought it amiss, for example, that though we had a public relations office, we had no overall plan for projecting the image of the college. Nor did we know what the present image was, or even what we wanted it to be!

It took a long time to make converts. Some of them never came around, even after our committee began to show recruitment gains as a result of the application of standard marketing principles.

A PERSONAL PROJECT

Is your college reaching its alumni? Although most universities have a very active alumni office, a surprising number of smaller colleges, particularly community colleges, do not.

If your college does not have an office of alumni affairs, why don't you evolve some simple techniques for keeping graduates informed, interested, and supportive? I trust you will find that the administration will welcome your efforts.

READING TO BROADEN UNDERSTANDING

The Advancement of Understanding and Support of Higher Education (American College Public Relations Association). See particularly p. 23, "The College and Its Public Relations."

CONROY, PAT. *The Water Is Wide* (Boston: Houghton Mifflin, 1972). The story of an off-beat white guy teaching in an all-black South Carolina sea island school. Talk about p.r. problems!

KOBRE, SIDNEY. *Successful Public Relations for Colleges And Universities* (New York: Hastings House, 1974). High-level text that covers the subject in detail. Good reference.

MOVSHOVITZ, HELEN. *What Every School Board Member Should Know about: Press and Community Relations* (Trenton: New Jersey School Board Association, 1975). A practical "how to" book.

15

PRODUCT PUBLIC RELATIONS

OVERVIEW AND GOALS

There is a point at which public relations and product promotion join hands. We are now going to see how this happens. There are four branches of promotion, the overall effort to sell goods and services: mass selling (advertising), personal selling, sales promotion, and publicity. This is a different kind of public relations than imagemaking. As you will see, it is intimately associated (as it should be) with the selling process itself. When you have finished this chapter, you should be able to

> *Appreciate* the importance of publicity in the selling effort.
>
> *Understand* how "tie-ins" are used in the promotional effort.
>
> *Recognize* how people of various kinds are used to promote and publicize products.

Very early in this book we observed that everything that happens in business happens against a backdrop of public relations. You have seen that good public relations—that is, good attitudes, perceptions, and images—make a company's products more acceptable to the public, and therefore more salable. In the last four chapters, you have seen how this works. Whether you are engaged in "positioning" a corporation, selling seats to a soccer game, soliciting gifts from alumni, or getting people to turn out for a musical concert, it all takes place before a backdrop of public relations. Now we come to something slightly different—the point where promotion and public relations begin to blend. This takes a little understanding.

When one sells a quart of oil or a gallon of gasoline, the sale takes place against a background of corporate public relations. How favorable an attitude do we have of Texaco, or Gulf, or Shell? But in addition to the corporate attitudes and perceptions, the product *may have a separate public relations life of its own.* You may have a very high regard for Westinghouse, a company that has worked hard for years to gain your trust. But that new toaster of theirs you just bought may have been discovered as a result of a story that appeared recently in your local newspaper.

The fact that corporate public relations and product public relations run along the same roadbed but on different tracks is a relatively new concept. Public relations began as corporate public relations. Bernays, Ivey Lee, and others, began as defenders of corporations against the attacks of reformers and "muckrakers." They dealt directly with the giants of industry—the Mellons, Rockefellers, and Harrimans. As might be expected, later public relations practitioners sought to hold their own image as high as possible. They did not wish to be seen as mere publicity flacks, but as important and trusted corporate advisers (as in fact most of them were) whose positions were very close to the chief executive officer's on the company's organization chart. Indeed, the autobiographies of those early public relations people tell of frequent luncheons and intimate meetings with "the boss." That is the way it was with public relations advisors for many years. And then something happened—modern marketing was born.

The Place of Public Relations in Marketing

Today we find a great many public relations people whose most immediate concern is that of enhancing the image of the company for which they work. But you will also find people who are essentially a part of the marketing effort. They are engaged in one of the great basic marketing activities, promotion.

Promotion, as the term is understood in marketing, consists of several different facets: personal selling, sales promotion, advertising, and publicity. The marketing function of publicity has been defined as

> *. . . nonpersonal stimulation of demand for a product, service, or business unit by planting commercially significant news about it in a published medium or*

obtaining favorable presentation of it upon radio, television, or stage that is not paid for by the sponsor.[1]

Where Publicity Moves in with Promotion

First of all, perhaps we should remind ourselves of the nature of product promotion. When someone puts on an after-Christmas sale, that is a promotion. When a sports star demonstrates his technique in a sports department, or an omelet maker demonstrates how to flip an omelet, that is promotion. A company-sponsored golf tournament or a store window, or two-for-the-price-of-one sale all fall under the heading of promotion. It is well to remind ourselves of the infinite variety of promotions. The fact of the matter is that publicity can help any promotion, simply as an alternative way of calling attention to the promotion itself, as well as the product being promoted.

When the promotion involves a sporting event such as the Kemper Open or the Murgani WTZ Championships, the job is relatively simple. Reams will be written about both events, and inevitably the company name will be mentioned time after time. In fact, the company picks up the tab for these events because they are good public relations. But not all sporting events, though sponsored, are participated in by champions, and are thus assured of wide press coverage. Sometimes it is necessary to fight your way onto the sports pages. The techniques of publicity are often used to turn the trick.

Let us say you are doing public relations for a boat show, an annual event in your city. Although all the best-known boat builders and engine manufacturers will be present as usual, the sports editor has a definitely "ho-hum" attitude. Even the stories about the biggest boat have not moved him, and it is beginning to look as though your boat show might slip in and out of town almost unnoticed.

It is now up to you to produce the person or thing that is most likely to provide a nice long feature article for the Sunday edition. Having done your homework, you know that most boat people are romantics at heart. (They've sailed around the world many times in their imaginations.) The very essence of romanticism is, of course, sunken treasure. The mention of pieces-of-eight, golden ingots, and silverplate starts every heart beating a little faster.

You have located a treasure hunter who has had some success and have given him a booth where he can sell books and trinkets and exhibit some Spanish gold. We can predict he'll be a hit with the guests at the show—everybody will stop and look. But it is before the show opens, when he begins whispering his tales of the Spanish Main into the ears of the feature editor,

---

[1]See Kotler, *Marketing Management* (Englewood Cliffs, N.J.: Prentice-Hall, 1976), p. 337, for his definition of marketing publicity and also a good list of promotional activities of various kinds.

FIGURE 15-1   Like the triple play in baseball, it is great when you can pull it off—and this one worked. Here a men's cologne, a soccer club, and a department store put it all together. Promotions are often based on mutual aid, as was this one. The product gets great exposure, the store gets a sensational advertisement, and the soccer team gets great publicity. The whole thing is an eye catcher. A break of this kind does not happen every day.

Credit: Furchgott's of Florida.

that things begin to happen. As the editor dreamily fingers the pieces-of-eight, she learns from our treasure hunter that there is more out there—*lots more*— and a king's ransom awaits the person with a little nerve, luck, and a good wet suit. Now that is the stuff dreams—and feature articles—are made of. Our editor can hardly wait to get to the typewriter. The day after the article appears, attendance jumps. You would be surprised how many people there are in this world who cannot wait to see a pile of glittering pieces-of-eight.

Publicity Tie-Ins

In addition to using publicity to enhance the value of your own promotion, you can score points by joining others in their promotions. These are the tie-ins so beloved to every promotor or creator of store windows. What tieing-in means, in effect, is that I will *lend* you the publicity engendered by my own promotion to help *your* promotion.

Let us say a big football game is scheduled to be played in your city. The committee in charge of promoting the game has been hard at work generating news stories and events to encourage ticket sales and interest in the game. How can I, as a retailer of men's clothes, put some of that publicity to work for me? I do it by means of a tie-in. I tie-in your promotional efforts for a football game with mine in behalf of men's clothes, to our mutual benefit. I know that the people doing publicity for the game are eager to help me in every way they can. They will supply banners, action photos, football equipment, and, of course, posters advertising the game. I decorate my windows with the colors and banners of the two teams. I use pictures of the rival coaches and scenes from games of the past. All this is used to enhance a display of colorful knitted caps, stadium coats, and other articles of men's wear worn by "sportsmen."

The Author as Publicist

Publishers' marketing people use normal promotional devices to increase the sales of books. Direct mail and sampling is very popular, especially with textbook publishers. Newspaper advertising, particularly in the book review sections, is widely used in promoting fiction and nonfiction designed for the general public.

But it is the author who often provides tremendous publicity impetus to the sales of the book. We mentioned in an earlier chapter the use of TV talk shows and interviews. A publisher can get considerable mileage out of an author who is attractive and articulate. The publicity received by a new book, when discussed in a half-hour TV interview, is almost incalculable.

But it works both ways. The talk-show host is anxious to have guests who will keep ratings high. He or she cannot afford to have people who are inarticulate and unattractive, no matter how many best sellers they have written. Since many prolific writers are, unfortunately, not particularly articulate in front of a camera, it limits the use of authors in this kind of publicity effort.

Another way the author can be used to generate publicity for the book is through lectures and autograph sessions (the two usually go together). It is amazing how many authors will subject themselves to the rigors of the "one-night stand." The publisher's public relations department may book the author for a series of lectures, often on college campuses or before literary organizations. The author will also be booked into one or more local retail outlets for an hour or two of autographing and chitchat. The retailer, of course, loves this, since the presence of the author increases store traffic and sells books. The reader, on the other hand, has the fun of walking out of the store with an autographed first edition.

Counselors and Advisors

As you have already seen, someone like an omelet expert is great for promotion. But when the counselor or advisor is a well-known figure, the publicity opportunities are greatly increased. The specialist, who is a well-known authority on whatever subject, usually has something to say. And what he or she says can be newsworthy.

The author of a diet book or cookbook is a logical subject for an interview in the section of the paper devoted to women's interests. The fact that he or she happens to be in town as part of a promotion for a new line of low-calorie diet foods is neither here nor there as far as the interviewer is concerned. The reporter is seeking to produce a readable story.

There is hardly a "sportsman's show" (a show in which hunting, fishing, and outdoor equipment is displayed for the trade and public) that does not have an expert fly-caster demonstrating his skill. Now *you* may never have heard of this expert, but you can bet every fly-fisherman who ever pulled on a pair of waders knows him and looks upon his skill with awe. They flock to see him and increase the size of the "gate"—and therefore the value of the show to the individual exhibitor.

Testimonials

In the early days of advertising and promotion, testimonials were usually the "before-and-after" type, or statements by anonymous characters who reported, "Yes, my headache is all gone." It never occurred to anyone to ask a really *famous* person. It was assumed they would refuse. But to the promoters' surprise, they said yes. In fact, it turned out that there were a surprising number of society figures and foreign nobility who would speak up for a given product and get their picture taken for a fee. Promotion took a new twist with the appearance of these well-connected and famous people. It now became possible to exploit these figures in a public relations kind of way.

From the appearance in the advertisement it was but a step to personal appearance. The countess would be invited to show up at a cocktail party at which some of the company's best customers would be present. No big deal—just show up, shake a few hands, chat with "the boys" for a moment. The exploitation of these figures became even more rewarding as they were moved closer to the selling action. A famous beauty in a cosmetics department or a natty British nobleman in a retail menswear store could do wonders for sales. TV gave what had started out to be a straightforward testimonial another twist—the use of well-known figures as spokespeople for a product.

Spokespeople

A magazine or newspaper advertising testimonial is static—a picture of the person giving the testimonial, and a printed statement. But a testimonial as television commercial is something else again. Now the well-known figure comes into your living room in living, breathing color, speaking words of wisdom to you in a personal way. Viewers come to identify the product with the person delivering the commercial message. The personalities and stars become, in effect, more than just commercial announcers; they are spokespeople for or representatives of the product *and* its producer. H. G. Marshall, a famous actor, speaks up for a stomach remedy. Bill Cosby is on the Jello team, and Sandy Duncan, stage and musical comedy star, chomps away cutely on her favorite cracker. Of course, when there is a big dealer or sales meeting, you can hardly leave these people behind. Besides, it is all in the contract.

Among a minority of stars and famous people, there is sometimes an irresistible temptation to exploit their fame and gain space and time in the local media. Usually it is a cruel hoax and takes the form of "something wonderful is going to happen to you on account of me." The people in the press *have* to fall for it, even though they know they are being exploited. Here are a couple of examples: A boxing promotor appeared in town, proclaiming that he was going to bring a championship fight to town. The casino with which he had a contract expressed mild surprise and amusement when it heard the story, which made the sports pages and evening news. We did not get any championship fight, and aside from an ego trip, I do not know what the boxing promotor got out of it. Here is another case: An old-time Hollywood star arrived in town for a two-week stand at the local dinner theater. Just before his opening, he called a press conference to announce he was planning to build a repertory theater here and to live here at least six months of the year. The reporters raced for their typewriters, and the dinner theater show got its share of the publicity. But we never got our theater, and though his show played to capacity audiences, he has not been back. No wonder reporters get cynical and sometimes difficult to deal with.

There is nothing very mysterious about the business of ethics. In every business and profession, most people play by the rules of the game. A few do not. Those few hurt all of us, and we do our best to exclude them. Most public relations people operate under the Code of Professional Standards for the Practice of Public Relations adopted by the Public Relations Society of America, April 29, 1977. It contains a declaration of principles and a 14-article code covering every aspect of public relations. Every local public relations society knows this code and insists that its members adhere to it.

Sports Idols

There are millions of Americans who would consider it a rare privilege to shake the hand of Mickey Mantle, have a picture taken with Joe DiMaggio, or receive an autograph from Chris Everet Lloyd or Nancy Lopez. These people, and hundreds more like them, have achieved the status of living legends. The fees they demand for their promotional-publicity services are sizable. With the rewards of outstanding ability in the sports field come the rewards of commercialization. In some cases, the "retirement income" of an ex-idol of the millions may be far more per year than he or she earned as an active athlete.

The producers of the Miller High Life television commercials seem to have taken the commercial exploitation of prominent sports figures about as far as it will go. In just one of those commercials, you can count a baseball manager, an ex-NFL coach, a great college fullback, a pool hustler, a Las Vegas odds-maker, a karate black belt, and goodness knows who else. It's a convention, and the talent fee for those commercials must be enormous.

Many of these figures are under exclusive contracts to their sponsors, but many of them find it more profitable to operate on their own in a freelance capacity. As you may know from reading the sports pages, the "personal representation" is of growing importance in the sports field. It is the personal representative who negotiates the player's contracts or who, after retirement, helps handle business affairs. This is the person you will contact if you want Mickey Mantle to appear at your next fund-raiser or opening day game. The "rep" will know if Mickey is available and what fee he will charge. Not all sports figures use business representatives. Many college football coaches have lucrative local radio and TV contracts, but can be contacted directly for appearances and speaking engagements.

The public relations fallout from these celebrity appearances is likely to be very rich. When the word gets around that Woody or Bear or Lou is

FIGURE 15-2   The manufacturer-sponsored athletic event can generate reams of publicity for the backer. What is more natural than a cosmetic manufacturer sponsoring an all-women tennis tournament?

Credit: Madison Square Garden.

coming to town, the press will be there to meet him at the airport. Some of these sports stars have developed routines that enhance the interest—and therefore the value—of an appearance. A baseball star will give the kids a demonstration of hitting and fielding and then line them up for autographs, or pose with them for pictures.

These personal appearances often test the public relations person's mettle. After all, it is his or her job to see that things run smoothly—something things do not always do. When the situation gets out of control, usually because of poor planning, the result can be disaster. We had a case here in town awhile back that was pretty scary. A famous star brought hundreds of kids out to the ball park. When he tried to line them up for autographs, a near-riot occurred. He was mobbed and had to scramble for the press box. Most public relations people have their favorite horror stories of the guest who got off the plane at the wrong city, or said something juicy into an open microphone that everyone assumed was dead. Public relations people have a tendency to go gray early.

The Product as Personality

Though live people—beautiful, talented, and socially well placed—play an important role in publicizing and promoting products, it is often the product itself that proves to be the star. Famous names and popular stars can call attention to a product. But very often it is wise for the public relations person to let the product "speak for itself." Of course, products have been doing just exactly this for ages. The modern public relations person just gives them all the help he or she can. This "speaking for yourself" can take many forms.

1. *Demonstrations.* One basic way to show a product's qualities or superiority is to demonstrate them. Certainly one of the most primitive examples is the fabled "pitchman" of street corner and county fair. In carny language, a "pitch" is a crowd. The pitchman gets his crowd curious by deftly demonstrating, with real fruits and vegetables, the remarkable usefulness of a kitchen gadget that slices, peels, grates, dices, cores, and a few other things. The pitchman's deft hands make it all look effortless.

   When a salesperson has something to sell that is portable, he or she usually carries it on a call. The chances of making a sale are greatly enhanced if he or she can get a prospect to try the product. We try to get you to try the nonportable things, too—vacuum cleaners, automobiles, sewing machines.

2. *Tasting.* This is a form of demonstration. That is why, in almost every supermarket you will find an attractive person offering you a tidbit of this or that for your tasting judgment. In these demonstrations, the product is also publicizing itself. For each person who tries the new cheese dip, there are dozens passing the demonstrator's table who become conscious that there *is* a new cheese dip.

3. *Shows and trade fairs.* One of the greatest vehicles for product publicity is *trade shows*—events in which an entire trade field will show its wares to potential buyers. Display booths provided with displays of the product, literature, and slide films attract the attention of potential users.

   As a product publicity event you are probably most familiar with foreign and domestic new car introductions. The new model lines and features are a carefully guarded secret until the great day of the unveiling. New automobile models *are* news and generate many lines of print in newspapers

FIGURE 15-3   Just as in store promotions, an "occasion"—Mother's Day, Christmas, etc.—often provides the public relations writer with the "hook" on which to hang the story. In this case Easter and all those leftover eggs from the neighborhood Easter egg hunt.

Eggs make Eggs Florentine and Eggs Florentine take butter. Notice that the copy not only provides the recipe, but the "reward" in the last paragraph.

Land O'Lakes, Inc.

4001 LEXINGTON AVE. N., ARDEN HILLS, MINNESOTA

Mailing address: P.O. Box 116, Minneapolis, MN 55440
Telephone: (612) 481-2222

Land O'Lakes Foods

SOLVE THE EASTER EGG DILEMMA WITH EASY EGGS FLORENTINE

Leftover hard-cooked Easter eggs will no longer be a problem when this recipe for Easy Eggs Florentine is in your recipe file. The sliced, cooked eggs are combined with Process American Cheese, spinach, onion, cream of mushroom soup and sour cream to produce a flavorful after-Easter main dish.

Simply layer chopped spinach, onion and eggs in a casserole dish and top with a mixture of shredded cheese, undiluted mushroom soup and sour cream. Melted butter and crushed herb seasoned stuffing mix form the tasty topping over all. Bake Easy Eggs Florentine uncovered, for 35 to 45 minutes, serve and congratulate yourself for solving the leftover Easter egg dilemma.

Once your family samples this simple dish with all the tastes they love -- they'll be asking for it again and again! You probably won't get by with waiting for another hard-cooked egg season to roll around to serve Easy Eggs Florentine

-more-

1281C

FIGURE 5-3   *continued*

EASY EGGS FLORENTINE

6 hard cooked eggs, sliced 1/8"
10-oz. pkg. frozen chopped spinach, thawed, <u>well</u> <u>drained</u>
1 tbsp. instant minced onion
1 c. (4 oz.) shredded LAND O LAKES®
    Process American Cheese
1/2 c. condensed cream of mushroom soup, undiluted
1/2 c. LAND O LAKES® Sour Cream
  2 tbsp. LAND O LAKES® Sweet Cream Butter
1/2 c. crushed herb seasoned stuffing mix

Heat oven to 350°. Have hard cooked eggs ready. In 1 1/2-qt. casserole
layer spinach, onion and sliced eggs. In 1 1/2-qt. bowl stir together cheese,
soup and sour cream. Spread cheese mixture over eggs. In 1-qt. saucepan melt
butter. Stir in stuffing mix until well mixed. Sprinkle stuffing mix on
cheese mixture. Bake, uncovered, for 35 to 45 min. or until heated through.
YIELD: 6 (1 c.) servings.

Credit: Reprinted by permission of Land O'Lakes, Inc.

and trade and specialty magazines. The public relations person's problem is not so much in generating publicity. The question is, what *kind* of publicity? Here, again, we see the product take over and generate its publicity through its own inherent qualities. When there is good news to tell, the automotive writers shout it to the housetops. The product is what makes the story outstanding.

Innovations

The great world of product making changes all the time. To remain static is to fall behind. Digital watches, pocket calculators, homogenized milk, surfboards, and a great many other products had to be thought up and introduced, *with attendant publicity.* Fortunately for us in public relations, there are thousands of journalists and broadcasters out there whose job is to bring us the news about the newest. If there is a new and interesting way to cook with walnuts, food editors are interested in hearing about it and passing the word along to their readers. When new *uses* are discovered (such as putting an open package of baking soda in the refrigerator as an odor absorber), editors pick it up and publicize it. In fact, the pages of trade magazines are packed with stories of people who have perfected a better product or have discovered a better way to do innovative things with the products they have.

The wise manufacturer's public relations people never lose sight of the fact that while they may be the mid-wives, it is the *product* that is the baby!

SUMMARY

Product public relations refers to the kind of publicity that is directly associated with the promotional effort. Thus, it is an integral part of marketing.

The commonest forms of product public relations involve people, and the product itself. The people who generate publicity are those who give testimonials, act as spokespeople, or otherwise appear on behalf of the product. They are usually famous people whose names and accomplishments are well known to the public. Sports stars are particularly effective in creating publicity for products.

Products themselves are publicity makers. New products and innovations and developments are newsworthy items which, in many cases, generate great amounts of publicity for the product.

KEY TERMS

Product public relations	Autograph session
Mass selling (advertising)	Testimonial
Personal selling	Personal appearance
Sales promotion	Spokesperson
Tie-in	Counselor, advisor
Sampling	Sports idol

THE WAY IT HAPPENED

Bourbon whiskies, as you may have noticed, depend to a great extent on the image they project. The law makes it difficult to say much about a whiskey, so the image that is projected is down-homey and sippin-good. Actually, most bourbon distilleries do have a romantic background and a long and honorable history.

I became involved with the rebirth of one from Nelson County called J. W. Dant. Whoever the original J. W. Dant was we never found out—some Kentucky farmer whose local distillery produced a product that pleased his friends, no doubt. With a brand name like J. W. Dant, we knew we needed a *character* to go with it—a Colonel J. W. Dant, suh.

But where to find him? We finally decided to use the president and chief promotor of the brand himself. After all, his face was the one that was going to be most familiar to the trade.

So we dressed the president up in a planter's hat and a string tie and ran his pictures in all the promotion. He looked great, too—not at all like a short, fat guy whose parents came from a small town in middle Europe, and who spoke with a rich, ripe Jersey City accent.

A PERSONAL PROJECT

Let us take two difficult to promote products—say, cosmetic surgery and personal injury legal services. Choose one and show how you would create a promotion-publicity campaign built around a famous character.

READING TO BROADEN UNDERSTANDING

KOTLER, PHILIP. *Principles of Marketing* (Englewood Cliffs, N.J.: Prentice-Hall, 1983). See pp. 552–55. Read particularly "A Publicity and Promotion Genius—Bill Vieck."

NORRIS, JAMES S. *Selling: The How and Why* (Englewood Cliffs, N.J.: Prentice-Hall, 1982). Chapter 6, "The Role of Advertising and Sales Promotion," helps tie it together.

Sales and Marketing Management (New York: Bill Publications). See any issue of this excellent "trade publication" for real-life stories of promotion-public relations. For example, "Marketers Turn on the Lights," p. 25, July 10, 1978.

16

IS THERE A PUBLIC RELATIONS JOB IN YOUR FUTURE?

Where Are You Going?

This is the final question: Is a career in public relations one I might like to pursue? Obviously this was a question you must have had in the back of your mind when you signed up for the course.

In the preceding chapters you have seen the kinds of disciplines and practices that are required of the public relations person. You have also seen, in a few of the many fields in which public relations plays a part, many examples of the creative work done by p.r. people. By now you should have a pretty good grasp of the big picture.

In this chapter we will combine fact and opinion to aid you in arriving at the answer to the question of the chapter title. This is not a "sell." Trying to force a square peg into a round hole is a disfavor. A great many people have neither the inherent talent nor the personality to be happy and successful in this field. It is better to find out now, rather than later. We want this chapter to help you do just that.

The Opportunities

There are a great many of them. As compared to advertising, which requires many of the same skills, the public relations door is wide open. It is recognized as a field with an increasing potential for growth.

As you saw in the opening chapter, public relations was once regarded as something reserved for the very rich or successful. Indeed, for many years, the practice of public relations was confined to business corporations and other large enterprises. Not so today! As you have seen from the illustrations in the text, there are many small, local enterprises with well-designed press releases.

Today, the practice of public relations is pervasive throughout our economy. There is hardly a public or private enterprise that does not practice some form of public relations, though it may be as basic as sending out an occasional release. The job often falls to the director or secretary of the organization. But this does not mean the organization cannot use all the professional advice it can get.

The practice of public relations counseling was formerly confined to a few large cities. Today, smaller cities regularly list a number of public relations firms. Here are a few examples:

Montgomery, Alabama	13	Clearwater, Florida	7
Hartford, Connecticut	40	Oklahoma City, Oklahoma	42
Toledo, Ohio	21		

These firms, employing varying numbers of people, are exclusive of the enterprises that have their own public relations specialists. Business enterprises, colleges and universities, sports enterprises, charitable institutions, state and federal government offices, travel firms, and entertainment enterprises all employ public relations people. And there are many more. The important point is this: When choosing a career in public relations, you also have the opportunity of choosing the field in which you can practice your profession.

This is important and will have a lot to do with your future happiness and therefore your performance. What kind of a public relations person do you wish to be? A job in a corporate public relations department may suit your personality just fine. Interested in travel? Try departments of tourism and the airlines. Maybe you would like to stay right on campus and work for the school—there are jobs in both the alumni and athletic office. For socially minded and outgoing types, work at a hotel, resort, or resort community can be stimulating and a lot of fun. I know no other profession that offers so many alternatives as to the area in which it may be practiced.

Compensation

Good public relations people are well paid, and topnotchers are very well paid. Obviously a corporate public relations executive occupies a very important position and is compensated accordingly. One of the best pieces

of advice for the young person starting off in any profession is this: Do not be concerned about starting salary. Develop your skills, and the money will follow. In public relations, you can be sure the high-salary potential is there.

However, the fact must be faced that, in a profession that employs a great many women, salaries can often be on the low side. We talked to one woman with 10 years' experience in the field, a master's degree, and a job in an educational institution's public relations department. She reports her salary at $16,000 per year, less than many high school teachers earn.

The *Occupational Handbook* issued by the U.S. Department of Labor's Bureau of Labor Statistics lists starting salaries in public relations as running between $9,600 and $13,000, with those holding a graduate degree making more. It lists top salaries in the field as $36,000 for presidents of public relations firms, $31,200 for those in top government posts, and $25,000 for those in educational institutions. In the federal government, holders of master's degrees may expect to start at $15,300.

Talents

If you are a writing type, this is one of the areas you will want to look into. "Writing type" is not a facetious phrase. There are those who are blessed with this kind of talent. You will find them in the short story class, working on the college newspaper, or just scribbling poems for their own amusement. For those who have writing skills and can develop them, there are a lot of job possibilities. Public relations is one of them. Since poets are vastly underpaid, and the great American novel may take a few years to develop, it may be well to look around at ways to keep bread on the table.

Preparing news releases *does* require writing skill. As I hope you have seen from the examples in the text, the ability to be interesting often makes the difference between whether you get published or not. Creative writing does not consist just of putting words together skillfully. It also means coming up with interesting ideas and angles. As was pointed out in the illustration on p. 259, the writer could have simply made an announcement. Rather, his creative ability provided him with an interesting angle that made the story more attractive to the editor.

Almost all practicing public relations people strongly advise a writing background. Or maybe it is the other way around: People with writing skills naturally gravitate toward public relations. Doreen Daly, a university public relations assistant, recalls that she found herself working on her high school and college newspapers, "and soon I was doing everything." She has an interesting observation to make. "When I advise students to do as much writing as possible, their faces sometimes fall. They seem to think public relations is mostly cocktail parties and entertaining events."

Kimberly Kelly, whose work for the Clemson Athletic Department appears in Figure 11–2, has a number of interesting things to say about your education:

In order to prepare for a career in sports information specifically and the advertising/public relations field in general, I would advise a solid liberal arts education in a communication arts type of program. A bachelor of arts degree in this area coupled with a minor or a major in a second subject of interest should provide an adequate foundation for gaining entry level positions in the above mentioned fields. (I obtained a BA in Communications Arts and a minor in sociology from St. Mary's College, Notre Dame, Ind. in 1980.)

Whatever the secondary course of study pursued may be, make sure that it is not closely related to your communications degree. There are two reasons why one should safeguard against this: (1) a closely related major carries too many content similarities and thus much theoretical material is a repeat; (2) a similar major doesn't broaden one's education/intellectual horizons but rather stockpiles one's knowledge onto a narrow base.

Regarding more specific course selection advice, I would recommend as many speech and writing courses as possible. Any courses that stress interpersonal communication such as those offered in the sociology, psychology, and education departments would also be beneficial. Finally, investigate the business department offerings, as a course in marketing, finance, business ethics/communications, and/or personnel training may also prove worthwhile. In short, take advantage of your liberal arts education to the fullest. Experiment and experience as many electives as your major will allow, for in the long run they will enhance your education and make you a well-rounded individual. And remember, it is the well-rounded liberal arts graduate who knows where to find and how to adapt to a wide variety of employment opportunities.

If you are going to be a public relations writer, you will want to be a master of styles, too. Much of your writing, of course, will be "news style"— the who, what, when, and where. But there are many other things you may be called upon to do: a brochure for a vacation resort, an appeal for a hospital fund-raising, an invitation to a children's Christmas party, the obituary of an important member of your firm. The ability to "shift gears" creatively is very important to the public relations person.

Joe Luter, who now runs his own public relations firm, arrived via the small town newspaper and ad agency route. A stint on a newspaper is great preparation for a public relations career. Hundreds of releases cross your desk each month, and you learn at first hand the good and the bad of p.r. writing.

Personality

As a teacher, I sometimes get tired of this business of the ideal personality for such-and-such a job. The description always seems to end up ". . . thrifty, brave, clean, and reverent."

Let us begin by noting that on any job you are expected to be courteous, cooperative, and reasonably easy to get along with. I have known a lot of public relations people, and it has always seemed to me that their personalities were much more geared to the type of public relations job they were in.

I knew a fellow who worked for one of the great public relations firms in New York. I'd say his personality was more of the stereotype of the newspaperman. Few public relations people fit the popular image of the flamboyant "press agent" who will do almost anything to get a line for a client. But these people *do* exist.

If you should land in the field of tourism or resort promotion, you are going to have to be outgoing and have social skills. Part of your job will be to behave charmingly with a great many different kinds of people. I have had several friends who were in the specialized field of financial public relations on Wall Street. They seemed to have assumed the coloration of those they dealt with: quiet, conservative, thoughtful, and not given to rash statements. All this business of "personality," it seems to me, often works itself out. If you want to be happy in your public relations job, you will go wherever, as a person, you fit in best.

The Job Hunt

Unless you are picked off the campus by a corporation looking for promising junior executives, the first job is often tough to get. Luck often plays a big part. So do persistence and hard work. Sometimes we have to sneak into public relations through the back door. I know one person who spent a couple of years in what amounted to solitary confinement, copyreading for a printing firm. Another sold time on a small radio station, and still another taught grade school for several years.

Most charitable, art, and theater organizations are delighted to get all the volunteer help they can. Work as a volunteer can teach you a lot and also enable you to meet some very helpful persons. Very often the public relations chairperson of these organizations is totally lost and has not the slightest idea of how to carry out his or her responsibilities. Your help will be more than appreciated. I know a young woman who rescued the distraught public relations chair of an arts festival. The woman's husband was chair of the trustees of the largest hospital in town. Guess who became an assistant in the hospital's public relations office? One person told me, "I was the last of the great volunteers, I think. As a student I was involved with the Notre Dame Sports Information Office for four years, the campus radio and television stations, my hometown radio station and newspaper, and currently I am a class reporter for my alma mater's alumnae magazine."

A number of successful public relations people have gotten their first jobs through a traditional method—they have answered ads or run ads themselves. Answering ads, of course, involves the harrowing experience of "Many are called, but few are chosen." Many public relations people have told me that they are *still* wondering why they were the ones selected from all that mob.

Do not be afraid to cultivate those who can help you. Get to know as many people in the field as possible. Whatever you do of a creative nature, be sure they see it. Make up a brochure of your college and volunteer work and take it around. Be persistent. Job needs pop up in funny ways. Someone may know someone else who needs a person like you right away. Sometimes jobs take a long time to mature. I knew one fellow who was told, "We like you and your work and there will be a job here for you one day." It was with the top agency in the business, and the person, fortunately employed, waited 16 months for it to come through. Your first job in this interesting and rewarding business will probably come through a lot faster.

INDEX*

*Pages in *italics* denote figures.

Dat